The Multimedia Library

MATERIALS SELECTION AND USE

The Multimedia Library

MATERIALS SELECTION AND USE

James Cabeceiras

Division of Library Science and
Department of Instructional Technology
San Jose State University
San Jose, California

ACADEMIC PRESS   New York   San Francisco   London   1978

A Subsidiary of Harcourt Brace Jovanovich, Publishers

ACADEMIC PRESS, INC.
111 Fifth Avenue, New York, New York 10003

United Kingdom Edition published by
ACADEMIC PRESS, INC. (LONDON) LTD.
24/28 Oval Road, London NW1 7DX

Library of Congress Cataloging in Publication Data

Cabeceiras, James.
    The multimedia library.

    (Library and information science)
    Bibliography: p.
    1. Selection of nonbook materials. 2. Book
selection. 3. Audio−visual library service. I. Title.
II. Series.
Z689.C12   025.2'1   77−11209
ISBN 0−12−153950−4

To Chris

While there was light,
So brilliantly did it shine,
That I will forever bask,
In the radiant afterglow.

Contents

3
Selection Aids

4
Library Media: Developing Bibliographies

5
Periodicals, Newspapers, and Pamphlets

6
Microforms

7
16-mm Films

8
8-mm Films

9
Filmstrips and Slides

10
Audio Recordings

11
Television

12
Globes, Maps, Models, Realia, Games,
and Simulations

13
Programmed Instruction

14
Books

15
Learning Centers

16
Local Preparation of Information Materials

17
Selecting the Proper Medium

Preface

In our current technological society, changes in practically every aspect of our lives are occurring at a rapid pace. The twentieth century has undergone an evolution unprecedented since the dawn of mankind. Discoveries in medicine are curing diseases, improving health, and extending the length of life. Transportation has progressed from the primitive horseless carriage to interplanetary travel. Man–machine systems have greatly increased productivity of goods. And the computer coupled with the science of cybernetics is accelerating the rate of change in just about everything we do.

One of the more evident changes that affects our lives is in the area of communications. Not only do we rely heavily on traditional print media as a source of information, but we are also becoming increasingly aware of and dependent on nonprint communication forms. Television, for example, will, by the time the average American reaches the age of 65, occupy 9-waking years of his or her life.

Libraries, because of their ubiquitous involvement in the selection, acquisition, control, and circulation of information, are vitally involved in the rapid communication evolution. The librarian needs to be aware of the many characteristics of the multitude of communication forms available. This book organizes and investigates the prevalent communication media worthy of inclusion in the modern library in an effort to assist the librarian in becoming more knowledgeable about them and in being able to make intelligent decisions regarding their unique contributions to the library goal of providing appropriate information forms to its patrons.

This book is intended primarily for the student of librarianship. In addition, many of the communication media investigated in this book are only now being discussed in schools of librarianship, and as libraries begin to acquire a greater variety of communication forms, the information in this book could well serve as a convenient handbook to the in-service librarian with limited experience in the area of nonprint media. Furthermore, the book is intentionally written to be of service to all types of libraries—public, private, special, academic, and school.

Bearing in mind that many librarians, whether by desire or circumstance, may have reservations about becoming involved with newer communication forms, Chapter 1 analyzes present and future trends in the field of librarianship with the purpose of orienting the reader toward a philosophy to which he or she can conscientiously subscribe and, in turn, make this book more meaningful. Chapter 2 explores the systems approach, so essential to the organized growth of the present-day library. Chapters 3 and 4 discuss the use of selection aids as invaluable tools and their use in the construction of bibliographies. Chapters 5–14 examine the various media found in libraries with an emphasis on identification and application, as well as developing criteria for selection and evaluation. Chapter 14 on book selection presents a basic overview of the book medium and is included to achieve completeness in the coverage of the multimedia library. Chapter 15 studies the role of the learning center as part of the library's function. The local production of materials is covered in Chapter 16 since many libraries want to become involved in making some of their own special materials to better service patrons' needs. Chapter 17 takes into account that being aware of the properties of various communication media is beneficial only if applied to selecting the proper medium for a particular task. Finally, I have presented extensive bibliographies at the end of most chapters for further reading.

I sincerely hope that this book efficiently and effectively enlightens the reader in the area of selecting materials for the multimedia library.

Acknowledgments

I wish to recognize Mrs. Mildred Chatton, with whom I team-teach a selection of materials librarianship course at San Jose State University, and whose critical comments have been invaluable to me in the arduous construction of this book. Also, I wish to thank Daryle Webb for his assistance in the design of the graphics appearing in this book and Sharon McCann for her skill and contribution with the photography. And special thanks to my wife, Helen, and my sons, Steven, Chris, and Brian, who provided the moral support so necessary in accomplishing this task.

1

Trends, Present and Future

Implication of Trends

"Change Is the Only Constant"

It is essential for the professional librarian to be able to identify with the institution—the library—where he or she dedicates a career to the performance of library service. He or she must know that the field of librarianship is not now, never was, nor ever will be in any kind of steady state. The profession is an extremely important entity within an ever-changing society and must be responsive to its needs. The librarian must realize that the library itself is in a constant state of metamorphosis. Oftentimes change and innovation in the library occurs almost imperceptibly, and as a result trends too often are assimilated but not appreciated. Frequently the librarian is aware only of the present time frame, the here and now. Such a myopic perspective tends to obfuscate the fact that the library of even the recent past was not what the library is today, and obviously the library of the future will be quite different from what it is today. Given these circumstances, it would clearly be valuable for the librarian to take the time and effort to analyze the phenomenon of change in the library and the demands it places on the library profession.

Perhaps one of the best ways to analyze current and future library trends is to put them on some kind of time-line continuum that includes not only present and future but the past as well. If we took the time to identify library changes since World War II, it would become apparent

1

that changes have occurred in both degree and kind. Often we are so busy with day-to-day operations that we fail to see change taking place. Unfortunately, with such a narrow time perspective we are not cognizant of the changes that have been assimilated, and we are hasty to criticize the library as an antiquated book museum that has not changed in over a century. Such criticisms are unwarranted, and worse, the people making them are neither aware of nor ready for future changes. As librarians, we need to examine carefully our own philosophy and decide whether we are going to be in the vanguard making changes or in a position further back adapting to change. Either way, the process is irreversible; changes have taken place and will continue to take place.

Ancient Carthage had a library of scrolls; the medieval monks had libraries of hand-written manuscripts. In the fifteenth century, Johann Gutenberg invented movable type and thus ushered in the era of mechanical printing, and a relatively short time later in 1658, John Amos Comenius published his *Orbus Pictus,* considered to be the first illustrated textbook. As time progressed, more efficient methods of printing, the advent of photography, and the use of color resulted in more, better, and less expensive books. In an examination of changes since World War II, we find libraries providing information in many different media: Libraries now circulate books (both hardcover and paperback), microform, art prints, periodicals, disc records, audiotapes, games and simulations, motion picture films, slides, filmstrips, models, realia, animals, and minerals. With the exception of four or five of the items listed, none were even available in libraries prior to 1945. Currently, we are beginning to witness the introduction of videotapes and computer terminals into the repertory of services provided. This extremely abbreviated chronology obviates the need for librarians to defend their institutions on charges of being static and archaic. Instead, emphasis needs to be placed on how to accommodate for change.

What is needed is an examination of the basic social and technological factors that are affecting our lives and in turn affecting the services provided by libraries. There is a constant shift in American demographic patterns; the shift from rural to urban to suburban living. Currently, some futurists are predicting a reverse change from suburban back to large metropolitan or megalopolitan living. Educational attainment, which vitally affects a person's need for and attitude toward libraries, is continually expanding. Earlier retirements are generating a group no longer in the labor pool but still mentally and physically active and desirous of more education. A new awareness of the symbiotic relationship between man and his environment is changing attitudes toward the exploitation of nature for personal profit. The future may find man concerned not with the puritan work ethic but rather with a communal effort toward group preservation. Financial status may no longer be the determinant of social rank, leading to a reduction of gaps between the current socioeconomic levels of American society. The family unit is undergoing change as well: The nuclear family is replacing the extended family; while at the same time people are living longer, entering the labor market later, and leaving it earlier. The country is presently experiencing an erosion of the control traditionally ascribed to family and religion. Social, moral, and religious mores are experiencing accelerated and sometimes traumatic changes. These are only some of the more visible societal changes taking place, but they are not the only arbiter of change.

Concomitant to social change is technological change. American society is rapidly evolving from the industrial, machine age to the era of electronics. There is a continuing logarithmic increase in the use of cybernetics. It is astounding to ponder that in less than three-quarters of the twentieth century man was able to proceed from the first heavier-than-air flight to walking on the moon. Not as dramatic, but perhaps more important, is the progress in medicine and health care. Many of the killer epidemics that plagued man are today virtually nonexistent, an achievement not without price. The world, for the first time, is faced with the critical problem of global overpopulation, which generates a whole new set of survival problems. We are now witnessing the emergence of genetic control and manipulation, biochemical regulation of the brain and intellect.

We are immersed in the epoch of electronic communication which is changing the concept of the library's role in society. Television as a form of mass communication has resulted in a decline in person-to-person communication, which will be further reduced by electronic information display devices used for one-to-one, man–machine communication. This access to electronic communication implies a myriad of both advantages and problems. Accumulated information available to man is presently doubling every 12 years, and it is projected that by 2000 it will be doubling in 1 year's time. This vast storehouse of information can be handled electronically, but some group will be responsible for its management. Librarians are the obvious choice for this task, and the responsibility and its inherent power are awesome. The librarian in a management capacity will have influence on the type of information produced and control of its selection, storage, retrieval, and discard. Information control requirements will require the librarian to be a finely trained information technologist. Being in control of this vast amount of information, the librarian will be required to perform greater service. The librarian must assist society by maintaining and supplying whatever information is needed. But who is to decide what is needed? This requires that the librarian be a skilled, responsive humanist able to assess individual needs and reply with the information that serves mankind. The problem of verbal illiteracy will be replaced by a demand for a higher and more efficient communication literacy. The librarian technologist will keep information available for all of society; the librarian humanist will prescribe it to the benefit of the individual.

Types of Materials Circulated

Having established that libraries are in a state of continual change within a changing society, it would be appropriate to examine more closely the changes taking place in the materials circulated. It is in the area of materials and material selection that the library justifies its existence, for if the materials selected are not the best that can be provided and are not in demand or needed by patrons, then the library becomes a warehouse of unneeded, unwanted information. Added to this is the concern that whatever acquisitions are made must prove to be economically valid.

There is much academic discussion as to whether the prime function of the library is to be a conservator or a disseminator of information about civilization. This book supports the latter position. If the library were only a conservator, then all information would best be acquired on some type of microform and stored in a safe place. But of what use is information if it can not be disseminated in its most appropriate media? Such information needs to be used effectively and efficiently. For this reason, the librarian needs to be aware of the various forms, how they are disseminated, and how they best serve a particular information need. An examination of the types of materials currently being circulated by libraries provides vivid evidence that change is taking place. Furthermore, some of the newer media forms being acquired are a positive indication that what is happening is not for the sole purpose of keeping the library modern, for if this indeed were the case, then libraries would only take collections of these newer media forms. The truth of the matter is that some of the newer forms provide a valuable service and holdings in many of these areas are growing as fast as, if not faster than holdings in the book area. An examination of some of the newer media will give an idea of the unique characteristics that make them popular and justify their selection.

A tremendous growth in the acquisition of paperback books is an indication of wise selection. With the advent of the paperback, the library can take advantage of what it offers. Being considerably less expensive than a hardcover book, a paperback is an ideal medium for acquiring a book of transient value. Not only will the book be in demand for a relatively short time span, but multiple copies can be inexpensively purchased if the demand is great. Also, with the proliferation of books being published, more titles can be purchased in paperback form. The lower price of paperbacks, however, does not give the librarian license to buy haphazardly. If the material is not being used, regardless of cost, its acquisition cannot be justified.

Microforms are becoming more prevalent in libraries, but here the librarian must consider a machine system that makes the information available in a readable form. When microforms were first acquired by libraries, it was done with the rationale that they resulted in tremendous savings in space. Now it is being realized that there are other benefits. The savings in binding costs of periodicals is considerable; and perhaps even more important, the microform is an inexpensive medium in which to acquire copies of printed matter in their original form. Also available in microform are books printed in the eighteenth century or earlier which would otherwise be quite expensive (if indeed they were even available for purchase); microform helps to make them both available and economically affordable.

New techniques in photocopying make it practical for libraries now to distribute art prints. The high reproduction quality of art prints is indeed admirable—and appreciated by the patron.

Improvements in the fidelity of audio recordings, on both disc record and magnetic tape, have resulted in an increase demand for information in this format. It is exceptional to find an American home, especially one with teenage children, that has neither a record player nor a tape recorder. The librarian needs to be aware of the demand for information in an audio format and of exactly what kind of audio information needs to be made available.

Packaged games and simulations have opened a whole new vista in information processing. They are becoming extremely popular as group learning and group experiencing activities. Games and simulations require active participation, for not only are the users acquiring information but they are emotionally relating to it as well.

The enormous growth of (and reliance on) visual literacy is resulting in a population that has a preference for the picture over the printed word. The librarian must be skilled in evaluating visual media and ascertain their communication effectiveness. Knowledge of how and under what circumstances the material will be used will determine whether it should be in print, slide, filmstrip, or motion picture form.

Models, maps (in many forms), and realia are also being acquired as a means of providing information in the best form possible. Again, the librarian must bear in mind that the criterion for determining the best format is that the item is being used by the patron.

Electronic information in the embodiment of the computer and television is making its appearance in the library. It is opening a new era of information service, evidencing a need for a whole new set of media selection skills.

These various media, their introduction, growth, and use by the library, are prima facie evidence that the library is in a state of metamorphosis. It is essential to remember that today's library patron is continually exposed to a wide variety of communication media forms and selects those he personally considers best for any particular information need; therefore, the librarian must select and have available those media that best serve those needs.

Trends in Library Service

Concomitant with the types of materials provided by the library are the services it provides. Here is another indication that the library is not a static institution. Because many of the newer materials require some type of device to gain access to their information (e.g., to listen to a disc record requires a record player), the library provides a service by having the necessary equipment available either for loan or for use in the library. This means that the library is now a facility that provides the properly designed space for using the new media. No longer are there just tables for reading; now we see the learning center concept where the patron can use a whole array of media in an ideally designed environment. Private spaces for individual or group use are becoming prevalent.

A library provides a vast array of community information services in a wide assortment of dissemination forms. Mobile and branch libraries are now accepted forms of service. Among other services provided by the library are booktalks to stimulate patrons into reading the best books, story hours for children to help explore the world of literature, interviews with authors to help appreciate works of literature, discussions and debates on popular issues to support free and critical inquiry, community bulletin boards to inform the public of items of general interest, reference services to aid in the dissemination of information, public service displays to advertise information about the community, film festivals to appreciate film as an art form, and art shows to foster cultural growth.

Cable television is making its appearance as a library service. Many of the services listed in the preceding paragraphs can be transmitted via cable television directly into the homes and businesses of the library service area. The ever-growing electronic refinements in television, with the use of such exotic devices as laser beams and holography, will generate a still greater expansion of library services. Eventually the library will be able to transmit, via television, information requested by individual subscribers. It is anticipated that such service will be common before the end of this century, i.e., within the next 2 decades.

In summary, the library is capable of providing just about any type of information service in any media format currently available in a technological society. This is not to imply that the library is the community's temple of omniscience. Rather, in concert with educational institutions, mass communication institutions, and centers of entertainment, a community has access to veritably all the information in the treasury of mankind. It is for the librarian, by the judicious accession and distribution of information, to provide the information services needed by the community and best obtained from a library. Such a task can only be accomplished by a highly skilled professional librarian.

Impact of Electronic Technology

Possibly the greatest change to occur in libraries is presently on the horizon of information science. It is conceivable that in the near future (i.e., within 20 years) libraries will be interconnected with a vast electronic information network. Electronic devices in local libraries will have direct and immediate access to information stored in regional, national, and international centers. This information will be retreivable and transmittable directly to the patron's home or place of employment. Furthermore, this information will be reproduced on a cathode ray tube (CRT) or in some form of hard copy, e.g., paper, videodisc, or microform.

The patron's access to the entire world's storehouse of information will be attained via the local library. Libraries will be responsible for analyzing requests for information and having the expertise to interpret them by using a man–machine interface system as a means of retrieving the exact information needed. This task cannot be performed by the unskilled patron, as it requires knowledge in the operation and efficient use of information systems.

Retrieving electronically stored information will be only part of the library profession's task. It will also include determining what data are to be entered into the information bank, what media format it is to be committed; what, if any, information is to be rejected or discarded. The system will include a feedback loop whereby there will be a two-way flow of information between the smallest library and the largest information bank. Obviously such a system will involve a highly sophisticated electronic network managed by capably trained professionals. Incidentally, these systems are not in scientists minds—presently they are leaving the laboratory, and early prototypes are being field tested.

It is difficult to comprehend the impact electronic technology is having and will continue to have on the library. The library could become the manager of all of mankind's recorded information worthy of being preserved, able to make it directly accessible on demand to any patron anywhere.

Although there will be many stages or plateaus of development prior to the realization of the ultimate electronic information bank, to say that such a phenomenon is unrealistic is to deny what is currently happening. The library has always been changing, although at times the changes seem imperceptible, but libraries are presently using sophisticated forms of television, and computer terminals are being installed in increasing numbers. The time has long passed when a library can accept or reject the idea of incorporating newer types of media into its repertory of services; rather a situation exists wherein the library must plan on how soon and to what degree it can provide all the information services demanded by society.

Adaptable Philosophy for the Present and Future

Every librarian, whether new to the profession or enjoying many years of service. should take time to postulate a philosophy and periodically evaluate it in order to determine if it is still providing the guidelines for fulfilling professional goals. Actually, there is no one best philosophy for the librarian, for in the final analysis, "best" is measured by its usefulness in attaining goals. Perhaps at this point it would be beneficial to stop reading this text-book and prepare a written statement of your personal philosophy for being a librarian. Can you work with your philosophy? Can you derive daily work goals and objectives from it? Is it a true statement? Can you defend it? Does it make a genuine contribution to the profession? Finally, is your philosophy compatible with the particular institution by which you are employed or from which you are seeking employment?

Too often librarians and other professionals as well perform their professionel obligations without concern for a philosophy or perhaps reflect a philosophy formulated by someone else that may provide little or no guidance for achieving personal professional goals. The librarian must be aware of how society is functioning. investigate the needs of the particular community in which he or she functions, know the goals of his or her particular library, and do a critical, introspective analysis of himself as a person and librarian.

This entire chapter has been devoted to present and future trends in the library. It has irrefutably stated that the library is a dynamic, evolving institution involved with change within a changing society. Granted the rate of change varies among libraries, the librarian must nevertheless ask, "How well do I cope with change?" Some people are always eager to adopt every new innovation that arrives on the scene; others prefer adhering to the "tried and true." Obviously such a statement is dichotomous; but regarding it as a continuum with innovation on one end and tradition at the other, place your own philosophy and that of your institution on it and see if this is where you feel they both belong (Figure 1.1). Bear in mind that this is not a "goodness" measurement, it is only an objective examination. All media, regardless of whether they have been around for centuries or are new, exotic, and futuristic, must meet the criterion of being the best means of serving the patron's needs. The printed book is not about to, and perhaps never will, disappear from the library; it is much too valuable, for it contains a treasury of information and enjoyment unobtainable in any other form. However, there is an ever growing demand for information in other media that cannot be overlooked.

In formulating or reviewing your philosophy, you will find other continua that can be objectively used (Figure 1.1). Where would you place yourself as regards being a technologist or humanist? Do you think that the library should direct society or serve it? Grant that directing and

Innovator	. . . . Traditionalist
Technologist	. . . . Humanist
Direct society	. . . . Serve society
Provide all that is available	. . . . Provide best that is available
Specialist	. . . . Generalist

Figure 1.1. Philosophical analysis continua.

serving society are both honorable endeavors, but ask yourself truthfully where you would place yourself on this continuum. Should the librarian in selecting materials provide the patron with everything available for a particular need, or should only the best materials be provided? Do you perceive yourself, on the basis of your training, ability, and attitude, as a highly skilled, narrow specialist or as a competent, broad generalist?

Your philosophy must measure up to or even exceed your professional goals. The library is a mainstay of society and must be in the control of people who can guide its destiny. There is an ever growing reliance on the library as the institution for preserving all information and making it available on demand. The growth of the library parallels society's ability to generate new information. The Library of Congress has over 336 miles of shelves and is still growing. The librarian is responsible for analyzing the needs of society as regards information and having a philosophy that allows for the design and implementation of a complete information system. It is both a difficult and a delicate task. It can only be delegated to the type of leadership that knows precisely where it is going—and how it is going to get there.

Selected Bibliography

Application of Automation in American Libraries. Peoria, Ill: Library Automation Research Consulting Associates, 1970.

Asheim, L., ed. *Library Manpower, Needs and Utilization*. Chicago: American Library Association, 1967.

Atkinson, F. *Librarianship: An Introduction to the Profession*. Hamden, Conn.: Shoestring Press, 1974.

Benge, R. *Libraries and Cultural Change*. Hamden, Conn.: Shoestring Press, 1970.

Buckland, M. K. *Book Availability and Library User*. Elmsford, N.Y.: Pergamon Press, 1975.

Carey, R. J. *Library Guiding: A Program for Exploiting Library Resources*. Hamden, Conn.: Shoestring Press, 1974.

Chandler, G. *Libraries in the Modern World, 2d ed*. Elmsford, N.Y.: Pergamon Press, 1965.

Dougherty, R. M., and Blomquist, L. *Improving Access to Library Resources*. Metuchen, N.J.: Scarecrow Press, 1974.

Enright, B. J. *New Media and the Library in Education*. Hamden, Conn.: Shoestring Press, 1972.

Ford, S. *Acquisition of Library Materials*. Chicago: American Library Association, 1973.

Garrison, G. *Total Community Library Service*. Chicago: American Library Association, 1973.

Goldstein, H. *The Changing Environment for Library Services in Metropolitan Areas.* Champaign: University of Illinois Library Science, 1966.

Grove, P. S. *Nonprint Media in Academic Libraries.* Chicago: American Library Association, 1975.

Heiliger, E. M., and Henderson, P. B. *Library Automation: Experience, Methodology and Technology of the Library as an Information System.* New York: McGraw-Hill, 1971.

Hicks, W., and Tillin, A. M. *Developing Multi-Media Libraries.* Ann Arbor, Mich.: R. R. Bowker, 1970.

Immelman, R. F. *Libraries and People.* Mystic, Conn.: Lawrence Verry, 1970.

Kies, C. *Problems in Library Public Relations.* Ann Arbor, Mich.: R. R. Bowker, 1974.

Kimber, R. T. *Automation in Libraries.* 2d ed. Elmsford, N.Y.: Pergamon Press, 1974.

Kujoth, J. *Libraries, Readers and Book Selection.* Metuchen, N.J.: Scarecrow Press, 1969.

Sanders, N. P., and Patrinostro, F. S., *Survey of Automated Activities in the Libraries of the World.* Peoria, Ill.: Library Automation Research Consulting Associates, 1971.

Shaffer, D. E. *Creativity for Librarians: A Management Guide to Encourage Creative Thinking.* Salem, Ohio: D. E. Shaffer, 1973.

Stone, Elizabeth W., ed. *New Directions in Staff Development.* Chicago: American Library Association, 1971.

Voight, M. J., ed. *Advances in Librarianship.* New York: Academic Press, 1974.

Wallace, S. L. *So You Want To Be A Librarian.* New York: Harper & Row, 1963.

Wasserman, P. *The New Librarianship: A Challenge for Change.* Ann Arbor, Mich.: R. R. Bowker, 1972.

Wheatley, Henry B. *How To Form A Library.* Folcroft, Pa.: Folcroft Library Editions, 1973.

2

Systems Approach to Selecting Materials

Need for a System of Media Selection

It is inadequate for the librarian to think that books, even though they are presently the mainstay of a collection, should receive prime acquisition consideration and that all other media should therefore be subservient. Selecting any one medium for acquisition is in itself a complete task if done properly, but when an entire range of media are involved, doing the task successfully can become all but impossible. It does not suffice for the librarian to assume that selection of media can be achieved by some subjective inner feeling for what a library should acquire. Attention must be given to a host of variables. The librarian must know all the intricate characteristics of the various media and how well they fulfill the library patron's needs. Cost-effectiveness factors must be considered. Availability of information from all sources has to be analyzed. The means by which the media are utilized is also an important factor. Finally, a decision on what is to be selected must be predicated upon how it affects the library's program. To do all these tasks requires an orderly procedure of investigation and furthermore a procedure that functions efficiently.

The problem confronting the librarian is to develop a procedure for materials selection that can be performed objectively, functions clearly for all involved, and results in the building of a well-balanced collection. When it comes to selecting various media, their interrelationships must be assessed. A particular kind of information might be available in a host of media, but the challenge is to select those that best serve the library collection. A book can be used conveniently by an individual and is quite durable; a paperback book containing the same information is less durable but also less expensive. A motion picture film, on the other hand, though more expensive has the advantage of sound, color, and motion and can be used with large audiences, but a motion picture requires projection equipment to make its information accessible. However, if motion is not vital to presenting a certain kind of information, then a sound filmstrip should perhaps be chosen in favor of a motion picture film. But again the problem remains as to how the librarian is to proceed to perform selection responsibilities time and again with accurate dispatch. Actually, what is needed is some method or system whereby the task of material selection is a formalized procedure. The formulation of such a procedure must be based upon the library's philosophy as to its reason for selecting information and also must reflect the policy of the institution. To perform these functions successfully, the librarian must have an operational knowledge of the systems approach or systems analysis.

Advantages of a Systems Approach

A systems approach is an activity involving the orderly, scientific analysis of all the components that can be identified with a functioning entity or contribute to its maintenance. This entity, or system, can be as microscopic as the electron or as macroscopic as the entire universe. *The American Heritage Dictionary of the English Language* (1976) defines a system as "a group of interacting, interrelated, or interdependent elements forming or regarded as forming a collective entity." Specialists involved in using the systems approach as a scientific method identify their activity with a host of synonyms. It is called systems analysis, operations research, operations analysis, systems evaluation, operations evaluation, systems research, and management science. Regardless of the synonym used, the function remains the same—the scientific investigation of the functioning of a system.

The systems approach is a worthwhile endeavor, for in any system the conduct of any element invariably has an effect on every other element and on the system as a whole. Some elements may be so insignificant that detecting their effect on the system is difficult, but a sufficient quantity of them could ultimately have a profound effect on the efficiency of the system. By using a systems approach, one initiates a systematic search for identifying and assessing significant interactions of the multitudinous variables that effect the entire system.

The scientific method requires that each discrete component or procedure in the system be identified, its purpose described, and its contribution evaluated. Alternative components or procedures are considered in an effort to evolve the most efficient system possible. The task of systems analysis involves: (1) formulating the problem; (2) constructing a model, formula, or equation; (3) deriving a solution; (4) predicting the impact of the solution (in solutions involving several alternatives, they are individually evaluated as to their consequences to the system); (5) simulating the solution(s) on a model of the system; (6) analyzing results; (7) making recommendation of course(s) of action; (8) evaluating the effect on the system.

The systems approach is worth the time and effort, for too often when a problem exists those responsible either become oblivious to it or assume the obvious and miss the subtleties causing the problem. Too often the problem is not obvious, rather it is an array of complex subtleties, hence a heuristic approach is used to help discover precisely what is happening. The librarian using the scientific method afforded by systems analysis no longer has to rely solely on subjective judgment in determining solutions to problems. Rather, decisions can be made based on empirical evidence accumulated by identifying, isolating, and testing every facet of the problem. It is a comprehensive approach that considers all the interrelated factors and generates results that are objective, quantifiable, and measurable.

The Systems Approach Applied to Library Operations

Because the systems approach is an orderly, scientific method of analyzing the components of any system, it can certainly contribute to improving the efficiency of a library operation. Before we proceed to its application to the library, a word of caution is warranted. Too often people doing initial reading on the systems approach treat the term as a euphemism for practical thinking. They claim that when a problem arises in the library it is discussed, thought, and resolved and that the discussing and thinking are essentially a systems approach. Such a simplification could not be further from the truth; indeed it is for just such reasons that a systems approach is needed. The systems approach is a research and development tool that can help improve library operations. Furthermore, its application is not restricted to management of the library as a whole institution, but in fact is perhaps best at providing service when used with the myriad of components or subsystems within the library.

Libraries are perenially struggling with problems of shortages of funds, staff, space, facilities, and materials. These problems are further compounded by ever increasing demands for services both in kind and in degree, and they can no longer be resolved in a piecemeal fashion. The traditional method of resolving a problem as an isolated entity may yield only artificial results; it is analogous to attempting to cure symptoms without regarding the disease. It would be well for the entire library professional staff to be skilled in using the systems approach. In this way, all the subsystems are analyzed, and the results are resolved within the context of the larger system which they ultimately effect. In reality, every subsystem is a component of a larger system, which in turn is itself a subsystem of a still larger system. It is characteristic of a pyramid concept, with each layer supporting what is above it. Through the systems approach, not only is the subsystem itself analyzed, but its effect to the rest of the system is ascertained as well. An accrued benefit is also realized: Communications are greatly improved, for now the staff has better understanding of how their respective components function and how they relate to every other component within the system. No longer are subsystems competing for budget priorities, instead needs are determined by how well they contribute to the operations of the entire system.

The library as a system is becoming ever more complex. The individual library building is becoming more diversified with regard to materials and services. Coupled with this is the increasing trend for local libraries to function as part of a state library system, which is part of a national library, which is in turn a subsystem of an international library system. With the continuing astronomical accumulation of information and the use of electronic data banks for its control, the era of isolated operations is rapidly disappearing.

With the aid of the computer, programs are available to assist in systems design and research. The librarian unskilled in computer technology can still apply some of the computer processes in resolving smaller subsystem problems. Concern must be given to voids or duplication of materials, breakdowns of operations, and bottlenecks in service. Plotting these problems and analyzing their causes and resultant effects will help to remedy shortcomings in the subsystem. Although ideally, these problems can best be handled by computer, the library without one can begin to use systems procedures and prepare for the time when a computer becomes available. It is not that the library cannot function without the aid of a computer, it is just that the computer can process data much more efficiently.

As an introduction to the library as a system, it would be best to identify the types of services or functions it performs; next, to generate a list of activities necessary to perform these services and functions; and finally, to prepare procedures for conducting these activities. The procedures, activities, services, and functions are diagrammed for purposes of analysis and decision-making.

Using one library building as a point for originating the systems approach, one can proceed upward and investigate how the library contributes to a larger system; proceed laterally and examine its function as part of a regional network of libraries; or proceed downward and examine the subsystems that affect its operation. (See Figure 2.1.) It is suggested that the downward approach be the first area of investigation, for in the pyramid concept it is best to start at the bottom and work up. If each small component is doing the job properly, then there is an assurance that the entire system is generally healthy.

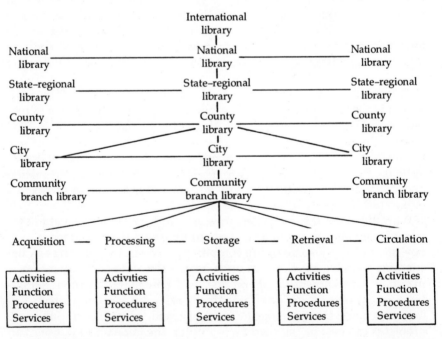

Figure 2.1. Diagram of a public library system (does not include interface with other types of libraries, i.e., academic, medical, industrial, private, etc.).

The library building as a system is responsible for administering to the information needs of a particular community. The major subsystems involved in achieving this objective are acquisition, processing, storage, retrieval, and circulation. Within these subsystems, other subsystems exists to the extent that some of them will appear in several subsystems. For the purpose of this discussion, we will examine only the area of acquisition, as the procedure for examining the other areas is basically the same.

Basic Flowcharting

To facilitate the process of synthesizing a procedure for selecting materials, the systems analyst uses the technique of flowcharting. Flowcharting is a process of diagramming all the procedures of a particular activity resulting in an easy to read, understandable visual display. It replaces the cumbersome, inefficient narrative procedure. All that is required of the user is an understanding of how to use some basic visual symbols.

The elements of the activity are diagrammed in a logical progression. The flow of activity can proceed either from top to bottom (vertical flow) or from left to right (horizontal flow) depending on the analyst's preference. Additional symbols are also used. Edward Chapman's *Library Systems Analysis Guidelines* (1970) treats flowcharting in greater detail and provides examples of greater complexity. However, with the basic symbols described in Figure 2.2, the reader has enough information to develop a primary flow chart.

Flowcharting does provide an orderly, disciplined approach to analyzing library procedural activities. It also provides an easy-to-read visual plotting that can be critically analyzed for any omissions or redundancies. Through its use, not only are existing procedures analyzed, but new procedures can be scrutinized prior to their implementation. New personnel in a library can follow flowcharts as a training aid or a checklist of the prescribed functions of an activity or procedure.

The novice to flowcharting may initially regard it as a cumbersome conglomeration of nonsensical doodles that poorly represent a schematic for intelligent, knowledgeable thinking. Perhaps this may be true, but even the most intelligent thinker must be able to communicate thought if it is to be of any benefit to the institution. The flowchart provides a most precise, both an efficient means of communication and a method for analyzing it. Examine Figure 2.2 and try to determine if the flowchart for selecting a film has any redundancies or omissions; examine it for ease of

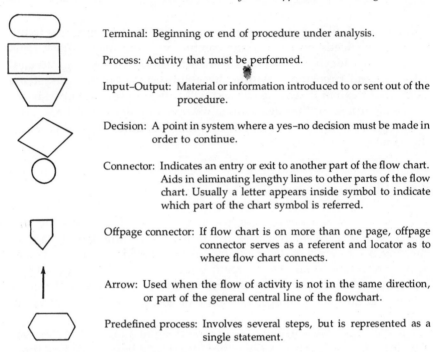

Terminal: Beginning or end of procedure under analysis.

Process: Activity that must be performed.

Input–Output: Material or information introduced to or sent out of the procedure.

Decision: A point in system where a yes–no decision must be made in order to continue.

Connector: Indicates an entry or exit to another part of the flow chart. Aids in eliminating lengthy lines to other parts of the flow chart. Usually a letter appears inside symbol to indicate which part of the chart symbol is referred.

Offpage connector: If flow chart is on more than one page, offpage connector serves as a referent and locator as to where flow chart connects.

Arrow: Used when the flow of activity is not in the same direction, or part of the general central line of the flowchart.

Predefined process: Involves several steps, but is represented as a single statement.

Figure 2.2.   Basic flow-chart symbols. (Data from Edward Chapman, *Library Systems Analysis Guidelines* © 1970, John Wiley & Sons, Inc., New York. Pp. 86–98.)

communication; consider whether if the same information were in verbal form only, it would be as easy to analyze; finally, examine it critically as to capability of defining a procedure in detail and providing a succinct decision-making process. Figure 2.3 is essentially a decision-making flowchart, similar charting can be done for workflow, organization of operations, time (clock–hour) procedures, and job function networks.

Selection of Multiple Media Forms

The major concerns in making the proper or best selection of information in a particular medium can be ascertained by making the following inquiries: (1) is the information suitable and presented in the best medium; (2) is the information in a medium that is best for the patron(s) who will be using it; (3) are facilities available, equipped, and needed to make the information accessible?

Determining which medium is best for a particular type of information requires that the characteristics of the information be carefully exam-

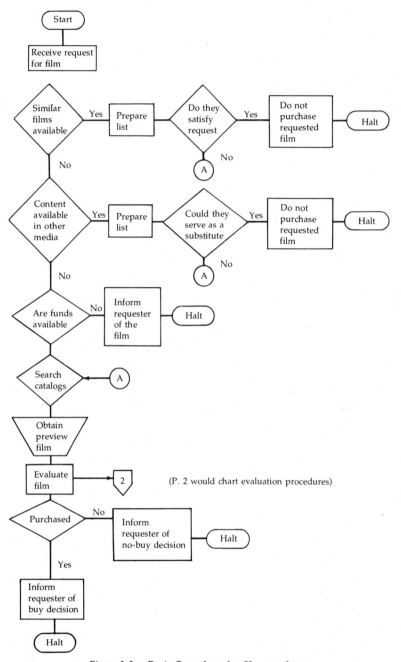

Figure 2.3. Basic flow chart for film purchase.

ined. An obvious example would be music, which is best presented in an audio form (audiotape or disc recording) in preference to motion picture or videotape formats. There are situations where different media have less subtle differences with regard to information content. Should a speech by a famous person be in printed form or audio form? Any decision regarding any kind of medium must be predicated on knowledge and not preference. The most beneficial method of making a determination would be to identify all the media formats applicable to a particular piece of information, list them in order of how well they present the information, and find if indeed the information is available in the forms identified. This task requires a knowledge of the characteristics of various communications media (see Chapter 17).

Having determined the best media and knowing their availability, the next step is to identify the various ways in which the patron(s) will most logically be using the information. It could be for independent use, small or large group use, cultural enrichment, entertainment, supplementary information, reference, research, or extensive study; the information may be used either inside or outside the library facility; the information, by virtue of format, could be of short- or long-term value (e.g., perhaps a film would be viewed only once by a particular patron whereas a book might be consulted on repeated occasions).

The final consideration in selecting a medium would be to examine how accessible it is to the patron. The library has a facility as well as a policy of how the facility is to be used that provides parameters to what media can be used and to what extent. A medium is of little use if it is inaccessible to the patron. A book is ready to use, but a film requires projection equipment. Conversely, a book can be read by only one person at a time, whereas a film can be viewed by one person or an audience of hundreds. Perhaps synonomous with accessibility is convenience of use, i.e., which medium would the patron prefer?

These three characteristics—suitability of medium, patron utilization, and accessability—are not investigated as discrete entities but rather are used as a means of examining all methods of determining which medium should ultimately be selected. This selection can best be achieved by developing a flowchart that provides a vehicle for logically, sequentially, and efficiently determining the merits of the various media being considered. The employing of flowchart techniques insures that the best decisions are made and that the selection process is accomplished by precise, thorough measurement. Because the emphasis in this textbook is on selection, greater stress is given to the use of systems analysis for acquiring materials; this is not, however, intended to negate the equally important areas of accessability and utilization. Ultimately, all the factors of selection, accessability, and utilization and their respective systems analysis are interfaced into an even larger system.

A Priori Considerations to Flowcharting

The flowcharting method developed earlier in this chapter introduced a procedure for selecting materials to make the selection process more accurate and efficient. It is also a method whereby any flaws or shortcomings can easily be detected and eliminated. In a situation involving the possible selection and consideration of more than one medium to satisfy an informational need, the process of flowchart analysis can make an enormous contribution. The flowchart will provide the valid visual proof necessary to substantiate a selection decision involving more than one medium.

When it has been determined that a need exists for information available in various media, the media can be processed through the flowchart to determine their contribution to the library collection. The procedure involves a flowchart for each type of medium. Incidentally, the media flow charts, once constructed, will be applicable in selection of a particular type of medium regardless of circumstance. In essence, the flowchart is a visual diagram of the library's selection policy, acquisition procedures, and utilization demands. Once it is prepared, flowchart revisions will be necessitated only if changes occur in the foregoing areas. The construction of flowcharts for each medium will be predicated upon well-defined criteria. Obviously, there will be a replication of many parts of the flowchart for all media, and indeed it is in the replicated areas that a one-to-one comparison can be made. In flowchart areas not replicated in other media flow charts, information is discovered regarding unique traits of a particular medium which further justifies its acceptance or rejection for acquisition.

Essentially, the flowchart for each medium will be of the criterion type whereby the areas of selection policy, acquisition procedures, and utilization demands can properly be analyzed. This is achieved by listing in sequence the criteria for each area as it applies to a particular medium and then plotting the criteria onto a flow chart. This can best be described by the following hypothetical example.

Cloverdale Library's Procedure for 16-mm Film Selection

A. Selection Policy

    1. Film should not be readily available from any other public institution (e.g., schools, local museum, etc.).

2. Film is not of the genre presented over broadcast television.
3. Film should culturally benefit library community.
4. Film should not cost more than 30 times the same type of information available in book form.
5. Film should not cost more than one-thirtieth of film budget.
6. Film must be requested or recommended by a patron and a librarian.
7. Film shall not be in an area representing more than 30% of library's current holdings.

B. Acquisition Procedures

1. All film titles pertaining or relevant to request must be listed.
2. Applicable titles shall be previewed.
3. Film evaluation committee must be unanimous in its decision to acquire the film.

C. Utilization Demands

1. Anticipated usage must be five times a year for a minimum of 5 years.
2. Must be applicable to an identifiable need of a particular community group that makes use of the library (e.g., elderly, hobbyists, vocational groups, etc.).

From these criteria, a flowchart can be generated that will attend to the various activities and processes necessary to select a film. Developing flowcharts for other media acquired by the library will result in a highly refined selection apparatus that is ready to assist in the selection process upon demand. When an information request is received for an item available in more than one form, it is subjected to the meticulous scrutiny of the flowchart. How well it survives the rigors of inspection will determine which medium is selected. It is possible to have a requested item accepted or rejected in all media available. Whatever the decision, it is justified upon a well-established, systematized selection process.

Selected Bibliography

Banathy, B. H. *A Systems View of Education*. Palo Alto, Calif.: Feavoy Press, 1973.
Boillot, M. H.; *Essentials of Flowcharting*. Dubuque, Iowa: Wm. C. Brown, 1975.
Benton, J. B. *Managing the Organizational Decision Process*. Lexington, Mass.: D. C. Heath, 1973.
Bingham, J. E., and Davies, G. W. *A Handbook of Systems Analysis*. New York: Halsted Press, 1973.
Chapin, N. *Flowcharts*, New York: Petroccili Books, 1971.
Chapman, E. A.; *Library Systems Analysis Guidelines*. New York: 1967.
Churchman, C. W. *Design of Inquiring Systems, Basic Concepts of Systems Analysis*. New York: Basic Books, 1972.
Cohen, L. J. *Operating System Analysis and Design*. Rochelle Park, N.J.: Hayden Book Co., 1971.
Coldicott, P. R. *Principles of Systems Analysis*. New York: Beekman, 1971.

Deutsch, R. *Systems Analysis Techniques.* Englewood Cliffs, N.J.: Prentice-Hall, 1969.

Elliot, R. E. *Problem Solving and Flowcharting.* Englewood Cliffs, N.J.: Reston Publishing Co., 1972.

Fitzgerald, J. M., and Fitzgerald, A. F. *The Fundamentals of Systems Analysis.* New York: John Wiley, 1973.

Lott, R. W. *Basic Systems Analysis.* Canfield Press, 1971.

McInerney, T. F., and Vallee, A. *Student's Guide to Flowcharting.* Englewood Cliffs, N.J.: Prentice-Hall, 1973.

Optner, S. L., ed. *Systems Analysis.* Baltimore: Penguin Books, 1973.

Ramo, S. *Cure for Chaos.* New York: David McKay, 1969.

Schriber, T. J. *Fundamentals of Flowcharting.* New York: John Wiley, 1969.

Vanduyn, J. *Practical Systems and Procedures Manual.* Englewood Cliffs, N.J.: Reston Publishing Co., 1975.

Wade, C. R., ed. *Introducing Systems and Control.* New York: McGraw-Hill, 1974.

Weinberg, G. M. *An Introduction to General Systems Thinking.* New York: John Wiley, 1975.

3

Selection Aids

Purpose of a Selection Aid

Whether employed in a professional or trade vocation, a person must have tools in order to perform properly. The lawyer without law books, the mechanic without wrenches would be rendered inoperative. Likewise, the librarian without reference tools would be unable to perform in a professional capacity. When deciding what materials will be in a library collection, the librarian must have access to a comprehensive set of tools referred to as selection aids.

Selction aids provide the necessary information as to what is available for the library collection, where it can be obtained, what it does, how well it does it, and its bibliographic characteristics, physical formats, and possible uses. Using parts or all of the information selection aids provided, the librarian can authoritatively select new materials and justify their inclusion in the library collection. Because of the huge proliferation of information in the world today, a growth that is increasing annually in logarithmic proportions, it is essential for the librarian to become an expert in using selection aids. If we consider that it took 1750 years to double the amount of information available at the birth of Christ, 150 years to double it again, only 60 years for the next doubling, and presently a short 12 years to double existing information, then we quickly realize that it is impossible, and perhaps unnecessary, for a library to acquire and house all the information generated. It is the selection aids that provide the best sources of information as to exactly what to acquire.

General Functions of Selection Aids

Knowing the various functions of selection aids facilitates categorizing them and provides the means whereby one has available the proper selection aid at the proper time. A selection aid, although primarily used for assisting in acquisition, also helps in locating sources of information. When used to their fullest potential, selection aids become primary locators of information, making them indispensable tools of the skilled librarian.

Selection aids perform the following general functions:

1. *Buying guide:* giving the cost of materials
2. *Reference tool:* to locate materials likely to contain information being sought
3. *Checklist:* to compare the completeness of a library collection to what is actually available
4. *Evaluate:* provides reviews and evaluations of material which give additional guidance in determining if it is what the librarian wants
5. *Precis:* provides content description
6. *Keeping abreast:* informs of new materials being produced
7. *Out of print:* informs of materials no longer being made
8. *Formats:* informs of the various formats, both print and nonprint, in which a particular item is available
9. *Categorization:* categorizes material for convenience in locating, by publisher, author, subject, age, suitability, medium, etc
10. *Indexing:* provides information on where an item is indexed

Obviously, there is no one selection aid capable of performing all these functions to the degree needed by each librarian. However, by having the right combination of selection aids, the librarian can have fingertip access to an astronomically large listing of sources of information. The proper combination can be achieved by performing an analytical evaluation of the selection aids acquired for your professional use. It is one thing to have the tools and know how to use them, but you must first know how valuable the tool is for your purposes.

Components to Be Examined When Evaluating a Selection Aid

Prior to evaluating a selection aid, you must determine what specific function you want it to serve. It is not fair to condemn a particular selection aid because it does not, for example, have complete bibliographical descriptions when indeed this is not its intended purpose. First, ascertain what information the aid claims to provide, and then evaluate how accurately, easily, thoroughly, and completely it is provided. Incidentally, it is for this reason that the librarian needs more than one selection aid tool; perhaps the evaluation should ascertain, when similar aids make identical claims, which one does the best job. If you have two similar selection tools and one is far superior to the other, then the poor one will never be used and would not have been acquired if properly evaluated. In evaluating selection aids, consider the adage: "If you can't use it—you don't need it."

Performing a systematic evaluation of selection aid components is essential. Never make prior assumptions; examine in detail those components you want included. The following components give an idea of what you should be evaluating in a selection aid; the degree to which it satisfies your particular need will determine its particular worth to you as a tool.

1. *Authorship:* Who selects entries? What are author's credentials? How does author select entries, e.g., uses committees, information from people in the field, etc.? Is there more than one author?

2. *Publication data:* Is the work new? How is it kept up to date? [Does it update by use of supplements, or does it produce entirely new editions?] Date first published? Are back issues available or necessary? What is the frequency of publication? Are new entries so indicated?

3. *Bibliographic entries:* Can list, author, title, edition, place, publisher, date, paging, volumes, illustrations, plates, portraits, maps, indexing, cost. Depending on the medium listings on nonprint materials would provide such information as color, black and white, speed, running time, format, captions, size and dimension, sound versus silent, etc.

4. *Scope and coverage:* What is the purpose of the selection aid? How wide is the range of subject matter included? To what type of library, information area, or patron is it applicable? How many different entires are listed? Does it include all materials available in a particular area, or does it only include those of a specific genre?

5. *Purpose:* What service is the selection aid suppose to provide? How well is the purpose achieved? Is the purpose expressly stated, and does it state parameters of coverage? Is the purpose too broad or too narrow? Is purpose consistent in the information it provides on each entry, and is it complete?

6. *Arrangement:* Is the information conveniently arranged for your purposes? Is the arrangement form dictionary, class, subject, age, or interest group? Are class numbers or LC card numbers given? Are index

tabs provided? Is any type of convenient color coding used, e.g., colored type or colored pages?

7. *Physical characteristics:* What is the type and quality of binding? Soft or hard cover? Quality and durability of paper? Is the layout of information consistent, orderly, and efficient to read? What about readability? Is the print large enough and easy to read; are devices such as bold type or italicized print used? If updated supplements are used, are they of the same quality as the original volume? Are the overall dimensions (size) of the selection aid practical?

8. *Uses:* How can it be used? As a buying guide? A reference tool? To construct bibliographies? As a primary resource? Can it be used to complement other selection aids? Who would use it; the acquisitions librarian, reference librarian, cataloger, or patron?

9. *Special features:* Does it contain articles of interest? Does it give procedures on how to locate information? Does it give suggestions on possible different ways it can be used? Does it contain advertisements? What kinds of indexing are used? Does it provide lists of suggested acquisitions? Does it use photographs or other graphic devices? Does it include actual passages from items it has selected?

10. *Cost:* Is the cost reasonable when compared to the price of similar selection aids? Are there discounts for multiple copies? Is the library required to purchase a subscription? Are replacement copies available, and if so, at what cost? Is it available in microform, and if so, at what cost?

All the foregoing considerations are helpful in determining and justifying the inclusion of a selection aid into your collection of professional tools. They also give assurance that you will have a valuable, useful selection aid.

Major Criteria Used in Comparing and Complementing Selection Aids

As previously described, the components of a selection aid can be assessed in determining its particular value to the librarian. Obviously, it is impossible for any one selection aid to be all things for all librarians; but the degree to which it satisfies your particular needs will determine its value. Being aware of what each component can contain, you should consider three major criteria when assessing how well a particular selection aid is suited to your requirements. Attention must be given to (1) completeness, (2) datedness, (3) evaluation.

Completeness

Once you have determined your needs, the first consideration will be that of completeness, which incidentally can have two different meanings. It can mean that an aid provides as much information as possible about a particular item, or it can mean that the aid lists every item available in a particular genre, topic, or area. The former characteristic is invaluable in investigating the merits of a particular item; the latter is indispensable as a locator. Here is obviously a situation where a combination of selection aids used in conjunction with each other, one for locating a particular item quickly and efficiently and the other to give detailed information about it, is ideal. Although it may be best to have both in combination, this often cannot be properly achieved: The proliferation of materials being produced daily would result in a rather large, unwieldly selection aid. Even selection aids published in multiple volumes ultimately reach a point of diminished returns. It becomes analogous to using an encyclopedia, i.e., exactly how much information do you really need at your fingertips.

Datedness

It is essential in selecting library materials that you be kept informed of current releases. The possibility always exists that what you are looking for is currently available in a more recent edition, a new revision, or even a whole new treatment. In the case of an item like a novel, of which the content obviously would not change, there may be recently released supplementary materials available (e.g., films, readings, etc.) that would greatly enhance the book. Also, being aware of what is recent, may lead you to modify what you are planning to acquire for your collection. At the opposite end of the datedness continuum is having selection aids of out-of-print materials which may now be available only in microform but nevertheless are available; the right selection aid is invaluable in locating an out-of-print item you may desperately need.

Evaluation

The third criterion to consider in selection aids is evaluation. Librarians are not omniscient about the different types of information a library may acquire; and even if they were, they would not have the time to preview all the materials available. Hence, the librarian must rely on evaluations to assist in acquisition. Evaluations vary greatly in scope: One can be nothing more than a simple annotation telling what the item is about; another can be a review conducted by a single critic; another an appraisal performed by a select group using some type of objective criteria; or still another can be a subjective evaluation performed by people from various walks of life and compiled by a central agency.

Regardless of what form the evaluation takes, it is essential to know the credentials of whomever is performing the evaluation. The evaluator's credentials are the best measure of the evaluation's validity and reliability. Furthermore, an evaluation should inform the user clearly, precisely, and succinctly. As an added feature, evaluations should have some type of uniformity. They should all be constructed in the same way so that the librarian does not have to decipher each evaluation as to format and approach.

Through the use of these three criteria—completeness, datedness, and evaluation—selection aids can be acquired that complement and enhance one other. All that is needed is for the librarian to develop the professional skills in utilizing them to their optimum potential. To this end, the librarian should continually ask, "Are the selection aids I am using keeping me completely informed in the most efficient way possible?" Ideally, it would be wonderful if the librarian could design his or her own unique selection aid format whereby only the exact information needed would be immediately accessible. Perhaps the day is not too far off when such information will be stored in a computer which will in turn not only provide the information needed but also make all the selections for any particular library. In the meantime, however, the librarian needs to have access to the right combination of selection aids which, in the hands of a knowledgeable professional, become the tools for doing an excellent job in the area of acquisitions.

Evaluation Grids for Examining Selection Aids

To determine which selection aids are needed for your particular task, a system should be devised that permits an easy, accurate analysis of any group, genre, or combination of selection aids. An easy method of achieving this is to construct grids that can be used to plot the values of selection aid characteristics being examined. Separate grids for completeness, datedness, and evaluation provide a graphic assessment. Furthermore, the grids, once completed, can be used in the future when different combinations of selection aids may be needed for different acquisition purposes. The result is having, in graphic form, an evaluation of all your selection aid tools which you can use for (1) determining what if any additional types of selection aids you may need; (2) assessing the strengths and weaknesses of selection aids; (3) deciding which combinations of selection aids are needed for a particular task; (4) providing a method of introducing a new librarian to the value and purpose of a particular selection aid; and (5) establishing a method of evaluating any new selection aids produced against your current selection aid holdings.

There are no particular standards for selection aid grids. Therefore, you must design a grid that best serves the needs of the particular library in which you are working. Because you are designing your own form, you may make it anything from a series of number values all the way to a plotting of subjective statements. The grid becomes a personal type of tool and should reflect whatever works best for you. The following are two different types of grids that it is hoped will give you that direction in constructing your own grid. (See grids 1 and 2.)

With this type of rating system, specific criteria are available for assessing a selection aid. It is for the librarian to determine which criteria should be assessed. Incidentally, if a selection aid should happen to score very low on a particular criterion, this would not be justification for rejecting, rather it would be an indication that another selection aid may be needed to complement it.

The overall rating gives the general value of the selection aid, but identical scores could very well have been achieved on entirely different criteria. The librarian may also assign a priori, a cut-off number on the overall rating, and any selection aid receiving an overall score below a particular assigned number would automatically be rejected.

Selection Aid Grid No. 2 (see pp. 32–33) provides space for comments that can be extremely helpful in ascertaining why a particular score was assigned to a feature of the selection aid. The last column, "Notes," provides space for comments that are perhaps not applicable to a particular criterion. This grid also involves a weighting system for use when it is determined that different aspects of a selection aid are not equally important. In the case of this grid, scope has a weighting of 5, but price a weighting of only 1. Computing the score for selection aid A you have $3 \times 5 = 15$ for scope; $4 \times 1 = 4$ for price; $2 \times 4 = 8$ for arrangement; $2 \times 3 = 6$ for annotation; and $4 \times 3 = 12$ for authorship—yielding a total score of 45 $(15 + 4 + 8 + 6 + 12 = 45)$.

Both grids achieve the same purpose, i.e., they provide a tool for assessing selection aids. Grid No. 1 uses a point system for each category with a possible maximum of 5 points. With this system it is possible to vary the point system so that a particular category would have a total of more than 5 points if indeed one category should have a higher point

General Selection Aid Grid No. 1

Selection aid	Scope	Arrangement of information	Special features	Treatment	Authorship	Format	Overall rating
A	5	4	3	3	4	5	24
B	5	3	5	5	5	5	28
C	2	3	0	2	4	1	12
D	3	4	4	2	5	3	20
Y	4	4	3	2	3	4	20
Z	3	5	4	5	5	3	25

Rating system: (Maximum points for any particular category = 5)

Scope:

1. Are the materials included relevant for library use?	1 point
2. Is the aid comprehensive enough to give the selector an adequate picture of what is available?	1 point
3. Are the materials listed recent enough to be useful?	1 point
4. Are materials in all different media listed?	1 point
5. Does the aid cover the necessary subject areas?	1 point

Arrangement of information:

1. Is information arranged concisely?	2 points
2. Is information cross-indexed?	2 points
3. Are easy symbolic devices used (e.g., stars, asterisks, etc.)?	1 point

Special features:

1. Does it contain informative, interesting articles?	1 point
2. Does it contain advertisements?	1 point
3. Does it give suggestions on methods of selecting?	2 points
4. Does it list special collections?	1 point

Treatment:

1. Does it provide enough information to justify acquisition?	1 point
2. Is bibliographic data complete?	2 points
3. Does it refer to other bibliographic sources?	1 point
4. Does it include footnoted information?	1 point

Authorship:

1. Are the authors reputable?	3 points
2. Are critical reviews signed?	1 point
3. Does aid use expertise of librarians in the field?	1 point

Format:

1. Is the aid easy to use and handle?	2 points
2. Print easy to read?	1 point
3. Is page layout convenient?	1 point
4. Is the binding and paper durable?	1 point

Selection Aid Grid for Selection Aids Dealing with Nonprint Materials, No. 2

Weighting	5^a	1	4	3	3		
Selection	Scope	Price	Arrangement	Annotation	Authorship	Score	Notes
A	Reviews hardware and software 3	$12/year 4	Index of reviews 2	Very little but complete 2	Official publication 4	45	
B	Reviews of all media. Directory of producers and distributors 5	$5.50 + subscribers. 5	Each medium appears in table of contents. Items arranged by 4	Reviews are critical. Give extensive information 5	All critical reviews are signed 5	76	Exceptionally good price. Print is too small
C	Reviews motion picture films only 2	$8/year 4	Poor table of contents 1	Description of most media not critical 2	Editorial board 2	30	

	Lists films only	$14. Has quarterly supplement	Arranged by curriculum subject and is cross-indexed by author, title	Descriptions too brief	Many consultants		Revised quarterly
D	1	5	4	2	5	47	
Y	All media extremely comprehensive 5	$150/5 volumes 1	Multiple listing with cross-references 5	No annotations. Simple line entry 1	Editorial board 2	55	Contains reference to primary aids for further information
Z	All media 5	$40/2 volumes 3	Confusing 0	No consistent format 1	Field editors 2	37	Reused yearly.

aWeighting range is from 1 low to 5 high.

value than another. Grid No. 2 achieves this result by assigning weighting values to each category. Either method achieves the same result, and you should use the type of grid that works best for you. As stated earlier, you should design your own unique grid; the two grids are presented here to give you an idea of the many possibilities.

Using selection aids properly is not a haphazard process of collecting all the selection aids available to have them at your disposal. Rather, it is a process of acquiring those needed for your particular professional application and knowing exactly what each is capable of doing. It must be remembered that selection aids are professional tools designed to assist the librarian in getting the job done accurately and efficiently and to provide the library with the materials it needs best to serve its patrons.

Selected Bibliography

Chisholm, M. M. *Media Indexes and Review Sources.* College Park: School of Library and Information Services, University of Maryland, 1972.

Cox, C. T. "Filmstrips: Selection, Evaluation, Cataloging, Processing." *Wilson Library Bulletin* 38:(Oct. 1963)178–182.

Easen, T. "A Selected Bibliography of A-V Media in Libraries." *Wilson Library Bulletin* 44:(Nov. 1969)312–319.

Grove, P. S., and Clement, E. G. *Bibliographic Control of Non-Print Media.* Chicago: American Library Association, 1972.

Lieberman, I. *A Working Bibliography of Commercially Available Audio-Visual Materials for the Teaching of Library Science.* Urbana: University of Illinois Graduate School of Library Science, 1968.

Meirhenry, W. C., *Mediated Teacher Education Resources.* Washington, D.C.: American Association of College for Teacher Education, 1970.

Molstad, J. A. *Sources of Information on Educational Media.* Washington, D.C.: U.S. Dept. of Health, Education and Welfare, 1963.

Multi-Media Reviews Index. Ann Arbor, Mich.: Pierian Press, 1970 and annual.

Perkins, R. *Book Selection Media.* Champaign, Ill.: National Council of Teachers of English, 1967.

Quinly, W. J. "Selection, Processing and Storage of Non-Print Materials: Aid, Indexes, Guidelines." *Library Trends*, 13:(April 1965)503–516.

Rufsvold, M. I., and Guss, C. "A Proposal Method for Establishing Bibliographic Control of the Newer Educational Media for the Purpose of Informing Teachers Concerning Available Materials and Their Educational Utility." Mimeographed. Bloomington: Indiana University, 1960.

Rufsvold, M. I., and Guss, C. *Guides to Educational Media.* 3rd ed. Chicago: American Library Association, 1971.

Selected List of Catalogs for Short Films and Filmstrips, New York: UNESCO, 1965.

Stone, C. W. "Development of Professional Tools for the Materials Center." *School Library as a Materials Center*, Washington, D.C.: U.S. Office of Education, 1963.

Tauber, M. F., and Lilley, O. L. "Feasibility Study Regarding the Establishment of an Educational Media Research Information Service." Mimeographed. New York: Columbia University, 1960.

Thomas, R. M., and Swartout, S. G. *Integrated Teaching Materials: How to Choose, Create, and Use Them.* New York: David McKay, 1963.

Wynar, B. S. *Introduction to Cataloging and Classification.* 3rd ed. Rochester: Libraries Unlimited, 1967.

4

Library Media: Developing Bibliographies

Major Categories of Media

Libraries are involved in a wide range of media, and the librarian needs to be aware of the various media categories. No longer can it suffice for materials to be classified simply as print or nonprint, or mediated or nonmediated. Classifying material as print or nonprint is ambiguous and not very helpful, print information can be found in many media, e.g., paper, microform, computer, videodisc. Mediated, as opposed to nonmediated indicates only whether or not it is necessary to have some device or piece of equipment to gain access to information, e.g., a book does not require any device whereas a film requires a piece of projection equipment. But with the proliferation of information available today it could well be that some information items are available in both mediated and nonmediated forms. A book can be available in a bound copy, or it can be available on microfilm. It is still a book, however; but in the latter form it requires the use of a microfilm reader in order to be read. Considering whether an item is mediated assists the librarian in a search. There would obviously be no need to search for a videotape if the library does not have access to videotape playback equipment.

The task of categorizing media appears to be quite simple, and indeed it is for the librarian who has a working knowledge of the various kinds of media and can categorically define how they are used. If you are requested to construct a bibliography in microform media only, then an awareness of the various microform formats would be critical in making intelligent selections. In fact, much of this book is devoted to an examination of the various media currently found in libraries.

The task of learning the various media categories is quite simple, and indeed most people are familiar with most of them as they are an integral part of their everyday lives. The benefit of such learning is realized when the library becomes involved in selection and needs to know what medium is best for a particular need or situation. The categories are not finite or closed, and it is possible that some information forms could be assigned to more than one category, but again knowing the various categories, the librarian will know what a particular medium does and how it can be used. The following list of 20 categories is based primarily on the physical characteristics of the items.

1. *Art Prints:* An art print would be either an original work of art (a painting) or a facsimile. It can be either framed or unframed. Being a work of art, an original can have any width or length and can possibly pose a storage problem for peculiar or odd-sized paintings. A reproduction on the other hand, can be available in the same size as the original or can be enlarged or reduced to a more manageable size, e.g., 20 × 24 inches. The value of art prints is basically twofold: They can be used for studying the styles and techniques of various artists, but where the general public is concerned they can be loaned out simply for esthetic appreciation. Patrons once accustomed to having art prints available in their own homes quite often become regular users of this type of library service. Some libraries integrate art prints into the picture file collection (Category 12); but if the art print collection is of any substantative size, it should be regarded as a specific category.

2. *Books:* Most books in libraries are *bound with hard covers;* however, *paperback* books are becoming more prevalent. *Reference* books, and more specifically *encyclopedias,* are generally available in hard cover. *Selection aids* are also available in book form, in both hard cover and paperback. Books are also classified as *fiction* or *nonfiction.* A more specific classification is a *textbook,* whose definition (depending on the situation) can become quite nebulus. Some librarians consider any book, even a novel, as a textbook if it is required reading and study for a particular course of instruction. Under a more specific definition, a *textbook* would be a book that investigates a particular area of study and organizes information in a concise format by which the reader can receive instruction and learn and verify information by virtue of its accuracy and authenticity. Quasi types of textbooks would be *dissertations* or *research papers* which, though

not primarily intended to instruct, do inform and provide scholarly information.

3. *Community resources:* Community resources include things available in or from the community and fall into two major areas: (1) Things in the community that cannot be brought to the library but must be seen on actual location and would be classified as *field trip items;* and (2) things from the community that can be brought into the library would be called *local realia* (see Category 12). A subarea or type would include *resource persons,* people available to the library who can make a contribution to a topic for which the librarian is preparing a bibliography.

4. *Computers:* Although it is unlikely that individual libraries will be housing their own computers, there is a growing number of computer terminals available to the library patron. The computer terminal is the means by which the user can introduce, obtain, and interact with information stored in a computer. Basically, the computer terminal looks like a combination typewriter and television screen. The keyboard is the channel whereby the user can communicate *to* the computer, and the plasma screen (which looks like a television tube) is the source from which the user gets information *from* the computer. The information appearing on the screen can be either print or graphic, and with some computer terminals there is a light-sensitive pen that the user can touch against the screen as a means of *responding* to information generated and presented by the computer. The computer terminal is also capable of producing hard copy, i.e., a paper printout of information supplied to it by both the user and the computer. Computer programs are now designed for use by the novice and require no experience whatever. The librarian's prime task is to select, or contribute to the selection of, programs that will be stored in the computer for patron use. Because of extreme ease of operation, the computer requires very little instruction on its use, and usually a few typewritten directions will suffice. Although this application is not a patron use, the computer can also be used to handle administrative and recordkeeping functions.

5. *Filmstrips.* These require viewing equipment. A filmstrip is a continuous strip of photographic film containing a series of still pictures intended to be viewed separately. They can be either *captioned* or *uncaptioned.* Filmstrips are predominantly available in a *35-mm half, single, or double frame format* (half frame and single frame are synonomous terms). Some companies now have filmstrips available in a *16-mm format.* On occasion, books are accompanied with *shortstrips* which are small filmstrips usually only 8 to 10 frames in length. *Sound filmstrips,* as the name indicates, are filmstrips accompanied with sound by either disc

record or audiotape (reel or cassette). A few years ago, a filmstrip was marketed with the sound information right on the filmstrip, but it never gained wide commercial acceptance.

6. *Kits:* A universally accepted definition of the term kit is lacking because producers of kits do not use the term the same way. It will have to suffice to say that a *kit* is a collection or package of two or more items on a particular topic. Therefore, if a producer packages two or more items and calls it a kit, it should be so classified. As an example, a producer will package several filmstrips and call it a kit, whereas another producer will call it a series. Usually a kit must be purchased as a complete unit, but a series of filmstrips can be purchased separately. Perhaps a true kit would be a *multimedia kit* which contains a variety of media (books, recording, filmstrips, guides, dittoes, etc.) or realia (coins, artifacts, minerals, etc.) dealing with a particular topic.

7. *Maps and charts:* A map or chart, for the purpose of definition, would be identified as a single, unbound, discrete item capable of being examined as a complete entity. Maps and charts vary in size from items that can be held in one hand to panels mounted on an entire wall. Maps are usually identified as to the *type of projection* (Mercator, polyconic, orthographic, equal area, polar, etc.) and *purpose* (political, geographic, topographic, demographic, vegetation, economic, etc.). Some maps are *made of paper* and can be folded when not in use; others have *cloth backing,* and are intended to be rolled when stored. Still other maps are *textured or three dimensional* and made of plastic. Charts could be *pictorial, diagrams, floor plans, blueprints, layouts,* or *flowcharts. Atlases,* in a true meaning, are books of maps and as such could be categorized as books. Also, *globes* can be considered to be maps, but in reality they are models of the earth, satellites, solar system, or stars.

8. *Microforms:* These require viewing equipment. Microforms characterize any information that has been reduced photographically and requires the use of some type of magnifying device to be made readable. Microforms are available in a whole hosts of formats, physical sizes, and degrees of magnification. Most common is *microfilm,* available in *reel* or *cartridge* and in *35-mm* or *16-mm* formats. Microfiche refers to microform available on sheets of film (3 × 5 inch, 4 × 6 inch, 5 × 7 inch, etc.). *Aperture cards* are computer cards containing pieces of microform (usually 35-mm microfilm). A *micro-opaque* card is an opaque piece of cardboard on which photographically printed information has been micrographically reduced. *Ultrafiche* is a microfiche with a very high micrographic reduction (50× to 210×).

9. *Motion pictures:* These require viewing and possibly listening

equipment. Although motion pictures are available in many formats, libraries are usually involved with *16-mm, super 8-mm,* and *standard or regular 8-mm formats.* (Commercial theatres use 35-mm, 70-mm, and 105-mm). Films are available as *silent* or with *sound tracks,* and the sound track is either *magnetic* or *optical.*

10. *Pamphlets:* The term *pamphlet* varies in definition among librarians, but generally one can be considered as an unbound work of one or more pieces of paper stapled together. Pamphlets usually provide information on topics of interest; and they are not intended to be exhaustive in their contents but rather to provide the reader with some specific information. Pamphlets vary in size from small *foldouts* to *stapled materials* printed in a variety of sizes.

11. *Periodicals.* Periodicals are not to be confused with pamphlets. Although in physical appearance they may look like some pamphlets, they are published on a regular or periodical basis; identified title; and classified by volume, issue, and date. It may be said that a periodical has continuity. Incidentally, accumulated periodicals can be bound, and many of them are available in microform.

12. *Pictures:* Pictures differ from maps and charts in that they are either photographs of objects or works of art that are drawn or painted. Pictures are available as photographs, various kinds of graphics, and illustrations. A librarian can inexpensively build a fine collection of pictures by clipping pictures out of discarded publications. Oftentimes these clipped visuals can be mounted on cardboard giving them quality worthy of display. The end product of this effort of clipping, mounting, and gathering various kinds of pictures will be a picture file which, when continually developed and built upon, will become a compendium of visuals used for study, the development of visual statements or stories, or pure esthetic appreciation. This is best exemplified by the compilation of pictures for use as study prints accompanied by textual explanatory materials on the subject. This is somewhat different from using art prints (Category 1)—(original art or reproductions, framed or unframed) for circulation to patrons for display and appreciation in their own homes.

13. *Programmed instruction:* This may require equipment. Programmed instruction includes those materials designed to instruct the learner in a prescribed sequence of (1) stimulus (giving information), (2) response (providing the learner an opportunity to answer or respond), and (3) reinforcement (giving the learner immediate feedback on his responses). Programmed instruction can be either of the *linear* or of the *branching* type either available in *linear texts* and *scramble texts* for use in *teaching machines,* or set up for use in *computers.* Programmed instruction

can be subcategorized as anything from a book to a host of media, both print and nonprint.

14. *Real things and models:* Real things and models cover a multitude of materials and can vary in size from very small to extremely large. Real things, also called *realia,* include items such as *live animals, animal specimens, minerals, plants, manufactured items,* and *works of art.* A model, on the other hand, is a representation of a real thing that has been enlarged or reduced, a cutaway or cross-section simplified or modified for easier viewing or understanding, or even a *replica blowup, miniaturization,* or *diorama.* A replica, of course, in some cases could be classified as a real thing.

15. *Recordings (audiotape):* These require listening equipment. Audiotapes are available in various speeds identified in inches per second (ips). The common commercial speeds are 1⅞, 3¾, and 7½ ips. Tapes are available in *open reel, cassette,* or *cartridge* formats. Recordings can be *monaural, stereophonic,* or *quadraphonic.* The major types of information found on recordings are *music, storytelling, reading, speeches, recitals,* and *sound effects.*

16. *Recordings (disc):* These require listening equipment. Disc recordings are available in various speeds or revolutions per minute (rpm). The speeds are 16⅔, 33⅓, 45, and 78 rpm. The 16⅔-rpm record is called a transcription, and 78-rpm recordings are obsolete and no longer in production. Information found on disc recordings is of basically the same type as that found on audiotape recordings. Recordings can be *monaural, stereophonic,* or *quadraphonic.*

17. *Recordings (videotape):* These require viewing and listening equipment. Videotape recordings are becoming more available to libraries. Libraries favor the *helical scan* format to the *quadruplex* format because helical scan equipment costs a fraction of the quadriplex equipment. Videotapes are available in *open reel* or *cassette* and range from ¼ to 2 inches in width. Recent developments have been made with videodiscs, and they will soon be available in libraries. Videotape programs can be purchased commercially or produced locally.

18. *Simulations and games:* Simulations and games are being packaged to provide the patron with a wide range of learning and recreatory activities. They can be as simple as a printed scenario, as complex as boxes with playing boards, counters, dice, spinning discs, etc. Simulations and games are intended to provide active participant behavior.

19. *Slides (photographic):* These require viewing equipment. Slides differ from filmstrips in that they are mounted individual photographs and not placed on one continuous piece of film. In this way, they can be rearranged, augmented, and deleted. The prevalent size is 2 × 2 inches,

which is a measurement of the entire slide including the mount. Greatest use of slides is in the area of *local production* and the *visual arts* (art, architecture, sculpture, etc.).

20. *Transparencies (overhead):* These require viewing equipment. Overhead transparencies are used extensively in education. They are usually mounted on 10¼- × 11¾-inch frames and contain a base transparency and possibly overlay transparencies. The major types of transparencies are *clear acetate* (on which information is drawn on with a pen), *thermal* (heat process), and *diazo* (low speed photographic). Polarized transparencies, using special materials and equipment, when projected give an illusion of motion.

The 20 categories listed can, if needed, be expanded or reduced depending on the type of bibliography being prepared. The list can serve as a classification guide in categorizing media. It can also be invaluable when the librarian must decide on exactly what kind of selection aid should be used in searching for a particular type of item.

Preparing a Multimedia Bibliography

A good way for the librarian to become acquainted with the many media categories is to prepare a multimedia bibliography. Doing so helps the librarian to acquire a precise perspective on his or her professional jurisdiction. Most important, the librarian is not an instructional technologist and is not therefore expected to know the technological and pedagogical uses of the various media categories. Librarians who perceive value in such a role usually enroll in some kind of university program involved with instructional media in order to acquire such expertise. The librarian's basic responsibility lies in the selection, storage, and retrieval of information; hence the value of being familiar with the preparation of bibliographies. Preparing a bibliography affords an opportunity to become oriented to the vast array of selection aids available for selecting information media. Furthermore, since you are a librarian, your administrator can rightfully expect you to be able to select, store, and retrieve any information media form. The patron can also expect the librarian to provide service in selecting the right information media for any requirement.

Preparing bibliographies is a vital service provided by the professional librarian. A bibliography is invaluable in the area of acquisitions, where the library needs to determine exactly what kind of collection in a particular area may be needed or updated. A library that wishes to embark on programs involving particular topics will have need of a bibliography in order to determine precisely what items should be made available for the program. In addition, many organizations, e.g., educational institutions, industries, clubs, etc., request lists of materials for topics they will be studying. When a patron approaches you and requests a detailed multimedia bibliography on Steinbeck, you must be prepared to analyze precisely what the patron wants and then be able to generate the information required.

Once a bibliography has been prepared, it can be kept on file for future reference and, if necessary, be ready, with minor modifications, to serve a different need from that for which it was originally intended.

In order to achieve success in preparing bibliographies, it is essential that the librarian become expert in using the many professional selection aid tools available for such a task. Knowing exactly which selection aids are available and needed, as well as knowing the purpose and scope of each, will greatly facilitate the search for information. Anyone can con-

---

1. Purpose

   a. Acquisitions _____
      For updating _____   Developing a new collection _____
   b. Program _____
      Specific topic(s) _____
   c. Patron request _____
      Type of patron _____
                       (e.g., industry, education, research, recreation, club, etc.)

2. Parameters

   a. Topic continuum

      Broad/General ⟷ Specific/In-depth
      Give a concise statement regarding topic investigation.

   b. Patron continuum

      Broad ⟷ Narrow (specific need)
      (in age, abilities, interest, need, etc.)
      Give a statement identifying patron and his need

3. Acceptable range of media to be considered (list types)

4. Type of bibliographic form requested
    Give all information needed (i.e., data needed in citation, annotation, reviews, selection aid, etc.)

5. Date to be completed _____
   Estimated time (hours) to prepare _____

Figure 4.1. Initial investigation checklist for preparing a bibliography.

duct a search through the selection aids on a hit or miss basis and come up with some type of bibliography, but it takes a skilled librarian to come up with the precise information required and to do it efficiently.

It would be best to undertake the task of preparing a bibliography by first defining the parameters of bibliography with regard to scope of a search. Primarily, there are two continua to function—topic and patron. The topic continuum ranges from a broad, general investigation to a specific, in-depth treatment. The patron continuum would range from general patrons, e.g., age, range, interests, and abilities, to a specific patron with a particular need. The continua can be used to determine how the bibliography will be treated and to guide your investigation. Next, attention should be given to the range of media formats that will be considered for inclusion in the bibliography. The last step to consider is the bibliographic form to be used in the construction of the entries.

By using the procedure of first determining purpose then constructing the parameters, you have a building block process to aid in specifying the procedure to be followed in undertaking the task, the particular selection aids to be consulted, and the goals the bibliography should achieve. Figure 4.1 should be used in establishing the scope of the bibliography being prepared.

Search and Selection Guidelines

A well-constructed bibliography should be able to be used by anyone (administrator, another librarian, or a patron) without any need of explanation. The scope of the bibliography and the extent of information in the entries should be described in detail in a preface. Essentially, the preface is a justification for the information included in, or deleted from, the bibliography. Not only does the preface guide you in your investigation, but it also will inform any future readers as to the scope and purpose of the bibliography. Using the preface as a descriptive vehicle, you justify how and to what extent the bibliography is to be treated. The following information should be considered for inclusion in the preface:

1. A brief description or overview of the topic
2. From the Initial Investigation Checklist (Figure 4.1) a statement can be drafted as to why the topic was chosen and how it is treated (e.g., introduction, scholarly, recreational, etc.)
3. The scope to which you intend to investigate the topic (i.e., breadth and depth)
4. Any areas (content area, patron area, media area) upon which a particular emphasis will be placed

5. Various ways the bibliography can be used (e.g., teaching, special programs, interest groups, etc.)
6. Description of the type of patron for which the bibliography is intended
7. Any logical combination of entries worthy of particular attention (e.g., by class of media, particular periods or topic areas, patron, levels of use, etc.)
8. Any substitutions, inclusions, modifications, or problems that may require special justification or explanation
9. Special features of the bibliography worthy of particular attention (e.g., unique arrangement, indexing, etc.)
10. Any special instructions or procedures on how mechanically to use the bibliography
11. Statement describing completeness of the bibliography, or directions for any further investigation that can be made on the topic
12. The number of entries, number of media categories, and number of selection aids used

Some of the information required in the preceding 12 steps to be considered for inclusion in a preface obviously will have to be added after the bibliographic search is completed. However, possible alternatives should be considered when you are conducting the actual search, and a variation in the content of the bibliography can (or must) be justified because of new information (or lack of it) revealed in the selection aids. The 12 steps also serve another, and perhaps more useful, purpose. They can be used to interrogate whomever is requesting the bibliography: Putting them into question form, you can ascertain precisely what types of bibliographic searches to undertake.

Constructing a Bibliography

Having used the Initial Investigation Checklist for preparing a Bibliography (Figure 4.1) and prepared at least a rough preface, you have set the groundwork for the actual construction of a bibliography. The key word to remember is *Consistency*. The following questions should be asked: Is the preface consistent with the actual bibliography? Does the arrangement of information follow a consistent organized form? Are the bibliographic entries consistent as to the amount and kind of information they contain? Is the bibliographic form consistent throughout the entire bibliography?

Information may be arranged by straight alphabetical, media category, chronological, or any other classification to suit your particular purpose.

At this point, it might be advantageous to consider the need for indexing whereby entires can be located quickly in any way desired.

You should strive for consistency, in the bibliographic entries, especially as regards information given. If, for example, the cost of items is essential, every entry should include cost; and where cost information is unobtainable, it should be so noted (n.a.) so that the reader will know it was not omitted through oversight. As different media may use different styles of entry, i.e., books are listed by author whereas films are listed by title, this should be so noted in the preface. If any kind of coding system is used in the entries, the directions for using the codes should also be given in the preface.

When annotations are provided, they too should be consistent in style. Do not mix annotations with evaluations. Be prepared to abstract annotative information from selections so that they are all approximately the same length. It is disconcerting to find one annotation that is only a brief sentence followed by one that contains several paragraphs.

Finally, a citation should be made of the selection aid from which the information for each bibliographic entry was obtained. Be complete with this citation; give the complete title, volume, date, and page numbers. This information is essential when the bibliography is used to locate the actual materials.

Consideration should be given to an appendix, especially in situations where complete address or other data may be needed to make the bibliography useful. The form of the appendix should be internally consistent. It is suggested that a block form be used, and perhaps a system of cross-indexing could appear here to indicate the specific bibliographic entries to which each applies.

Evaluating a Bibliography

The skill, time, and effort required to produce a bibliography dictate that it be well done. Pride of accomplishment should be reflected in every aspect of your bibliography. Actually, a developed competency in what has previously been discussed in this chapter will assure a high quality bibliography. The key points made there could also be used as evaluative criteria.

To be more specific, there are two major areas of evaluation: (1) physical appearance and (2) content. As regards physical appearance, be aware of neatness, arrangement of information, proofreading (spelling), grammar, organization, and consistency of presentation of information. The physical appearance or mechanical aspect of the bibliography does not require special skills to evaluate—which also means that imperfections are readily visible. The finest bibliography ever produced will suffer greatly if typographical errors detract the reader from the bibliographical content.

As regards evaluation of content, here is where the professional skills of the librarian come to the fore. Perhaps the best way to evaluate content is to challenge the various aspects of the bibliography with a barrage of questions.

Evaluation of Preface

1. *Specificity:* Does the preface specifically state what the purpose is of the bibliography? Verbosity has no place in a bibliography preface.
2. *Parameters:* Are the limits of the bibliography clearly defined? The parameters should be understood prior to reading the bibliography and reexamined after reading it to determine if indeed they are accurate.
3. *Cues:* Are any cues, directions, or hints given to facilitate the reading of the bibliography?

Evaluation of Bibliography

1. *Form:* Is the form or style consistent? The reader should be almost able to develop a cadence in reading the entries. Information should be in a consistent.sequence. This is especially true if a reader desires to know only a particular aspect of information from each entry.
2. *Accuracy:* Is the information true, accurate, and up to date? The bibliography is of little value if the information cannot be used because, for some reason, it is erroneous.
3. *Selection:* Are the items selected for entry the best available as justified in the preface? To list any books, or the first book you happen to come across, does not require much skill; to include the best books is the mark of a true professional.
4. *Quantity:* Are enough items listed? This should be considered as a two-edged sword, for a bibliography can contain too many entries as well as too few. Remember the bibliography is constructed to be used and not as an exercise in using selection aids.
5. *Balance:* Is there a good balance among the various types of items or media included? Again, this is justified in the preface and evidenced in the bibliography. If undue emphasis is placed on some types of entries at the expense of others, it clearly indicates that the

search was not conducted properly and could reflect lack of interest, time, skill, or accessability to the search tools.

6. *Annotations:* When included, do they inform or help the reader in making a decision?
7. *Selection aids:* Was a good variety of selection aids used: Were primary as well as secondary aids consulted? If, for example, only one selection aid was used, the assignment was merely a clerical task and did not require the skill and time of a professional librarian.

Evaluation of Appendix

1. *Arrangement:* If an appendix is used, is the information easy to locate? Are primary aids distinguised from secondary aids?
2. *Referencing:* Do entries indicate for which bibliographic entries they were used? This could save time in grouping entries for latter acquisition, especially if a list of publishers or distributors is included.

Evaluation of Index

1. *Cross-indexing:* Is the cross-index purposeful? Does it provide a needed service? Are there sufficient types of cross-indexing?
2. *Ease of use:* Can the index be used to provide needed information quickly? If codes, symbols, or numerations are used, are they easy to comprehend?

Using these questions for evaluating bibliographies can assist you in developing criteria that will not only give direction in constructing a bibliography but also determine if such direction was achieved. A bibliography is a scholarly task that reflects the professional knowledge, attitude, and skill of the librarian who prepares it.

Selected Bibliography

Boehn, E. H. *Cue System for Bibliography and Indexing.* Santa Barbara: American Bibliographic Center, Clio Press, 1967.

Carter, M., and Bonk, W. J. *Building Library Collections.* 2d ed. New York: Scarecrow Press, 1964.

Clarke, V. *Non-Book Library Materials.* Denton: North Texas State College, 1953.

Gambee, B. L. *Non-Book Materials as Library Resources.* Chapel Hill: University of North Carolina, 1967.

Grove, P. S., and Tolten, H. L. "Bibliographic Control of Media: The Librarian's Excedrin Headache." *Wilson Library Bulletin,* Vol. 44:299–311 (Nov. 1969).

Haines, H. *Living With Books*. 2d ed. New York: Columbia University Press, 1965.
Hicks, W. B., and Tillin, A. M. *Developing Multi-Media Libraries*. New York: R. R. Bowker, 1970.
McClusky, F. D. *The A-V Bibliography Revised*. Dubuque, Iowa: Wm. C. Brown, 1955.
Perkins, Ralph. *Book Selection Media*. Champaign, Ill.: National Council of Teachers of English, 1967.
Winchell, C. M. *Guide to Reference Books*. 8th ed. Chicago: American Library Association, 1967.

5

Periodicals, Newspapers, and Pamphlets

Characteristics of Periodicals

Periodicals are unique information forms in that they provide continuous, scheduled, and updated flows of information on particular topics. Of all print forms, periodicals excel in providing information of current value and interest. Briefly defined, *periodicals* are publications in serial form which can be produced daily, weekly, monthly, quarterly, annually, or on any other periodic basis. They are without a doubt the greatest single quantitative source of information being produced in the world today. In the area of science alone, there are over 100,000 periodical titles from which to choose. By virtue of their physical format and content, it is convenient to categorize periodicals as journals, magazines, serials, or newspapers. Within each category, there are specific characteristics worth knowing as a means of better understanding the function of periodicals.

Journals are professional technical or scientific publications. They are generally written in a scholarly style because their purpose is to inform subscribers of developments in a particular area of endeavor. The writing style and vocabulary used are predicated on the supposition that the reader has a knowledge of the information area treated and in all probability is professionally affiliated with the field. A journal is definitely not slanted toward the lay reader. Journals have their own staffs of editors and writers but rely heavily on members of the profession for the contribution of articles. In this way, subscribers know what members of their profession are doing, the periodical thus provides each member of a profession with a convenient means of disseminating information to other members. Many journals are available only to members of a professional association. When this is the case, the library, in order to be a subscriber, must join the association, which is usually possible through a special library classification.

Magazines differ from journals in that they are intended for general circulation and aimed at readers who are not required to possess professional knowledge of the information discussed. An individual reads a magazine because of interest and not necessarily to keep abreast of his or her profession. Even magazines that deal with specific topics or areas of interest handle their information so that it has appeal to the general reader. Magazine news articles place greater emphasis on what is happening and how it affects people while news articles in journals place stress on how and why things happen and their influence on a particular profession.

There is a trend in magazine publication away from the general pictorial type magazine that covers current events and toward special interest, nontechnical magazines. The 1960s and early 1970s witnessed the termination of magazines such as *Life*, which in its prime had a weekly circulation of well over 4 million copies. The demise of this type of publication has been attributed to television. Because the public can now see daily news events happen live, the interest in seeing them in print once a week waned. The nation's interest in news magazines is greater for those that treat news in greater detail than television and, although it is not always readily perceived, with a viewpoint that not only informs the reader but tends to think for him as well. Some news magazines arrange articles as regular features or sections, e.g., international, national, and regional news and art, science, education, sports, business, religion, and entertainment sections. *Time* and *Newsweek* follow this format and provide the reader with a familiar, structured smorgasbord of news. Other news magazines select only significant news topics and develop them in greater depth and detail. Such magazines do not attempt to disguise their biases on issues and generally advocate a particular viewpoint. This type of publication includes such magazines as *The Nation* and *New Republic*.

A large number of magazines appeal to a particular sex: *McCalls, Good Housekeeping, Seventeen, Glamour,* and *Cosmopolitan* are intended for females; and *True, Argosy, Popular Mechanics, Field and Stream,* and *Playboy* for males. The articles in these magazines are chosen, written, and illustrated in a style that is intended to appeal to a particular sex—as attested by the fact that readership of each is predominantly made up of one sex.

Some magazines are geared to a particular emotional or mental level. Such magazines are not derogatory but rather appeal to a certain type of reader, and their inclusion in the library should be seriously considered for recreatory reading. Included would be confession type magazines that are supposedly true stories; love stories that deal with sin, suffering, despair, love, joy, and happiness; movie magazines and magazines that deal with popular public figures reveal personal information about celebrities in an exposé, "behind the scenes" fashion; police and detective magazines that give information with shocking, terrifying detail; comic books in which each issue deals with a different situation but always involving the same characters or the same type of story. Because of their appeal to younger readers, many comic books now have genuine educational value and should not be overlooked as a supplement to learning.

Many new magazines restrict their content to a particular sport, hobby, or activity. They are not intended for a large circulation but appeal to special interests. These magazines are devoted to such topics are coin collecting, sailing, needlepoint, backpacking, organic gardening, antique autos, jewelry making, etc. Their success is attributed to the fact that they are often the only source of current information for people with special kinds of interests. Closely allied to these magazines are the popularized trade magazines that treat professional topics in a non-professional manner and are intended to be read by people outside a particular profession. A good example is *Psychology Today* which discusses psychology in terms that appeal to the lay reader. Still another type of magazine with tremendous appeal is the digest. The digest condenses and abridges human interest stories which have appeared in other periodicals for quick reading. Some articles are taken from the context of other periodicals while other are exclusively written for the digest. In either case, their success is attributed to the manner in which they abbreviate information.

A third category of periodical, the serial, would include such publications as *World Almanac* or *Farmer's Almanac*, reports or monographs from groups or societies that are published on a regular basis, and newsletters available on a subscription basis. Basically, serials contain an updating or expanding of a particular type of information that is published on a prescribed installment basis. In some cases, where there is a fine line of distinction as to whether a periodical is a journal, a magazine, or a serial, it is necessary to determine the prime objective of the periodical. If it is to keep a profession informed, it should be classified as a journal; if it is to cater to the special or broad interest of the general public, it is a magazine; if it is published to update, revise, or broaden existing issues, it is a serial.

In the last category of periodical fall newspapers; because they differ markedly from journals, magazines, and serials they are treated separately in the following section.

The scope, treatment, and intent of periodicals are so varied that it would be especially helpful for the librarian to spend time investigating the various periodical selection aids available with regard to developing and maintaining the periodical collection. The periodical selection aids listed at the end of this chapter are valuable for setting up a collection and evaluating periodicals worthy of subscription consideration.

Glossary of Periodical Terms

I. *Periodical:* Publication in serial form
  A. Journal: Designed for a particular profession; scientific, scholarly, professional, technical, trade
  B. Magazine: General circulation; appeal to general public; wide range of subject matter
  C. Serial: Updates an existing periodical

II. *Characteristics and examples of periodicals:*
  A. Journal: Written in technical language, keeps reader up to date; also called a trade journal. Examples: *Library Journal, Audiovisual Instruction, Harvard Library Bulletin, A.M.A. Journal*
  B. Magazine: Written in lay language, can provide news, entertainment, or information applicable to nonprofessional special interest
    1. News—departmentalized: Classifies news events in a tightly structured format, e.g.; international, national, regional, education, sports, arts, etc. Examples: *Time, Newsweek, U.S. News and World Report*
    2. News—extended: Explores significant news events in great detail, tends to adopt a particular position or bias. Examples: *The Nation, New Republic, American Legion*
    3. Confessions: Claim to be true stories but are written to a strict formula, e.g., sin and suffering, love and happiness. Examples: *True Romantic Confessions, Startling Confessions, My Romance*

4. Movie magazines: Personal behind the scenes information of popular people's private lives. Examples: *Modern Screen, Photoplay*
5. Detective stories: Shocking details of violent crimes. Examples: *Master Detective, Official Detective*
6. Females' magazines: Written with an emphasized appeal to females. Examples: *McCalls, Seventeen, Glamour*
7. Males' magazines: Written with an emphasized appeal to males. Examples: *True, Argosy, Playboy*
8. Popularized trade journals: Professional topic written in lay terms, informs and satisfies information needs of general public. Examples: *Psychology Today, Science for the People, Scientific American*
9. Comic books: Use cartoons to depict comedy, mystery, adventure, history, violence; many of them deal with same character in different situations; appeal to children. Examples: *Superman, Archie, Casper the Friendly Ghost*
10. Digests: Condense stories of current human interest, tend to capsulize information for quick reading. Examples: *Reader's Digest, Coronet, Science Digest*
11. Special interest: Devoted to a particular sport, hobby, or activity; not intented for large circulation, appeal to a special interest e.g., antiques, coin collecting, sailing, gardening, backpacking, etc. Examples: *Rock and Gem, High Fidelity, Popular Needlework, Model Airplane News*

C. Serials: Each issue contains essentially the same information, but it is updated; includes almanacs, transactions of societies, reports, and supplements. Examples: *Farmer's Almanac, Guinness Book of Records, Standard and Poor's*

Characteristics of Newspapers

Among the various information media available in libraries, the newspaper is relied upon to provide a steady flow of current, up-to-date information. Granted that most people in the United States rely on television newscasting as their initial source for news events, they do however depend on newspapers for obtaining details of news events, opinions from recognized experts, and the plethora of less vital news information not available on television. The use of newspapers is in a sense somewhat paradoxical. They must be read immediately while their information is still news. It is indeed a rare event when a person is interested in reading a newspaper that is several days old, for the information is somewhat stale. The newspaper is of value only to keep the reader informed of current news happenings, hence there is not any particular demand for an "old" newspaper. However, because newspapers are a daily record of significant events occuring throughout the world, they become an invaluable archival and historical resource. Because people do not save newspapers, they rely heavily upon the library to maintain and preserve a collection of out-of-date newspapers. In many libraries, perhaps the greatest use of newspapers involves requests of old issues. Therefore, the librarian must determine not only which newspapers should be acquired for immediate consumption but also those newspaper that need to be kept on file (perhaps on microfilm) for all kinds of primary historical data.

The historical development of newspapers as an information medium serves to illustrate their societal impact. Originally developed in the seventeenth century, the newspaper was called a "broadside," which was a large single page printed on one side only and issued weekly or biweekly. *The Oxford Gazette*, a biweekly printed in England, was the first newspaper to appear in the English language. The first issue came out in November 1665 and in 1666 the paper was renamed *The London Gazette*. It is still published biweekly but more as a record of official matters than as a newspaper. The first formal attempt at publishing a newspaper in America occurred in Boston in 1690 with a paper called *Public Occurrences, Both Foreign and Domestic*, of which only one issue was printed. It was not until April 1704, with the publication of the *Boston Newsletter*, that the American colonies had a continuously printed weekly newspaper. The first daily, the *Pennsylvania Packet and General Advertiser* appeared in Philadelphia in 1784. The *New York Times*, founded in 1851, is without a doubt the core of newspaper collections in libraries throughout the United States. The twentieth century has witnessed the growth of newspaper chains, as well as the decline of several different newspapers serving metropolitan areas with local ownership.

The modern newspaper provides a host of services. It is an invaluable source of up-to-date news. By its regular appearance, it provides subscribers with a constant, reliable flow of information including local, regional, national, and world news; special articles; matters of interest; syndicated articles; comics; and an abundance of advertisements. Actually, it is from revenues produced by solicitation of advertising that newspapers reap their profits; and for this reason they are sold at prices the public can afford and is willing to pay.

Newspapers profess to provide their readers with objective reporting and to present a wide range of opinions with a wide range of treatment for the purpose of providing enough information to allow uninfluenced interpretation and decision making on the part of the reader. Any influencing of opinion is assumed to appear only in editorials. However, this is seldom the case; newspapers acquire reputations for particular preferences and sentiments on various aspects of the news, especially on matters of politics and the function of governments. Many people read a newspaper because it supports their particular philosophical perspective, and they readily agree or concur with its opinions. In a sense, they rely on a particular newspaper to think for them.

To compile information for its editions, a newspaper maintains a staff of editors, writers, and photographers to gather information in the area it serves. If the newspaper is large enough or part of a chain, it will retain offices for its reporters in vital state, national, and international locations. It will also subscribe to the services of syndicated columnists whose writings support its views. The newspaper will also maintain a teletype connection with one or more news services such as Associated Press (AP), which is considered to maintain a conservative stance, United Press International (UPI), which is reputed to be somewhat liberal, or International News Service (INS), which is purported to pursue the sensational aspects of the news.

Because newspapers have tendencies toward slanting the news and have reputations ranging from conservative to liberal to radical, it would be well for a library to subscribe to several newspapers in an effort to provide an equitable balance of news information and news interpretation. It is not unusual for a large metropolitan library to subscribe to 80 or 100 newspapers in an effort to satisfy the needs of its patrons. Subscriptions should be maintained with local and regional newspapers as a means of providing a service to patrons who cannot afford them. In addition, a variety of major English language newspapers should be acquired that present various news perspectives.

The possibility also exists that a sufficient number of library patrons have interest in reading newspapers from a particular geographical area (e.g., newspapers from areas where they formerly resided) to justify subscribing to them. On occasion, temporary subscriptions can perhaps be started with newspapers located in areas of high news interest, e.g., Northern Ireland during its periods of political crisis, Alaska for local feeling regarding the Alaska pipeline. Not to be overlooked are foreign language newspapers, which include both those published in foreign countries and those printed in the United States.

The most important service a library can provide patrons with the newspapers to which it subscribes is to maintain a constant flow of news information from a wide range of perspectives and opinions. The styles, formats, and languages should be suited to readers' abilities and pro-

mote a knowledgeable, informed public capable of intelligently responding to the news events that affect their lives.

Newspapers, both those used for immediate consumption and those
used for archive purposes, are seldom if ever charged out of the library.
Therefore, it is essential that they be prominently displayed and that an
adequate reading area be conveniently available. The newspapers need
to be rotated daily, the most recent issue being the most physically
accessible. Depending on demand, it is generally convenient to keep
current newspapers on open shelves for at least four weeks, after which
they can be either stored or destroyed. Depending on budget, use, and
space, a librarian may opt to keep a newspaper on an open shelf for up
to three months, after which it would be available on microfilm and can
be destroyed. The transition of the newspaper's function from current
news to archival information requires careful consideration as to which
newspapers are to be retained and in what format. Newspapers can be
kept until such time as they are available to the library in microform
(usually 16-mm or 35-mm microfilm), when the original newspapers can
be removed from circulation.

When determining which newspapers are to be available in microform, it usually becomes apparent that not all newspapers taken on a
daily basis need to be available in microform. The newspaper in microform is used for archive purposes, providing the reader with a record
of past events. As an archive, its prime purpose is no longer to influence
and shape public opinion but rather to preserve news events in a
chronological, time-line sequence. The interest to the reader is now on
"when" and "what" was said of a particular event and not on its importance and influence as a current event.

Most public libraries deem it adequate to subscribe to microforms of
The New York Times and a local or regional newspaper; academic libraries,
by virtue of requests, may need to subscribe to several national and
foreign newspaper microform services. A major problem with newspapers in microform is indexing. Having a complete collection of every
issue ever printed by a newspaper is of questionable value if information
therein cannot be conveniently retrieved. This makes *The New York Times*
an excellent selection as a newspaper to be kept for archive purposes.
The New York Times maintains an index of its newspapers from 1913 to
the present which is published semimonthly and annually. *The New
York Times Index* also has a secondary benefit by acting as a psuedo index
for other papers. Much of the information appearing in *The New York
Times* undoubtedly appears simultaneously in other newspapers
throughout the United States. Therefore, to locate a news item in a local
newspaper, one can check the date of its occurrence in *The New York
Times Index*. Unfortunately, the index would not include news items of

purely local value. Another index of news events is the *London Times Official Index*, and complementing it is *Palmer's Index to the Times Newspapers*, 1790 to date. *Palmer's Index*, although less detailed than the *Official Index*, does cover a much longer period of time. Many local newspapers, becoming aware of the need to prepare indexes for their microform subscribers, are now producing them. Some private companies are also compiling indexes of newspapers of a particular region, e.g., since 1970 the *California News Index* has published an index for six major newspapers and seven magazines available in California. This index covers California affairs and indexes information by subject, name, organization, and state geographic location. Thus by using the *New York Times Index* and the *California News Index*, the user has complete access to all information appearing in the six major state newspapers. The *California News Index* is also useful in locating information (of state and national interest) in other newspapers published in California.

In maintaining the library's newspaper collection, there are guides for locating back files of newspapers. To assist in this task are Clarence Brigham's *History and Bibliography of American Newspapers 1690–1820*, which lists and gives the locations of 2120 newspapers; *American Newspapers 1821–1936*, which is a union list of newspaper files available in 5700 United States and Canadian libraries; and the Library of Congress *Newspapers on Microfilm*, which contains a list of 12,000 American and 4000 foreign newspapers available on microfilm.

Most libraries allocate space for current newspapers near or convenient to the front entrance of the library. When assigning space for reading newspapers, consideration needs to be given to privacy and comfort. Newspapers are oftentimes shelved with other current periodicals and used in the same area. Although located in a prominent place, the newspaper reading area should not be disturbed by heavy traffic to and from other areas of the library. Lounge chairs are especially well suited to this area, and many libraries attempt to create a homey atmosphere by allowing smoking in restricted areas. Use of newspapers in microform quite often involves a patron undertaking research, and for this reason writing surfaces are generally made available for note taking. Newspapers in microform are usually housed in a different part of the library and considered to provide a service different from that provided by the current newspapers found in the reading or lounging area.

Characteristics of Pamphlets

A valuable resource in any library is its collection of pamphlets, or what is more properly called the vertical file collection. Pamphlets are unique in character in that they are printed material that cannot be classified as books or periodicals. The truth of the matter is that pamphlets are somewhat amorphous items that are not physically designed in a standard, prescribed format. The American Library Association (1973) provides the following definition of a pamphlet:

> Pamphlet: 1. In a restricted technical sense, an independent publication consisting of a few leaves of printed matter stitched together but not bound; usually enclosed in paper covers. While independent in the sense that each pamphlet is complete in itself it is a common custom to issue pamphlets in series, usually numbered consecutively. In local library practice, there is variation in the number of leaves or pages allowed under the term. For the purposes of statistics and method, some libraries set the limit at 80 pages (originally based on the equivalent of 5 printed sheets folded to octavo); others consider "about 100 pages" sufficient restriction. From the bindery point of view, a pamphlet is any collection of leaves, paper-bound or self-covered, consisting of 64 pages or less. 2. A brief controversial treatise on a topic of current interest, usually religious or political; common in England from the sixteenth to the eighteenth century [pp. 96–97].

The ALA definition places emphasis on the physical characteristics of pamphlets. It is valid to proceed on the premise that they are neither books nor periodicals but unique enough in makeup to warrant their own classification. It is a sound definition, for the librarian can use it as a primary identification for that wide range of materials available to libraries that cannot be classified as either books or periodicals but exist somewhere between them.

Perhaps it would be more advantageous to expand the ALA definition to include the kinds of information found in pamphlets and the function the vertical file provides. Pamphlets cover an extremely wide range of subjects, but their uniqueness is that an individual pamphlet contains concise information on a specific topic. A pamphlet is an ideal resource for anyone desiring to obtain concise information about something without being required to search through a book to locate it. Furthermore, much information appears in pamphlets before it is incorporated in books, and pamphlets are thus often primary resources of current information. For this reason, the vertical file provides an excellent reference service. The task of the librarian is to specify the function of the library's vertical file and then proceed to work within it. Some libraries have outstanding vertical file collections because they have a precise knowledge of what kinds of pamphlets they are to contain.

In building and maintaining a vertical file, one should not consider it a catch-all or junk pile containing every scrap of information that comes across the librarian's desk. Basically, there are two approaches to building a vertical file: one is to have a little bit of everything; the other is to develop a few topical areas thoroughly. It would do well for the librarian to consider patrons' needs before subscribing to either approach. A knowledge of the library community's needs and an awareness of information trends is invaluable. Some information is so new or unique that it can only be found in a pamphlet. It is for the librarian to determine what is worth saving.

The librarian does well to consider the merits of pamphlets. Actually, they are a source of free or relatively inexpensive up-to-date information. Many pamphlets are prepared by people with expertise in a particular topic. Industries are always producing pamphlet literature about the capabilities of their products and services, e.g., fertilizer producers have pamphlets on how to use fertilizers to grow beautiful gardens and fight garden pests. Associations and charitable organizations provide pamphlets as a public service, e.g., American Heart Association on how to prevent heart attacks. Local, state, federal, and foreign governments with their myriad departments have a bounty of information available in pamphlet form. Once the content scope of the vertical file has been determined, the harvest of pamphlet information can be easily gathered. The task is not where to locate pamphlets but rather which pamphlets should be acquired and which should be rejected.

Pamphlets should help fill existing gaps in a library's collection by providing information not available or readily accessible in any other format. This means that pamphlets should contain up-to-date information not presently available in books; information so narrow, unique, or brief that it does not warrant having a book written about it; or concise information appearing in a pamphlet that is the most convenient way for a patron to obtain it. In building the vertical file collection, one must exercise caution with regard to information bias. If a pamphlet is selected because it fulfills the criterion of content scope, it should be carefully evaluated for unbalanced or extreme biases. These biases often consist of facts misused or taken out of context, giving only one side of a many-sided issue, giving undue emphasis to certain particulars, or even making unwarranted or unsubstantiated criticism of an opposing point of view. If a pamphlet reveals any indications of these biases but it is still the librarian's decision to place it in the vertical file collection, then every effort should be made to balance this information with information that subscribes to other or even opposing points of view. Biased material should always be identified by author and endorsing body along with date of publication as an aid to the reader in assessing content reliability and validity. It is a good practice with all material placed in the vertical file collection, whether or not it be biased, to be certain that the source and authorship of the information is available, for in the final analysis it is a prime means by which the reader can intelligently assess the value of information. It is a good practice to avoid anonymity.

Although the conscientious librarian is always concerned about censoring material on the possibility of imposing personal standards or depriving patrons of information which they have a proper right to assess for themselves, the responsibility of what is to be included in the collection ultimately resides with the librarian. For this reason, criteria need to be developed that are unique to selecting material for the vertical file collection.

The first task in developing these criteria is to prepare a statement of policy that precisely defines the purpose and scope of the vertical file collection. The policy statement should become the benchmark from which the following suggested selection criteria could evolve.

1. A pamphlet is selected because it fills a need or provides a service not presently available in other media forms (e.g., conciseness, specificity, datedness, authoritativeness).
2. The source of information is available and should include author, distributor, and sponsor.
3. Whenever necessary or possible, other points of views, or at least a bibliography of where other points of view can be obtained, should be available.
4. The pamphlet should be free from undesirable advertising. Many pamphlets are produced by the private sector of the economy, and a pamphlet whose sole purpose is to promote a product or service should be avoided. Note: Many companies that provide excellent public service with their pamphlets are often the most authoritative source of expertise.
5. The cost of the material must be minimal. (The cost criterion is one of the strengths of the vertical file collection. Most materials are free or relatively inexpensive; the library should nevertheless set a maximum price it would be willing to pay for any pamphlet.)
6. Limits should be placed on how much information should be housed in the vertical file collection.

These six criteria can serve as a basis for building a vertical file collection. Criterion 5 indicates that cost should be kept minimal because vertical file materials tend to be inexpensive and building a collection should not be a costly undertaking. Although subscribing to this criterion should not be difficult, Criterion 6 most often poses a problem. Because many materials are free, a librarian may tend to store every scrap of information that comes to the library in the vertical file collection. What is needed is a two-phase weeding process; one to weed what goes into the collection and the other to cull what should be removed from it.

With regard to weeding what goes into the collection, the material should first fit within the purpose, purview, and scope of the vertical file collection. The material should also be up to date, concise, and not readily or conveniently available in any other form. The vertical file collection should support, not duplicate, other areas of the library's collection. The process of weeding out materials can be done systematically. Many similar methods of weeding out materials are employed by libraries. A sound procedure is to stamp all materials with the date they are received and set a time-certain life value on the material, e.g., 1 year, 2 years, 3 years, or until replaced by newer information. The time-certain period can be implemented by color code. This can be done by using felt-tip pens and color striping marks across the top of the material whereby a blue stripe would indicate material to be removed at the end of 1 year, a red stripe 2 years, a green stripe 3 years, and a black stripe material to remain in the collection until replaced by newer material. In this way, the vertical file collection can be weeded annually by simply removing those materials that are out of date as indicated by the appropriate color code. Degeneration of the vertical file into an overstuffed, worthless junkpile that must laboriously be sifted through in order to find a worthwhile piece of information should be stringently avoided. The librarian should be aware that much of the material in the vertical file is ephemeral and should be discarded when it is no longer useful. Hence it is essential when working with the vertical file collection to get materials into and out of circulation as quickly as possible.

The librarian needs to be constantly aware of materials that can be placed in the vertical file collection. Again depending on the purpose and scope of the vertical file collection, information can be gathered from newspaper clippings, reprints of magazine articles, and the many new pamphlets being printed daily. To help in the selection process, there are many location aids that list titles and resources available. Among them are the *Vertical File Index,* which is a monthly (except August) periodical published by H.W. Wilson listing pamphlets arranged by subject and cross-filed in a separate file title index; the monthly catalog of *United States Publications;* the *Monthly Checklist of State Publications;* and the *Public Affairs Information Service Bulletin (PAIS),* which is published weekly. Not to be overlooked are reader services published in many periodicals, which oftentimes include a reader service card for checking off materials desired; the local chamber of commerce; local public service agencies; and of course the telephone directory, which contains a plethora of resources having pamphlets available. The pamphlet bibliography at the end of this chapter is worthy of added attention for additional resources on building vertical file collections.

Pamphlets can provide an invaluable service to the library, but in order to do so they must be handled with a specific policy that includes judicious acquisition and weeding of information and an awareness that they contain informational material not conveniently available in other media forms.

Selected Bibliography

American Library Association. *A.L.A. Glossary of Library Terms.* Chicago: American Library Association, 12th printing, 1973.

Ball, M. O. *Subject Headings for the Information File 8th ed.,* New York: H. W. Wilson Co., 1956.

Bruce Miller Publications. *So You Want to Start a Picture File: An Aid to Better Teaching.* Riverside, California: Bruce Miller Publications, 1968.

Condit, L. *Pamphlet about Pamphlets.* Ann Arbor, Mich.: University Microfilms, 1968.

Gould, G., and Wolfe, I. *How to Organize and Maintain the Library Picture-Pamphlet File.* Dobbs Ferry, N.Y.: Oceana Publications, 1968.

Ireland, N. O. *The Pamphlet File in School, College and Pub-Libraries.* Westwood, Mass.: Faxon, 1954.

Miller, S. *Vertical File and Its Satellites: A Handbook of Acquisition, Processing and Organization.* Littleton, Colo.: Libraries Unlimited, 1971.

SELECTION AIDS

Newspapers

American Newspapers 1821–1936; A Union List of Files Available in the United States and Canada. New York: H. W. Wilson Co., 1937.

Blum, E. *Reference Books in the Mass Media: An Annotated Selected Booklist Covering Book Publishing, Broadcasting, Films, Newspapers, Magazines and Advertising.* Urbana: University of Illinois Press, 1962.

Brigham, C. S. *History and Bibliography of American Newspapers, 1690–1820.* 2 vols. Worcester, Mass.: American Antiquarian Society, 1947.

California News Index. Claremont, Calif.: Center of California Public Affairs, 220 W. Foothill Blvd. 1970.

Editor & Publisher. *International Year Book.* Annual. 1920 to date. New York: Editor & Publisher, 1920–.

New York Times Index. 1913 to date. New York: The New York Times. Semi-monthly and annual.

Palmer's Index to the Times Newspaper. Quarterly. 1790 to date. London: Palmer, 1868–.

Times, London. *Index to the Times*. Monthly and annual. 1907 to date. London: Times Office, 1907–.

U.S. Library of Congress. Union Catalog Division. *Newspapers on Microfilm*. 5th ed. Washington, D.C.: Library of Congress, 1963.

Pamphlets

Aubrey, R. *Selected Free Material for Classroom Teachers*. rev. ed. Palo Alto, Calif. Fearon Press, 1972.

Bennett, W. *Occupations Filing Plan and Bibliography*. rev. ed. Danville, Ill.: Interstate Printers and Publishers, 1968.

Chamber of Commerce of the United States, Washington, D.C. *Guide to Foreign Information Services*. 1970. *Sources of State Information and State Industrial Directories*. 1971.

Dever, E. *Sources of Free and Inexpensive Educational Materials*. 4th ed. Grafton, W. Va.: Esther Dever, 1967.

Educators Progress Service Inc.; Randolph Wise. *Educators Guide to Free Guidance Materials*. Annual. *Educators Guide to Free Films*. Annual. *Educators Guide to Free Filmstrips*. Annual. *Educators Guide to Free Health, Physical Education, and Recreation Materials*. Annual. *Educators Guide to Free Science Materials*. Annual. *Educators Guide to Free Social Studies Materials*. Annual. *Educators Guide to Free Tapes, Scripts, Transcriptions*. Annual. *Educators Index of Free Materials*. Annual. *Elementary Teachers Goide to Free Curriculum Materials*. Annual.

Fisk, M., ed. *Encyclopedia of Associations*. 8th ed. 3 vols. Detroit: Gale Research Co., 1973.

Forrester, G. *Occupational Literature: An Annotated Bibliography*. rev. ed. New York: H. W. Wilson Co., 1971.

Free and Inexpensive Learning Materials. 15th ed. Nashville: Division of Surveys and Field Services, 1970.

Health Education Materials and Organizations Which Offer Them. New York: Health Insurance Institute, n.d.

Kenworthy, L. S., and Birdie, R. A. *Free and Inexpensive Materials on World Affairs*. 3rd ed. New York: Columbia University, 1969.

Leidy, W. P. *A Popular Guide to Government Publications*. 3rd ed. New York: Columbia University Press, 1968.

A List of Worthwhile Life and Health Insurance Books, Annual. New York: Health Insurance Institute.

Mechanic, S., comp. *Annotated List of Selected United States Publications Available to Depository Libraries*. New York: H. W. Wilson Co., 1973.

Monthly Catalog of U.S. Government Publications. Monthly. Washington D.C.: Superintendent of Documents.

Monthly Catalog of State Publications. Washington, D.C.: Superintendent of Documents Annual Index.

Nicholsen, M. E. *People in Books: A Selective Guide to Bibliographical Literature Arranged by Vocations and Other Fields by Reader Interest*. New York: H. W. Wilson Co., 1969.

NVGA Bibliography of Current Career Information. 5th ed. Washington, D.C.: American Personnel and Guidance Association, 1969.

Pope, T. *Free and Inexpensive Educational Aids.* 3rd ed. New York: Dover Publications, 1971.

Public Affairs Information Service Bulletin (PAIS). Weekly. New York: Public Affairs Information Service.

Public Affairs Pamphlets. 15 issues per year. New York: Public Affairs Pamphlets.

Salisbury, G. *Catalog of Free Teaching Materials.* 7th ed. Ventura, Calif.: Catalog of Free Teaching Materials, 1970.

Schmeckebeir, L., and Eastin, R. B. *Government Publications and Their Use.* 2nd rev. ed. Washington, D.C.: The Brookings Institution, 1969.

Schumn, P. *Materials for Occupational Education: An Annotated Source Guide* Ann Arbor, Mich.: R. R. Bowker Co., 1973.

Selected U.S. Publications. Bimonthly. Washington D.C.: Superintendent of Documents.

Sources of Free and Inexpensive Pictures for the Classroom. Riverside, Calif.: Bruce Miller Publications, 1968.

Sources of Free and Inexpensive Teaching Aids. Riverside, Calif.: Bruce Miller Publications, 1968.

Congressional Directory. Annual. Washington D.C.: Superintendent of Documents.

U.S. Dept. of Labor, Bureau of Labor Statistics, Washington, D.C.: Superintendent of Documents. *Occupational Outlook Handbook.* Biennial. *Occupational Outlook Quarterly.*

U.S. Dept. of Labor, Manpower Administration. *Occupational Guides.* Washington, D.C., n.d.

Vertical File Index. Monthly. New York: H. W. Wilson Co.

6

Microforms

Definition of Microform

Microform is a generic term which identifies visual information originally in paper form that has been photographically reduced. This includes books, magazines, newspapers, maps, charts, cancelled checks, etc. The magnification needed to read microforms ranges anywhere from 10 times magnification ($10\times$) to 210 times magnification ($210\times$). The resultant savings in storage space is hard to conceive. For example, the 20,000 volumes of the *Library of American Civilization* in book form occupy 2000 feet of shelf space, but on microform they can be stored in a single file drawer. Microform is indeed the "transistorization" of the printed page.

The advantages of microforms are numerous. They are a way of preserving information contained in rare documents; microform copies are easy to make; they save space; with them, binding problems are eliminated; they are less expensive than books; microform editions are never out of print; and they are tough and durable.

But before you commit yourself to a microform system, consider their possible disadvantages. Microforms require some type of machine or device to enlarge them to readable size; because of their small size, they can easily be misfiled; a user must view them in the library proper rather than elsewhere because that is where the viewing machinery is located. There is a whole array of microform standards, each involving its own system of equipment, storage, duplication and retrieval. The patron who is not familiar with microform tends initially to be a little reticent to use this medium, but this problem is usually temporary.

Physical Features of Microforms

Microforms come in four basic physical arrangements: (1) microfilm, (2) microfiche, (3) micro-opaque material, and (4) aperture card. (See Figure 6.1.)

Microfilm identifies that microform stored on a roll or reel of film. If the film base is made of acetate, a reel will hold 100 feet of film; if it is a polyester type, the same reel will hold 200 feet of film.

Microfiche, or *fiche* as it is commonly called, is a single piece of film about the size of a postcard. Incidentally, the term *fiche* is a French word meaning card.

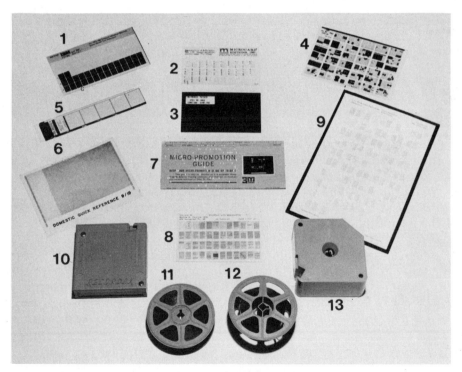

Figure 6.1. Assorted microforms: (1) 3- × 6-inch negative microfiche; (2) 3- × 5-inch positive microfiche; (3) 3- × 5-inch negative microfiche; (4) 4- × 6-inch positive microfiche; (5) 1⅜- × 7-inch ultrafiche; (6) 4- × 6-inch ultrafiche; (7) aperture card; (8) 3- × 5-inch positive micro-opaque; (9) 6- × 9-inch positive micro-opaque; (10) 16-mm microfilm cartridge; (11) 16-mm open-reel microfilm; (12) 35-mm open-reel microfilm; (13) 35-mm microfilm cartridge.

A *micro-opaque card* is similar to microfiche but instead of being film it is a white opaque card. Fiche is similar to a film negative whereas the micro-opaque card is analogous to a photographic print.

An *aperture card*, as the name indicates, is a card with an aperture or cut-out hole which has a piece of film bonded to the aperture.

Bearing in mind the physical features of these several microforms, we must next consider the various formats and magnifications in which they are available. Microfilm is available in both 35-mm and 16-mm formats, with or without sprocket holes and with or without self-threading cartridges, in color or in black and white. Microfiche is made in a 3- × 5-inch or 4- × 6-inch format, the latter being more prevalent. Micro-opaque cards are prepared on 3- × 5-inch, 4- × 6-inch, 5- × 8-inch, and 6- × 9-inch white cards. An aperture card is a standard electric accounting machine card, what is commonly called a computer card, and as such can be stored and retrieved electronically. The aperture is usually the size of a single frame of 35-mm film.

Image Magnification and Storage Capacity

Along with the wide array of physical features and formats available in microforms, consideration must be given to image magnification. In order to view microforms, you must have a lens magnification system to enlarge information to a readable size. Magnifications usually range from 10× to 40×; 19× and 21× are the most common. There is also in the microfiche format a still greater image reduction on what is called super or ultrafiche, which requires anywhere from 50× to 210× magnification. Ultrafiche is generally available in 60×, 150×, and 210× magnification.

As an indication of how magnification affects the amount of material stored on a 4- × 6-inch card, up to 60, 90, or 98 pages of information can be stored on a single microfiche but with ultrafiche, up to 3000 pages.

Positive versus Negative Microforms

Microforms are available on either positive or negative film. If you are viewing a positive microform on a reader, the information looks just like the original. Conversely, if you are viewing information on negative film, the type is white and the background black, and a photograph looks like a photographic negative with black and white reversed. There are two underlying purposes for libraries having positive or negative collections, both relating to reproduction equipment. If a patron wants to take information out of the library but does not have equipment for viewing microforms, then photographic equipment is available to reproduce the information on paper.

Unfortunately, the equipment produces paper copies in a form opposite that of the film, i.e., positive film gives negative paper copy and vice versa. Recent technological developments have produced equipment able to produce paper reproductions in the same form as the original, but at present this equipment is still relatively expensive.

Selecting Microforms

The librarian must decide just what type or types of microform should be in the library collection. Of course, the needs and applications of patrons should serve as a guide, as well as the current state of the art. If the bulk of the requests from patrons are for paper reproductions to use outside the facility, then it is best to have the collection on negative film, unless you can afford the more expensive positive to positive reproduction equipment, in which case you can have the collection on positive film. If patrons make the most use of the collection on the equipment in the library, then by all means have the collection on positive film.

Micro-opaque cards are inefficient and may soon be obsolete. The opaque cards are thicker than microfiche film and (more important) the image produced on the viewer is generally not as brilliant as that produced by film. This is caused by the fact that the projection light is reflected off the opaque card but passes through the film, giving the latter generally a better image. A library would have occasion to acquire micro-opaque cards only if they were the sole microform format in which the information was available. Incidentally, there are still some periodicals available only on micro-opaque cards. This is true of some European scientific publications.

Periodicals, especially newspapers, are available on 35-mm microfilm. It is a convenient form for low-access information (which does not require immediate or frequent access) because several months of periodical information can be stored on one reel of film.

Polyester film is preferred to acetate film solely because a reel will hold twice as much polyester film, but the librarian must be certain that the equipment in the library can accommodate polyester film. As polyester film is also relatively new, the librarian must know to what extent information is available in this format.

In making a decision between 35-mm and 16-mm microfilm, the librarian should ascertain first of all if the 16-mm reel holds as much information as a comparable 35-mm reel. If this is true, then an examination must be made of the magnification differences—16-mm will require greater magnification to give the same size image as 35-mm film. The librarian should make a side-by-side viewing comparison of 16-mm and 35-mm before making a decision.

Whether to use open reel or cartridge microfilm can best be determined by the extent patrons use the facility. If patrons are occasional users, then cartridge is better. This eliminates the need to instruct the patron every time he uses a machine. If the patron is a frequent user, then open reel is satisfactory because the machines are not difficult to thread once a person knows how. Open reel is more difficult to thread, but the machine does not require a self-threading device that can break down. Not requiring a cartridge or a self-threading device, the open reel has a lower cost of equipment acquisition and maintenance. The film in a cartridge is never handled, which is a plus for a cartridge system.

A final consideration in favor of microfilm is that the reels are relatively large in comparison with other microforms. This does permit an open shelf policy which is not too practical with other microforms, which being so thin can easily be misfiled. Imagine what would happen if you allowed patrons to remove and return cards from the card catalog.

Microfiche is well suited for high-access information. Where a reel of microfilm can store several months of periodicals, more than likely a fiche would store only a single issue; therefore, a patron would not tie up several months of periodicals while examining one issue. Fiche also has the advantage of rapid access to information because the user can go directly to a particular page without winding through a reel. Actually, information can be located as quickly as it can in the original paper document. With microfiche you need to purchase only the information you actually need. Single manuscripts are best acquired in the fiche format. Documents reproduced on fiche are easily identified: Labels are provided on the fiche that can be read with the naked eye. This feature greatly facilitates accessioning and storing.

Aperture cards require the use of a card sorter if they are to be utilized to their best advantage. Usually the information, because of the relatively small aperture, is limited to a few pages. The aperture card is well suited for applications which require access to complex cross-indexed information because patrons have computerized access to many combinations of aperture cards. Because of computer accuracy, aperture cards are always refiled in the proper place, eliminating human error in filing and doing it much more rapidly.

The majority of information on microform is available in the 10×–40× range of magnification. Ultra magnification of the 60×–210× range requires equipment that is extremely critical as regards alignment. A slight misalignment will render the machine unusable. Presently, ultra magnification is available only in some types of fiche and short strip and only in black and white. But the reduction of space required for storing information is tremendous. As a comparison, envision the amount of space thirty 100-page periodicals would occupy; they could be all stored on approximately thirty standard magnification 4- × 6-inch fiches or on one 4- × 6-inch ultrafiche. Ultrafiche is obviously ideal for institutions requiring the storage of tremendous amounts of information or of extremely low access but extremely valuable information that can be stored in a vault.

Normal 10×–40× range magnification is presently the standard for libraries serving the general public. The quality of magnified images is generally good, and equipment is relatively simple in design. An attractive feature for normal magnification is the availability of color on reels of microfilm. The film used is 35-mm sprocketed film. Results are excellent, and color film is ideal for magazines.

Trends in Microform Selection

One particularly irksome problem that confronts librarians with respect to microforms is the multitude of standards. Institutions that rush headlong toward every microform innovation usually end up with a crazy patchwork quilt of incompatible systems. Other institutions adopt a "wait and see" or "wait till it is perfected" attitude, and as a result, the microform world passes them by. Perhaps the best solution to this dilemma is to investigate alternative systems, near future trends, and the particular needs of your institution; then commit yourself to a system that can serve you at least 5 or 10 years. In this way, you can evolve a plan of amortization that can justify your microform system over a given period of time.

Present trends appear to be toward 35-mm open reel, positive black and white microfilm in the 10×–40× magnification range. A probable cause for this is that many newspapers and magazines are available in this format and will be for many years. The availability of newspapers and magazines on microfilm has also relieved librarians of a tremendous storage and retrieval problem. Still a third reason is that the machinery used for viewing this type of microfilm is fairly simple to operate, low in maintenance, rugged and durable, and not too expensive.

Following closely behind 35-mm microfilm is the 4- × 6-inch positive microfiche in the same 10×–40× magnification range. The popularity of microfiche is attributable to the demands for high-access materials stored on a quick retrieval single sheets of film; in addition, many professional periodicals, books, and research papers are stored on this format.

Many institutions are committed to a combination of the 35-mm microfilm and 4- × 6-inch fiche system. This gives them the versatility of storing information on high- or low-access modes, plus a format on which the bulk of material that a library usually uses or wants on microform is commercially available.

Because most patrons view microforms in the library, the microfilm and fiche systems provide the best control, fiche being a closed-shelf collection and the possibility of microfilm being an open-shelf collection.

Within the next few years, many patrons will own their own microform readers. When this becomes more prevalent, then the trend will be toward 10×–40× magnification fiche readers. With the added feature of fiche reproduction, the patron can pay a small fee to purchase a fiche and add it to his own collection.

Note that the magnification has been in the 10×–40× range. The viewing equipment in this range for both library and home use, when compared to ultra magnification viewing equipment (50×–210×), is less expensive, less complicated, less delicate, and easier to operate.

The trends just stated are immediate future trends. This means they are actually happening now or will be prevalent within a few years. Well before 2000, microforms will be computer stored, and the patron sitting at home with a computer terminal will request information from the library collection to appear on television and, if he so desires, obtain a permanent paper or magnetic-tape print-out. Such systems are already in prototype stages, it will take only proper marketing to make them available in American homes. Therefore, the library that is moving in the direction of the microform trend will be ready for the technology available to citizens of the near future.

Knowing which kinds of microforms are available, the librarian can now intelligently use the selection aids. It is essential to know if the particular microform being selected is in the format being used by the library. There are several selection aids particularly designed to assist the librarian in locating information on microforms. In some microform selection aids, information is often minimal; therefore, it is well to bear in mind that materials available in microform were formerly available in a printed format and that additional data can be obtained from selections aids prepared expressly for the printed version.

Selecting Microform Viewers

Along with the trends of microforms, the librarian needs to be aware of viewing and reproduction equipment. For every microform format, compatible viewing equipment is required to read the material. Furthermore, as new format refinements and changes have occurred, a host of adapters have been designed for existing equipment, but modifying existing equipment has created more problems than it has solved. The best equipment program is one tied into the library's 5- to 10-year commitment to a particular microform in which the equipment is also included in an amortization plan. The librarian in this way can periodically justify new equipment requests without the need for jury rigging existing equipment.

If only one or at best two microform formats are used, then it is possible to need only one or two types of viewing equipment. When selecting viewing equipment, consider cost, warranty, ease of operation, ease of maintenance, versatility, quality of projected image, noise, cooling, lamp size and ease of replacement, and physical dimensions.

Consider the following questions when selecting equipment:

Does the equipment require a darkened room for adequate viewing?

If microfilm, does the equipment make considerable noise when winding or rewinding film?

Does equipment require a fan to cool the lamp; if so, is the fan quiet?

If equipment is to be moved frequently, what is its portability?

What is the length of lamp life, and how expensive is a replacement lamp?

How much space does the equipment occupy, and can you afford the space?

Can you find out where the equipment is currently being used?

Is the equipment easy to focus, and is the image brilliant, crisp, and sharp?

Can the patron learn to operate it without assistance from the librarian?

Can it be serviced locally; how long will it take; and are loaners available?

Does it provide for a varied selection of lenses in the $10\times$–$40\times$ range?

Is it adjustable to material stored on both a horizontal and vertical
format?

If the unit is motorized, does it require a special electrical outlet?

Is construction and alignment of parts sturdy and durable?

What safeguards does it have for preventing damage to the film
(e.g., tears, burns, scratches)?

Is it equipped with or does it require a dust or storage cover?

Along with these questions, there may be concern for speed of operation. Some types of viewing equipment are motorized to give rapid
access to information on microfilm. Motors can turn microfilm reels at
much higher speeds than hand cranking, and keyboard devices permit
the user to punch a few keys to display information automatically on the
screen. If the time of the patron is quite valuable, these motorized features should be considered.

If paper reproductions of information will be requested, then a microfilm reader will have to have print capabilities. Be aware of the following:

Does it require use of chemicals?

Does it make a wet or a dry copy?

Does it reproduce positive copy from negative film (or vice versa),
or can it give positive copy from positive film?

If necessary, can an attachment be added to make it coin operated?

Can the patron operate it without assistance?

Can it accommodate various microform formats?

A major premise for using microforms is that of tremendous space
saving, and this premise must extend to the equipment selected to store
it. Here is one instance where standards are prevalent. Regardless of the
particular microform used, there is one set of physical dimensions for
that form. For example, all 35-mm reels, and of course all 4- × 6-inch
fiche, are the same size. This means that storage equipment should be
acquired that is exactly the same size and designed for a particular microform. When selecting storage equipment for fiche, closed file drawers
should be chosen as a means of reducing the accumulation of dust. If
there is a possibility of water on floors being splashed during janitorial
service, then storage should be high enough from the floor to prevent
this problem.

Basic Microform Selection Aids

There are several selection aids available to assist the librarian in locating information on microforms. The five aids described here are basic

tools which tell if the information is on microform. Further information about any particular selection can be obtained from aids that list, annotate and review the item in its original paper format.

Books on Demand: A Catalog of OP Titles: published by University Microfilms, Xerox Company, 300 North Zeeb Road, Ann Arbor, Michigan 48106.

> Scope: A comprehensive listing of domestic and foreign books that are out of print and available in microform.
>
> Entries: By author, title, publisher, and date of publication in original form.
>
> Special features: Contains a section on Slavic language titles. A supplement, *The O-P Bookfinder*, is available bimonthly and is free to librarians on request.

Guide to Microforms in Print: published by Microcard Editions, National Cash Register Company, 901 Twenty-sixth Street N.W., Washington, D.C. 20037.

> Scope: Annual cumulative guide in alphabetical order to books, journals, and other materials which are available on microfilm from United States publishers. Theses and dissertations are not listed. Prices of materials are given.
>
> Entries: Books are entered by author. Author entries include title and date of publication of work in its original form.
>
> Newspapers are entered by state, city, name.
>
> Archival materials and manuscripts are entered as listed by the publishing organization.
>
> Projects (e.g., publishing all the works cited in a bibliography) are entered under the compiler of the bibliography and/or the subject.
>
> Special features: Alphabetical listing of publishers and a directory of publishers by alphabetical designation. Has pertinent advertisements.

Newspapers on Microfilms and Special Collections: published by Micro Photo Division, Bell & Howell Company, Old Mansfield Road, Wooster, Ohio 44691.

> Scope: Annual publication of over 5000 newspapers (domestic and foreign) and a list of periodicals available from Bell & Howell Company. Also has a listing of special interest collections and special educational products. Gives information on microform related equipment.
>
> Entries: Newspapers are entered by state, city, name and available dates.
>
> Periodicals are entered by title, dates available, and price.

Special Interest Collections have a full page description.

Special features: Information on obtainable newspaper facsimilies.
A section on special newspaper collections.

Serials in Microform: published by University Microfilms, Xerox Company, 300 North Zeeb Road, Ann Arbor, Michigan 48106.

Scope: Lists the largest and most comprehensive selection of periodicals, documents, newspapers, and other serial literature available anywhere in microform. Has titles from 1669 to the present. Has nearly 7000 listings.

Entries: Alphabetically by title in the main section. Section of subject categories. Each entry has an order number, title, city of publication, backfile listings, current volumes, external and publisher indexes.

Special features: Backfile and current publications available in *Serials Bulletin*, available bimonthly and free on request.

Subject Guide to Microforms in Print: published by Microcard Editions, National Cash Register Company, 901 Twenty-sixth Street N.W., Washington, D.C. 20037.

Scope: A biennial, comprehensive guide by subject classifications to materials which are available on microform from United States publishers. Theses and dissertations are not listed.

Entries: Books are entered by author. Author entries include title and date of publication of work in its original form.

Newspapers are entered by state, city, name.

Archival materials and manuscripts are entered as listed by the publishing organization.

Projects (e.g., publishing all the works cited in a bibliography) are entered under the compiler of the bibliography and/or the subject.

Special Features: Alphabetical listing of publishers and a directory of publishers by alphabetical designations.

List of subject classification and index to subject classifications.

One step beyond the use of selection aids would be consideration by the library of having some of its own material committed to microform. Many companies provide this service, and it is suggested that the librarian consult the publisher of the local newspaper for further information about this service. With the information in this chapter, the librarian can provide specifications to the microphotographer as to the exact kind of reproduction services desired.

Microforms are here now. Their use is increasing at an accelerating rate. A strong possibility exists that sometime in the near future microforms will be the major format on which most information in the library is stored.

Selected Bibliography

Introduction to Micrographics. National Micrographics Association, 1973.

Lee, T. G. *Microform Systems: A Handbook for Educators.* 5th ed. National Microfilm Association, 1971.

Lee, T. G. *Microfilm Technology Primer on Scholarly Journals.* Princeton, N.J.: Princeton Microfilm Corp., 1969.

Nelson, C. E. *Microfilm Technology.* New York: McGraw-Hill, 1965.

Veaner, A. B. *The Evaluation of Micropublications: A Handbook for Librarians.* Chicago: American Library Association, Library Technology Program, 1971.

Zummo, R. M., and Tofquist, W. S. *Microforms: A Growth Industry.* Pamphlet. Washington, D.C.: U.S. Government Printing Office, February 1969.

SELECTION AIDS

Books on Demand: A Catalog of OP Titles. Published by University Microfilms, Xerox Company, 300 North Zeeb Road, Ann Arbor, Michigan 48106.

Guide to Microforms in Print. Published by Microcard Editions, National Cash Register Company, 901 Twenty-sixth Street N.W., Washington, D.C. 20037.

Newspapers on Microfilms and Special Collections. Published by Micro Photo Division, Bell & Howell Company, Old Mansfield Road, Wooster, Ohio 44691.

Serials in Microform. Published by University Microfilms, Xerox Company, 300 North Zeeb Road, Ann ARbor, Michigan 48106.

Subject Guide to Microforms in Print. Published by Microcard Editions, National Cash Register Company, 901 Twenty-sixth Street N.W., Washington, D.C. 20037.

7

16-mm Films

16-mm Film in the Library

The 16-mm film makes a unique contribution to the library collection as a medium of entertainment, education, and cultural enrichment and as an art form. It is essential for the librarian to be aware of why 16-mm films are currently the most prevalent form of sound–visual–motion media in the library and perhaps more important, have an appreciation of how motion picture films in general are capable of enhancing information effectiveness.

Motion picture films are presently available in predominantly three formats, 8 mm, 16 mm, and 35 mm (mm stands for *millimeter*, a measurement of the actual physical width of the film). Eight-millimeter film is produced in both standard 8-mm and super 8-mm formats. (Eight-millimeter film is treated in greater depth in Chapter 9.) Eight-millimeter films are extremely popular with the amateur or home moviemaker, and commercially produced 8-mm films are being acquired by libraries to satisfy information requests limited to individual or small group viewing. At the other extreme of motion picture film formats is the 35-mm film. This format is intended for professional use only for theater or large audience viewing. The cost of production and production equipment limits the feasibility of 35-mm film to large film producers who must aim their productions toward large audiences in order to insure a return from their large investments. In a ever increasing search for better quality, producers are making film spectaculars in 70-mm and 105-mm formats. The costs of producing 70- and 105-mm films are obviously even greater than those of producing comparable 35-mm films. Needless to say, the acquisition of films in the 35-mm (or larger) formats is well beyond the range of the library in both cost and need.

Sixteen-millimeter film format is the mainstay of the library collection. There are four main reasons why this is so: (1) historical development; (2) cost; (3) capabilities of 16-mm film, and (4) availabilities of titles.

Historical Development

Motion picture film development began in 1894 with the invention of Thomas Edison's Kinetoscope and the first motion picture and continued through the advent of the sound motion picture film, which by 1930 was hailed as a new form of entertainment. This period witnessed major cinemagraphic milestones (for example: the nickelodeon; the film, *The Great Train Robbery*, set filmic standards for shooting and editing films which are still used today; *Birth of a Nation*, which is recognized as one of the first successful feature length films ever made; and the evolution of the movie mystique, which includes Hollywood, motion picture stars, and the recognition of motion pictures as a legitimate art form). Early motion picture films were made of a highly flammable nitrate material, and because of several disastrous fires, legislation was passed requiring motion picture films to be projected from within specially designed fireproof projection booths. With the eventual development of safety or fireproof film, the path was clear for films to be used in a nontheater setting. It immediately became evident that the nontheatrical film was being viewed by audiences considerably smaller in size than those who viewed theater productions. This sparked development of 16-mm film, which if limited to small audience viewing, produces results in quality of projection comparable to those of a 35-mm film being projected to a large audience. Early developments of 16-mm film were rather slow, productions being aimed at short, one-reel (11 minutes approximately) cartoons, recreation of historical events, and travelogues. The 1940s saw a growth of educational films which gave the 16-mm filmmaker the necessary impetus for producing films. Sixteen-millimeter films were now recognized as a valuable means of presenting information. They contained sound–visual–motion information in the only format available to schools and libraries which was both manageable and economically feasible. By virtue of this acceptance, 16-mm films are currently the sound–visual–motion format that offers the greatest number and variety of available titles, which in turn makes them the mainstay of the library for information in this format.

Cost

The consideration of cost as a reason for libraries to become predominant users of 16-mm films was originally a help but now may be a hindrance. The help aspect is evident; the hindrance aspect is a factor each librarian must carefully evaluate. First, to consider the help aspect of 16-mm films, the equipment used to produce 16-mm films is far less expensive than 35-mm equipment and permits more people to be filmmakers and make more low budget films that libraries can afford to buy. There is also a significant savings in the actual cost of 16-mm film in comparison with 35-mm film. When 16-mm film became the standard for the nontheatrical film market, 16-mm projectors were mass produced at a fraction of the cost of 35-mm theatrical projectors. This resulted not only in less expensive projection equipment, but because of the competition in the American free enterprise system, many improvements were made in projection equipment. Today, 16-mm motion picture projectors project brilliantly sharp images, reproduce sound of highly acceptable fidelity, are compact and lightweight, function quietly, and are extremely easy to operate, for example, improvements are still being made to self-threading projectors. Because of these cost factors, the 16-mm format is the standard sound–visual–motion medium of libraries.

In regards to cost being a hindrance, many librarians presently believe that for the largest portion of their sound–motion–visual projection requirements, super 8-mm film more than adequately fulfills their needs. For small audience viewing (20–30 people) or individual viewing, super 8-mm film performs as well as 16-mm film. Both super 8-mm film and its projection equipment cost less than 16 mm. However, because libraries have invested heavily in 16-mm films and equipment, they are committed to them, and any gradual transition to super 8-mm film is neither practical nor economically feasible. For the super 8-mm format to make a penetration in the library requires what may be considered as plateau decisions. As an example, all films that are to be viewed primarily by one individual at a time should be acquired in the super 8-mm format only. The next plateau would be to determine if there are large groups of audiences in the 20–30 people range served by the library; and if so, films for these groups should also be in super 8-mm format. The final plateau would be to become aware of new technological developments in both super 8-mm and television projection that could make 16-mm films truly obsolete. Many film distributors now provide the librarian the option of purchasing materials in either super 8-mm, 16-mm, or videotape format. Sixteen-millimeter film has the provident virtue of providing the librarian a means of acquiring a sound–motion–visual medium, but it is for the prudent librarian to know to what extent to become involved and when to make the necessary transition to a new and better format.

Capabilities of 16-mm Films

The capabilities of 16-mm film are not solely inherent in 16-mm film, but rather are prevalent to it. As previously stated, in the historical development of 16-mm films, the early films were cartoons, historical events, and travelogues. Upon this foundation, a whole genre of 16-mm films was produced that capitalized upon events that could best be portrayed by combining sound–visual–motion and color—films intended to provide a common experience; films from which viewers with a wide range of abilities and interests could benefit; films that require the use of such techniques as the montage, time lapse, slow motion, flashback, microphotography, and animation. Besides entertaining, 16-mm films are also capable of educating, informing, persuading, and testing the viewer. Many contemporary social issues such as drugs, ethnic problems, ecology, futures, etc. are finding an effective vehicle of expression in the 16-mm film. Although these issues are more than adequately developed in print form, the 16-mm film serves as a catalyst for small group identification, discussion, persuasion, and reaction.

Availability of Titles

Of all the sound–visual–motion formats, the 16-mm film has the greatest number of titles commercially available to the librarian. Coupled to this are "free" films distributed by government, nonprofit institutions, and industry that are presently available only in the 16-mm format. A brief perusal of the 2 volume NICEM index to 16-mm films immediately reveals the number of subjects and titles available to the library. Because of the vast number of titles available in 16-mm format as compared to other film formats, the library is almost obligated to invest money in this medium. This being the case, the librarian is responsible for investigating the 16-mm medium in order better to understand how it can be used to its best advantage and truly to profit from its fullest potential.

Advantages of Motion Picture Films

An audience inquiry made after the showing of a fine motion picture about what impressed audience members most about the film typically elicits replies that extol the film's realism; that mention total involvement with the film; that claim complete understanding of the film; and that cite a genuine identification with the film's content. These comments are not platitudes, rather they are sincere expressions of the feelings a truly fine film can invoke within the viewer. Undoubtedly the key to classifying these comments is in the word *feelings*, for of all information media, motion pictures are capable of providing the *observer* with the greatest vicarious experience. The word observer is italicized to categorize an entire body of information media where the consumer is an observer rather than a participant. This category includes all types of print media (art prints, photographs, graphics), slides, filmstrips, and tape and disc recordings. By definition, the consumer of information is an observer because he does not actually handle, manipulate, or construct the information being consumed; in short he or she is not performing or doing. Of all the items in the observing category, the motion picture film is the least abstract or, stated positively, the most concrete experience. By virtue of its concreteness, it is also the most real. Considering the elements of the motion picture film, this is easy to understand: It can contain visuals (print and nonprint), motion, sound, and in many cases color. The other media in the observing category at most contain only two of these elements.

The librarian must critically analyze and synthesize the basic elements of visuals, sound, motion, and color of the motion picture as a means of indentifying its unique advantages in order to ascertain if it is a truly fine production. The motion picture is described as a medium which emphasizes picture primacy, and perhaps in most cases this is true. However, it is necessary to avoid the pitfall of becoming overly absorbed with picture and not maintaining an acute awareness of sound. Again it must be stressed that the librarian must attend to all the elements of the motion picture and be certain that they are meaningfully orchestrated into a truly fine production. The elements of the motion picture become means whereby the successful communication of its unique advantages can be carefully scrutinized.

There are several unique advantages to motion pictures. They can record, document, or preserve events in the most realistic form possible. These film events can take the form of the actual occurrence or a dramatization of it. The event can be staged or filmed on actual location. As a result, the past can be recreated, the future acted out. Because films involve motion, they provide a continuity of action; the viewer knows not only what is happening but how it is happening. Motion pictures do not require a high degree of intelligence or verbal ability in order to be understood. It is said that they provide a common experience whereby all levels of intelligence can derive something of benefit. It is for the librarian to determine if the advantage of common experience is suitable for the patrons for whom it is intended. It is conceivable that a film intended for viewers of high intelligence could be of such a kind that even when viewed by such a group, the range of ability within the group will cause some obviously to get more out of the film than others even though all will understand the film to varying degrees. Motion picture films remove the barriers of time, distance, size, and visibility. Time can be compressed, expanded, turned backward or forward, or held still. Distance is never a problem; the film can take the viewer to the other side of the earth or the far side of the moon. The smallest of objects can be microphotographed, or an entire planet can be seen in motion. Nothing is invisible to the motion picture film. The real invisible world can be seen by magnification, cutaway, or animation. The abstract invisible world can be viewed using such techniques as the flashback or superimposition, e.g., the viewer is able to see what the actor is thinking. Motion picture film has the unique advantage of providing a bird's eye view of the events being depicted. The viewer is "there," right in the heart of the action. Again, bear in mind that these unique advantages of the motion picture are achieved by the filmmaker skillfully combining the elements of visuals, motion, sounds, and color. The techniques the filmmaker uses when working with these elements are what makes the motion picture an art form.

Making a Motion Picture

Motion pictures involve more than a technique of recording moving visuals on photographic film. Motion pictures are truly an art form, and as such they suggest that it would be well for the librarian to be cognizant of how the film production crew employs the medium to achieve desired results. This cognizance can be invaluable when the occasion arises to select a motion picture for the library collection. The librarian needs a critical evaluative eye for motion pictures and should know not only if the film message is achieved but also how it was achieved.

Producing a motion picture is an art, and the filmmaker has at his disposal three techniques or devices through which to create his product. They are (1) camera manipulation, (2) sound recording, and (3) film editing. Bear in mind that filmmaking is a highly complicated art form, and narrowing down production to three major techniques appears to make it too simplistic. It is in the knowledge, ability, and skill of the filmmaker in successfully working with the various components in each technique that results in a great motion picture.

Camera Manipulation

By careful selection of lenses, camera position, and camera movement the filmmaker can capture on film precisely the information required from the script. Lenses can make objects appear near or far away, large or small; and scenes can have infinite degrees of focus. Zoom lenses can take the viewer into or out of a scene without a change in perspective. Lenses can also distort spatial relationships in an effort to achieve desired effects. Camera position can range from a very high to a very low level, can be very close to or very far from the subjects and scenes being photographed. Again, it is all in the effect that the filmmaker wants to create; e.g., a low camera very close to a subject, with the camera shooting up from a low angle, will make the subject appear to be huge and monstrous, the opposite set-up will make the subject appear small and diminutive. Camera movement creates a feeling of the viewer moving through the scene being filmed (remember the camera lens serves as the eye of the viewer when the film is being shot). The camera can be moved up or down (tilt), rotated on a fixed axis (pan), moved in or out of a scene (dolly), moved across a scene (truck), or any combination thereof. Camera movement is said to be successful when the viewer is unaware of it occurring, i.e., the technique should not detract from the content. All camera manipulation must be done under proper lighting conditions and perhaps should be considered as a major technique in and of itself.

Sound Recording

Too often the viewer takes sound for granted because, as discussed earlier, motion picture film relies on picture primacy. Nonetheless, if sound is poor, the film's message could become lost or obscured. Sound techniques employ such devices as music, either dominant or in the background, to create a mood or heighten visual effects; sound effects to add realism to the film; voice over or voice narration, whereby an off-screen voice is describing what is being viewed; live voice recording (lip synchronization) with the sound track actually being recorded while the scene is being filmed. The combining of sound with the visual and the action (motion) can result in the overall success or failure of the film.

Although the emphasis of picture primacy has been stressed, it is never-theless a fact that the viewer is less tolerant of poor sound than of a poor picture.

Film Editing

After the film has been shot, it is the film editing that puts the polish to the film by the skillful combining of all the scenes that were filmed. Many filmic effects are achieved in the editing room. Scenes are cut and tailored to appropriate lengths, and transitional devices are used to join scenes together. These include cuts, fades, dissolves, and special effects such as the montage, iris, and wipe. The cut is the straight splicing together of two scenes which directs the viewer to another scene occur-ring at the same place or at the same time. In a fade, one scene fades out to black and the succeeding scene fades in from black. This in effect denotes a change in time or place between scenes, the amount of change being controlled by the length of the fade. A dissolve, similar to a fade, occurs when two scenes overlap each other and conveys a gentle and easy transition from one scene to another; again the effect achieved is dependent upon the length of the dissolve. Special effects embellish the quality of production. A montage is a series of usually short but not directly related scenes which, when edited together, form a picture statement. It is analogous to a collection of words forming a sentence. An iris occurs when two scenes are superimposed with the main scene occupying the bulk of the screen and the secondary or superimposed scene appearing within a circle or iris, usually in the corner or center of the screen. A wipe occurs when one scene is replaced by another by sliding it across the screen on either a horizontal or vertical axis, i.e., as one scene is being "wiped" off another scene is being "wiped" on.

There are many other components to these three major techniques in producing a film, but it should suffice that filmmaking is a highly techni-cal art form. The librarian would do well to become knowledgeable in the techniques used in order to better understand and evaluate motion picture films (A good basic film on the topic is *Basic Film Terms: A Visual Dictionary*, Santa Monica, Calif.: Pyramid Films, 1970).

Cost Effectiveness of the Motion Picture

Too often the task of the librarian must be first to determine which information medium should be chosen and then, if the decision is for 16-mm film, to deliberate upon a whole set of criteria as to precisely which films to acquire and what, if any, are the acquisition alternatives.

Perhaps the first factor to be considered in the acquisition process should be that of cost effectiveness. More succinctly stated: Will the 16-mm film return more value per dollar than any other media format? There is no question that 16-mm film is currently the single most expensive information item that the librarian acquires. It is unfortunate to purchase a $10 book that receives little or no use, but it is barely short of catastrophic to purchase a $500 film that receives little or no use. Indeed, it is reasonable for a budget administrator to challenge a librarian's request for a $500 film when the same information is available in a $10 book. An answer to such a challenge must be predicated on a thorough knowledge of the capabilities of information media forms and in this case of the particular capabilities of 16-mm motion picture film.

A 16-mm motion picture can be viewed by an individual or by a large audience. When it is viewed by an audience, there is a commonality of experience—everyone is seeing it at the same time, and they can respond and react to it together. Presenting information to an audience accomplishes an objective more efficiently than the use of individual books. If the library were to buy 50 books (50 × $10 = $500), they would still only accommodate 50 people, whereas a film can accommodate several hundred people at one time. As a further comparison of the cost effectiveness of a $500 film compared to a $10 book: If each time the film is used it is viewed by an average audience of 50 people and the film is used 25 times, then the cost of the film is 40¢ per person [$500 ÷ (50 people × 25 uses) = 40¢]. Using the 40¢-per-person film cost and applying it to the $10 book, then the book too must be used 25 times [$500 ÷ (1 person × 25 uses) = 40¢)]. If the sole criterion for selection is per patron cost, then the purchase of the film or the book can equally be justified. Other criteria must also be considered in making a media selection determination.

As regards the actual cost of a film, it is best to use the 5–5 rule, which when applied to the purchase of a 16-mm film is interpreted to mean that in order to justify the purchase of a 16-mm film, it must be used a minimum of 5 times a year for 5 years, otherwise it should be rented instead of purchased. The 5–5 rule can be quickly validated by examining the catalogs of companies that rent and sell films. It immediately becomes apparent that the cost of 25 rentals (5 × 5) usually approximates the film's purchase price. Incidentally, many libraries have a policy of only renting films. The 5–5 rule still applies, and such libraries would do well to examine their rental records and determine if indeed their film rental policies are in need of modification.

Coupled to the factors of actual costs and numbers of patrons, the film presents its message in a fraction of the time it would take to obtain it from a book. Furthermore, the 16-mm motion picture film has the capability of providing for individual differences, in that both the slow and faster learner can benefit from it. Several factors become evident. For the slow learner, viewing a film is not predicated on an ability to read. Also, any vocabulary used in a film is augmented and reinforced with moving images, i.e., the viewer sees as well as hears how the vocabulary is used. On the other hand, the fast learner, or more knowledgeable person who comprehends the spoken word, is able to perceive visual subtleties that further enhance the understanding of the film's message.

Much research indicates that our society is gradually becoming functionally illiterate (i.e., 22 million Americans are unable to read a classified ad or fill out a job application). In inverse ratio to the decline in reading literacy is a growth in visual literacy. More people now acquire information via audiovisual channels, e.g., television and motion pictures. This does not mean that the librarian should condone reading illiteracy, but rather that having films available could be a means of furthering the cause of reading literacy. The film will provide information that the functional illiterate can handle and will get such a person into the library (which is still an environment conducive to reading), and the film could serve as a bridge to books. It could well be a case not of either–or, i.e., either the book or the film, but rather of both the book and the film.

Again as regards time, 16-mm films usually range from 10 to 60 minutes in length, therefore they do not require a long attention span. The film can be viewed in one sitting, which eliminates the need to retain information over an extended period of time. The film's message is presented succinctly in motion, sound, and color and does not require the time-consuming use of cues or lengthy descriptors. Film offers a concreteness and reality of experience that enhances retention of information. Because the film is a time saver, it is possible for an individual to view it more than once for different reasons, e.g., introduction of information, appreciation, review.

Along with the intellectual advantages of film are its psychological attributes. By providing a vicarious experience, motion picture film is able to shape behavior and attitudes. When a film is well done (an excellent documentary, for example), it can cause the viewer to react by wanting to do something. While being projected, the film requires the attention and demands complete control of the viewer's auditory and optic senses. Realizing the film is projected in a darkened room, the viewer is not distracted by the real environment and becomes immersed in the world of the film. When this occurs, the viewer "feels" the film, and the resultant psychological impact can be tremendous. To substantiate this, the reader need only view a film such as the classic documentary, *Harvest of Shame*. It is indeed a rare person who is not effected by it and does not feel and experience the futile plight of the United States migrant farmworker. *Harvest of Shame* is an excellent, moving documentary film; but the librarian in selecting film needs to develop an objective perspective. It must be remembered that the filmmaker lets the camera and audio recorders "see and hear" only what he wants them to "see and hear." Nevertheless, when properly used, the 16-mm film captures a sense of realism unachievable by any other information media form. (Note: Television producers use basically the same techniques as the filmmaker.) It would be truly wonderful if the signing of the Declaration of Independence had been recorded on film.

If the rationale described in this section leads to the decision to acquire films, the librarian can attend to the task of which particular films to acquire. For this purpose, it would be well to have some kind of understanding of the types or classifications of films.

Feature, Educational, and Art Films

There are many ways to categorize the 16-mm films in the library collection, but it is recommended that they be assigned to three major categories: the feature film, the educational film, and the art film. The reason for this classification is to provide the librarian with a means of ascertaining what proportion of the film collection is generally devoted to entertainment, information, and cultural enrichment. These three categories are not mutually exclusive, and a film could possibly be assigned to more than one category. To be able to utilize the three categories properly, it is necessary to have a working definition of the three terms.

To be classified as a feature film, a motion picture must display the following characteristics: It is usually a theatrical or dramatic production, and when compared to educational and art films, it has a much longer running time—averaging 90–135 minutes. Its purpose is to entertain and provide viewers with an opportunity to escape, if only for a short while, from their own daily routine existences. A feature film is usually associated with the Hollywood type production in that it has a story to tell. Feature films usually have well developed plots and tend to focus on people and the events in their lives.

The educational film should contain a learning objective. It is viewed for the specific purpose of learning something, whether a process, factual information, or an attitude. Although it can be entertaining, the purpose of the entertainment would only be as a vehicle for the learning that is expected to occur. The educational film makes extensive use of voice-over narration that informs the viewer of what is taking place and direct viewers attention to what should be observed. To be properly used, the educational film should entail pre- and postviewing activities, and many educational films are accordingly accompanied with teacher guides or instructional pamphlets. It is beneficial to the viewer if the learning objectives are explicit, but too often they are only implied. In either case, the learning objectives should be well developed in the film and should not be many in number. As a result, educational films average 10–30 minutes in length, a practice which serves two purposes: (1) it is an adequate time to present a limited number of learning objectives and (2) as the film is often used in a classroom setting, it allows time for pre- and postfilm activities during a normal class period. To be truly effective, the educational film should be made with the intent that it provide the viewer with the best way to achieve a particular learning objective. On occasion, the educational film will supplement, or be supplemented by, other forms of information media. The educational film will not replace the textbook, but it can certainly enhance it.

Without becoming mired down in a definition of what is art, let it suffice to say that the art film portrays a technique depicting a creative experience. The viewer sees the genesis of an idea evolve into a creative experience. By skillful use of camera, light, color, and sound, the filmmaker produces a work of cinematic art. Incidentally, an art film is not to be confused with a film about art, which is classified as an educational film. Rather, an art film uses the motion picture medium to convey its message, which in a pure sense means the film is the message. An art film cannot be translated to another media form without a tremendous loss of the total esthetic experience. Of the three types of films, the art film is usually the shortest, ranging from about 5 to 20 minutes of playing time. Art films are extremely popular in public libraries; they provide patrons with films that are unavailable from any other source. Furthermore, public librarians are assuming the role of purveyors of art films, citing as a justification that the library is the only community organization attending to art film masterpieces.

These in summary are the definitions of the three major categories of films. Subsumed under the categories of feature, educational, and art film are a host of film types, e.g., history films, science films, cartoons, mystery films, horror films, comedy films, biographical film, etc. These types obviously need not be defined, as the title of the type is in fact a definition of content. As stated earlier, a film or film type can be assigned to more than one of the three major categories, but fundamentally a feature film entertains, an educational film informs, and an art film provides an esthetic experience.

16-mm Motion Picture Selection Aids

Once you have made the decision to acquire a film or a particular type of film for the library collection, the next task is to find what films are available in any given genre. The knowledge acquired in the preceding sections of this chapter can now be applied to the actual selection process. The task of selecting a film is a demanding one, but in terms of both the film's relatively high cost and the number of film titles available for selection, it is a worthwhile endeavor. Thousands of 16-mm film are currently available, and each year hundreds of new films are produced that would enhance a library's film holdings. Unfortunately, there is always a financial limit on the number of films a library can acquire. Certainly, if the valid constraints of cost effectiveness are prudently applied, it is a skillful librarian who acquires that particular film which is just right for the library. To assure that the film search is properly conducted, the librarian needs to have access to the proper 16-mm film selection tools. Here again it is the professional ability of the librarian to know which selection aids are available and what information they provide.

Making a decision as to which selection aids to use becomes a case of knowing exactly what information is needed to make film selection decisions. A good film selection aid has some unique feature that makes it valuable, and perhaps several selection aids will need to be consulted in order to determine which films need to be previewed and ultimately acquired for the library collection. Unique features to look for in selection aids are those that list all films available, film of a particular genre, vital statistics (e.g., producers, cost, length, date, etc.), new films, free films, film evaluations and reviews, annotations, and cross-indexes. Obviously, no one selection aid could do justice to all these aspects in an easy to manage format, hence several aids may need to be used in combination.

As an aid in determining which selection aids to use, Figure 7.1 lists a cross-section of film selection aids and a predominant feature of each. Some of the titles of the selection aids are self-explanatory. Many selection aids provide more information than is indicated in the figure, how-

	Location	Evaluation	Review	Selection	Notes
Educator's Guide to Free Films	X				
Educator's Purchasing Master	X			X	
EFLA Manual on Film Evaluation			X		
8-mm Film Directory 1969–70			X		
Feature Films of 8-mm and 16-mm: A Directory of Feature Films Available for Sale and Lease in the U.S.	X		X	X	
Feature Films on 8-mm and 16-mm		X			
Films for Libraries		X	X		Supplemented by booklist
Film Review Index	X				Locates film reviews
Guide to Films about Ecology, Adaptation and Pollution	X				Special topic
Guide to Films about Famous People	X				Special topic
Guide to Films about Negroes	X				Special topic
Guide to Foreign Government Loan Films	X				Special topic
Guide to Government Loan Films	X				
Guide to Military Loan Films	X				Special topic
Guide to State Loan Films	X				
Learning Directory	X				
Multi-Media Reviews Index	X				Locates film reviews; Annual of AVI Review

Figure 7.1. 16-mm motion picture film selection aids.

	Location	Evaluation	Review	Selection	Notes
National Union Catalog: Motion Pictures and Filmstrips	X			X	
New Educational Materials: A Classified Guide			X		
New York Times Film Reviews			X		Feature Film
NICEM Index to 16-mm Educational Motion Pictures	X			X	
Olympic Training Film Profiles	X				Vocational films
Sources of United States Government Films and Audiovisual Materials	X				
United Nations 16-mm Film Catalog	X				United Nations topics
United States Government Films for Public Education Use	X				

Figure 7.1. Continued.

	Location	Evaluation	Review	Selection	Notes
Audiovisual Instruction			X	X	
AV Guide			X		
Booklist and Subscription Books Bulletin		X			
Business Screen Magazine			X		Special topic
Film Facts			X		
Film Library Quarterly			X		Research
Film Quarterly			X		Research
Film News			X		
Films in Review			X		
Film Review Index	X				Locates film reviews
K-Eight			X		
Landeis Film Reviews: Source Directory			X	X	
Media and Methods			X	X	
Previews			X		
School Library Journal			X		
Senior Scholastic		X	X		How to use film
Sightlines in Business and Industry			X		

Figure 7.2.   Periodicals helpful in film selection.

ever, they are considered excellent aids for the purpose(s) indicated. When using the chart, *Location* indicates a location tool that informs that there is a film available on a particular topic: *Evaluation* indicates that the tool evaluates films; *Review* indicates the film is reviewed (sometimes solely by virtue of being included in the publication as an indication that the editors deem it worthwhile); *Selection* indicates that the aid gives objective information and data about films, e.g., bibliographic entry, catologing information, subject heading, précis.

Figure 7.2 lists periodicals that contain information helpful in film selection. Some of the periodicals are devoted entirely to film selection, while others contain articles or sections devoted to film selection. The library involved in film selection should subscribe to some of these periodicals—they provide the best way to keep pace with new film releases.

Criteria for Selecting 16-mm Film

Motion picture selection aids tell the librarian what is available and something about the films, but criteria must be established in selecting a motion picture. Film selection must be accomplished in an orderly, systematic fashion that justifies acquiring certain titles while rejecting others. In the final analysis, the question must be asked, "Considering my library, did I purchase the right film?"

When establishing criteria for film selection, it is best to identify main areas of consideration and how they in turn affect the selection process. Three main areas would be (1) the library, (2) the film, and (3) the patron. Within this broad delineation criteria can be developed that insure proper attention is given to each of the areas. It is only by utilizing a systematic investigation through the use of specific criteria that the librarian will be assured that films being selected are best for the library's film program. The following criteria, though not exclusive, are worthy of consideration when selecting a motion picture film.

The Library

Before any film selection can be made, you must know your library and its philosophy, policy, budget, and current holdings.

1. *Philosophy:* What does the library regard as the purpose of having films? What kind of collection does library want (e.g., feature

films, educational films, art films)? What are the plans or goals of
the library for its film collection?

2. *Policy:* Who can use the films? When and where can films be seen
   (e.g., in the library only or can they be charged out)? What are the
   provisions for making projection equipment available?
3. *Budget:* How many dollars are available for purchase, rental, maintenance, repair? Does the patron pay a fee? Are any funds allocated for a special genre of film? Is it better to buy a long, expensive film or several short ones?
4. *Current holdings:* Is there a good balance in the collection? Do
   certain areas need rejuvenation with second editions or newer,
   up-dated topics? How large is the collection? To what extent are
   films being used?

The Film

Criteria developed for the actual selection of a film deal with the
specifics of the film and are concerned with obtaining films of the highest quality. If the right film is selected, it will be in agreement with the
library's program and worthwhile to the library patron.

5. *Content:* Does it have something to say and know how to say it?
6. *Authenticity:* Is it truthful? Accurate?
7. *Objectivity:* Is it biased or prejudiced? Does it present propaganda,
   or is it selling something?.
8. *Subjectivity:* Does it let the audience "get close" to the story?
9. *Relevance:* Does the film have any relevance to the patron?
10. *Specificity:* Does the film make a point and get to it? Is the film the
    proper medium (e.g., could it be better done as a filmstrip)?
11. *Technical quality:* How good is the photography, color, sound,
    lighting, continuity and organization of scenes, and camera tech-
    nique? What is the picture primacy (i.e., the emphasis in a film
    should be on the visual and not the audio). What is the rate of
    development or sequencing?

The Patron

You must know the patron who could or would use the film. The best
film in complete compliance with the library's policy is of no value if the
patron does not use it.

12. *Groups:* Are there any special interest groups or institutions that
    would make use of films?

13. *Programs:* Is there a library film program that the patron would attend to view the film?
14. *Interest:* Do patrons have the background, need, or interest to want to see the film?
15. *Other resources:* Can the film be seen elsewhere (e.g., local theatre or on television)? Is the film available in another medium (e.g., book)?

Although the 15 criteria are assigned to the three main considerations, it is only by using them in combination that best results can be obtained. Too often librarians place greatest concern on the second consideration and disregard the library and the patron. When this occurs, great films are undoubtedly acquired, but unfortunately they are of little value to the library and of less value to the patron. By giving equal concern to all considerations and employing the 15 criteria to accomplish the selection process, one employs a procedure that guarantees acquiring the best film for a particular library. Using the criteria as a guide, the next logical step is to develop a film evaluation form that will expedite the selection process and be congruent with the library's goals and objectives.

16-mm Film Evaluation Forms

When placed on a continuum, film evaluation forms can range from the highly subjective to the highly objective. A highly subjective form would contain very few questions and leave much space for narrative and subjective comments from the evaluator. At the other end of the continuum, a highly objective form would only provide opportunity for the evaluator to circle numbers or make appropriate checkmarks, which would make it somewhat of a rating form. Either type of film evaluation form can be respectable, valid, and reliable. The emphasis on a subjective form is to obtain quality information, i.e., to learn precisely what the evaluator thinks of a particular film. Unfortunately, subjective remarks are often difficult to quantify, and individuals, each having his own discrete value system, do not necessarily assign the same meaning or value to words. Perhaps one evaluator, who says a film is "terrific" or "great," in extolling its virtues, is using the terms somewhat hyperbolically and in reality means merely that the film is O.K. Another evaluator, who may use only short, terse remarks that do not reflect a high degree of preference for the film, may consider the film very worthy for acquisition. The task of the librarian in assessing remarks on a purely subjective film evaluation form is to quantify the various remarks from various evaluators and try to make valid interpretations as to whether the film should be acquired.

On the other hand, a highly objective film evaluation form can ask many more questions regarding the film being evaluated, but the respondent can only check off those remarks that appear to be closest to his or her reaction to the film. The objective form limits answers to yes or no or to some variation of a rating scale, e.g., excellent, good, fair, poor. No provisions are made for subjective remarks. A purely objective form is easy to quantify—all that is required is to total all the check marks and average them out. Unfortunately, there may be some characteristic about the film which the evaluation form did not attend to; and the evaluator is unable to provide a subjective insight which, in fact, may give an indication of the film's true worth. Therefore, most film evaluation forms employ some combination of subjective and objective statements. It is for the librarian constructing a film evaluation form to determine what information is needed from the evaluator in order to make an acquisition decision and which types of statements, subjective or objective, best achieve this end. In the final analysis, the librarian who ultimately makes the buy–no buy decision should work with the combination of subjective and objective information that best assists in making that decision.

Any film evaluation form must consider the respondent or person filling out the form. It helps to know the evaluator's expertise, how much time he or she can devote to filling out a form, and how frequently he or she will be using the form. Perhaps the evaluator is a professional librarian with facility in using evaluation forms, perhaps a patron with little or no experience. Depending on who will be using the form, one can determine if an explanation is necessary on how to use it. Terms should probably be simple enough to require no explanation or interpretation.

There should also be a concern for brevity. Being parsimonious has a distinct advantage: It does not tire out the evaluator by requiring responses to a lot of trivia. Regardless of the length of the form, there is one cardinal rule: "Ask a question only if you actually intend to use the information." Oftentimes, an elaborate form is used, and the only question the librarian looks at is the yes–no question on whether to acquire the film. If this is the case, save the evaluator's time and ask only one question, "Should the film be purchased: Yes—No?"

Another consideration in developing a film evaluation form is the use to which the form will be put. Is it to aid in selection and purchase; to develop a précis; to provide information to the potential viewer; or to be used for special classes of films? Whichever the case may be, the form must be designed for its particular application. A final consideration is "How is the form to be used?" Is it to be used by a committee who will engage in discussion after a group viewing or by an individual after a private viewing?

Basically, there can be six parts to a film evaluation form:

1. Vital information, or bibliographic entry, which should include title, producer, running time, color–black and white, cost, copyright date, distributor
2. Content information in the form of a 75-word précis
3. Content evaluation which examines how well the information is presented
4. Technical evaluation which examines the cinematic qualities of the film
5. Application, or who, why, or how the film can be used
6. A summary statement that should include, whether implied or specifically stated, a yes or no conclusion

The film evaluation forms shown in Figures 7.3 and 7.4 provide examples of purely subjective and purely objective forms that can be used as a basis for constructing forms for any institution. Depending on the needs of a particular library, the forms can be combined or modified in any way necessary, which would move them away from the subjective–objective extremes of the continuum. But keep in mind only to ask questions that will actually be used. In both forms, the bibliographic information, and possibly the annotation, depending on your viewpoint, can be modified

---

```
                                                          Date:

Title of film:

Annotation:

Content quality:

Technical quality:

How can film be used:

Conclusion:

Name of evaluator:                              Position:
```

Figure 7.3.   Subjective film evaluation form.

	Excellent 4	Good 3	Fair 2	Poor 1	Not applicable
Content:					
Authentic					
Biased					
Accurate					
Propaganda					
Up to date					
Enough information					
Length					
Technical quality					
Photography					
Editing					
Continuity					
Sound					
Cinematic technique					
Uses:					
Introduction					
Overview					
Stimulation					
Review					
Demonstration					
In-depth study					
Audience:					
Preschool					
K–6					
7–9					
10–12					
College					
Adult					
Does film					
Achieve its objective?					
Keep viewer's interest?					
Tell its story successfully?					
Have cross-discipline use?					

Evaluator's name: Position: Date:

Title of film: Distributor:
Producer: Date: Running time:
Color_____ Black and white_____ Cost:

Annotation (75 words or less):

Do you recommend that this film be acquired for the library collection?
Yes_____ No_____

Figure 7.4. Objective film evaluation form.

or even filled in by the librarian and not the evaluator, this not being evaluation information per se.

An interesting aspect of the objective form is the number under each evaluative category. Carrying objectivity to its extreme, the librarian should also be objective in analyzing the evaluator's response. This can be achieved if the librarian develops accept–reject standards prior to looking at the evaluator's response, which in turn can be achieved by setting acceptance levels for each category. For example, if the librarian makes a decision a priori that the content section must achieve a score of 21 or the film will be rejected and the evaluator checks three excellent (3 × 4 = 12), two good (2 × 3 = 6), and two fair (2 × 2 = 4), then the total score is 22 (12 + 6 + 4 = 22) and the librarian must accept the fact that the content is worthwhile. If this objective scoring system is followed throughout the entire form, decisions will not be influenced by the librarian's bias. Conversely, with the subjective form the librarian must put his or her own value on the evaluator's value statement.

It is not intended to say one form is better than another. The only good form is the one that works. Where it rests on the subjective–objective continuum is a decision only the librarian can make. It is to be hoped that the information in this chapter will result in intelligent, well thought out decision making in regard to developing the library's 16-mm film collection.

Selected Bibliography

Burke, J. G., ed. *Print, Image and Sound: Essays on Media*. Chicago: American Library Association, 1972.

Jones, E. S. *Manual on Film Evaluation*. New York: Educational Film Library Association, 1967.

Kuhns, W., and Stanley, R. *Exploring the Film*. Dayton: George A. Pflaum, 1968.

Spottiswoode, R. *A Grammar of the Film*. Berkeley: University of California Press, 1962.

Stephensen, R., and Debrix, J. R. *The Cinema As Art*. London: Cox and Wyman, 1969.

Tyler, P. *The Liveliest Art*. New York: Mentor Books, 1959.

SELECTION AIDS

Books

American Library Association. Audio-Visual Committee. *Films for Libraries*. Chicago: American Library Association, 1962. Supplemented by *Booklist*.

Educational Film Library Association. *Feature Films on 8 mm and 16 mm.* Annual. New York: Educational Film Library Association.

Educator's Guide to Free Films. Annual. Randolph, Wisc.: Educator's Progress Service.

Educator's Purchasing Master. 2 vols. Annual. Englewood, Colo. 80110: Fisher Publishing.

Film Review Index. 2 vols. Monterey Park, Calif.: 91754: Audio-Visual Associates, P.O. Box 324, 1970–1971.

Kone, A. *8 mm Film Directory 1969–70.* New York: Educational Film Library, 1969.

Learning Directory. New York: Westinghouse Learning Corp., 1971–.

Limbacher, J. L., ed. *Feature Films of 8 mm and 16 mm: A Directory of Feature Films Available for Rental, Sale and Lease in the United States.* 3rd ed. New York: R. R. Bowker, 1971.

Multi-Media Reviews Index. Ann Arbor, Mich.: Pierian Press, 1970.

National Audiovisual Center. *Sources of United States Government Films and Audiovisual Materials.* Annual. Washington, D.C.: National Audiovisual Center.

National Union Catalog. U.S. Library of Congress. *National Union Catalog: Motion Pictures and Filmstrips.* Quarterly. Washington, D.C.: U.S. Library of Congress, 1953–.

New Educational Materials: A Classified Guide. Annual. New York 10036: Citation Press, Educator's Service Division, Scholastic Magazines, Inc., 50 W. 44th St.

New York Times Film Reviews 1913–1968. 6 vols. plus supplements. New York: Arno Press, 1970.

NICEM. *Index to 16 mm Educational Motion Pictures.* 3 vols. New York: R. R. Bowker, 1973.

Olympic Training Film Profiles. 3 vols. New York: Olympic Film Service, 161 W. 22d St., 1968–1971.

Reed, S., ed. *United States Government Films for Public Educational Use—1963.* Washington, D.C.: U.S. Office of Education, 1964.

Sprecher, Daniel, ed. *Guide to Free Loan Films: About Foreign Lands.* Alexandria, Va.: Serina Press, 1975.

Sprechter, Daniel, ed. *Guide to Free Loan Foreign Government Films.* Alexandria, Va.: Serina Press. 1972.

Sprecher, Daniel, ed. *Guide to Free Loan Government Films.* 4th ed. Alexandria, Va.: Serina Press. 1976.

Sprechter, Daniel, ed. *Guide to Free Loan Military Films.* Alexandria, Va.: Serina Press. 1969.

Sprecher, Daniel, ed. *Guide to Free Loan Sport Films.* 2d ed. Alexandria, Va.: Serina Press. 1976.

Sprecher, Daniel, ed. *Guide to Free Loan Training Films.* Alexandria, Va.: Serina Press. 1975.

Sprecher, Daniel, ed. *Guide to Free Loan Films: On the Urban Condition.* Alexandria, Va.: Serina Press. 1976.

United Nations 16 mm Film Catalog. New York 10036: Distributed by Text Film
    Division, Contemporary Films, McGraw-Hill, 330 W. 42nd St., 1968. Free.

For Evaluation

Education Film Library Association. *Manual on Film Evaluation.* New York: Edu-
    cation Film Library Association, 1967.

Periodicals

AV Guide. (formerly *Educational Screen and AV Guide*). Blue Book Audio Visual
    Materials in December issue (formerly in July/August issue).
Audiovisual Instruction.
Booklist and Subscription Books Bulletin.
Business Screen Magazine.
Educational Products Report. New York 10016: Educational Products Information
    Exchange (EPIE).
Filmfacts.
Film Library Quarterly.
Film Quarterly.
Film News.
Film in Review.
Film Review Index.
K-Eight.
Landers Film Reviews: Source Directory. Los Angeles, Calif. 90069: Landers Associ-
    ation, P.O. Box 69760.
Media and Methods.
Previews.
School Library Journal.
Senior Scholastic (Teacher's Edition).
Training in Business & Industry.
Sightlines.

8

8-mm Films

Physical Features of 8-mm Film

When standard 8-mm film was originally designed, it was actually 16-mm silent film cut in half. For many years, standard 8-mm film was the only type of 8-mm film available. Unfortunately, the sprocket hole was designed for 16-mm film and equipment, and it became apparent that 8-mm film actually did not need such large sprocket holes in order to function properly. Hence, super 8-mm film was designed with much smaller sprocket holes and the extra space resulted in a 50% increase in the size of the picture area.

Carefully examine Figure 8.1. Note that both standard 8 mm and super 8 mm are the same width, but the sprocket holes of standard 8 mm (3 mm) are twice as wide as those of super 8 mm (1.5 mm). Observe that on standard 8-mm film the sprocket holes are located where the frames meet, whereas on super 8-mm film the sprocket holes are adjacent to the middle of each frame. Note also that the super 8-mm film frame is approximately 50% larger in area then the standard 8-mm film frame.

Physical Features of Optical and Magnetic Sound Tracks

As noted in Chapter 7, sound tracks are of two varieties, magnetic and optical. The magnetic sound track has a very thin strip, or stripe, of magnetic tape placed on the edge of the film. If you are shooting your

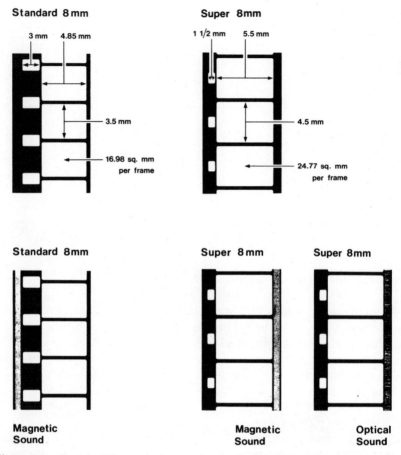

Figure 8.1. Standard 8-mm and super 8-mm film formats. Note location, physical dimensions, and shape of sprocket holes and location of frame lines and sound tracks.

own film, the magnetic stripe can be purchased on the original film or placed on the film after it has been exposed and processed. A major advantage of magnetic striped film is that with inexpensive equipment anyone can narrate or edit his own sound tracks. An obvious disadvantage is that information can be accidentally erased quite easily.

Putting an optical sound track on a film is a professional procedure. Because the optical sound track is produced by a photographic process not requiring additional striping for each film copy, production and process costs are reduced. An optical sound track is permanent and cannot be altered or edited. It is interesting to note that the majority of

8-mm films use magnetic sound tracks, but with 16-mm film optical sound tracks are overwhelming prevalent. This occurrence is attributed mostly to the fact that 16-mm films are used mostly by professional filmmakers but 8-mm film is the domain of the home filmmaker.

Look again at Figure 8.1 and examine the sound tracks closely. You can observe that the magnetic sound track is an extremely thin piece, or stripe, of magnetic tape whereas the optical sound track is photographed right on to the film and appears as variations of clear, transparent areas. If you could actually touch a piece of film with a magnetic sound track you would feel the additional thickness of the magnetic tape.

Comparison of Standard 8-mm and Super 8-mm Film

Setting up two projectors identical in every respect except that one accommodates standard 8-mm film while the other projects super 8-mm film, one notes immediately that the projected images are not the same. When both projectors are the same distance from the screen, the image projected by the super 8-mm film is 50% larger in area. This is obvious when you recall that the area of a super 8-mm frame is 50% larger to begin with. To make both images the same size requires that the projector with the standard 8-mm film be placed further away from the screen than the projector with the super 8-mm film. When both projected images are the same size, there is a deteriorization of picture quality with the standard 8-mm film. Obviously, the smaller standard 8-mm frame must have a greater enlargement in order to equal the projected area of the super 8-mm film. At close distances, the difference in quality is not too discernible, but as you continue to move both projectors further away from the screen, it becomes apparent that the standard 8-mm image is fuzzier, grainier, and less sharp. Although both images deteriorate in quality as the projectors are moved further away from the screen, it becomes more evident at a shorter distance and increases more rapidly with the standard 8-mm film. This fact is an important consideration when purchasing 8-mm films. If your 8-mm films are going to be used primarily for independent viewing (i.e., by one person), then it does not matter which type of film you acquire as the independent viewer will be viewing the film on a small screen. On the other hand, if your films are to be viewed by larger audiences, say 20–30 people, requiring the projection of a large image, then it is absolutely essential that super 8 mm be used.

In fact, selecting the proper film format can become a dilemma. Whenever possible, super 8-mm film should probably be acquired. Its better image has resulted in the gradual obsolescence of standard 8-mm film. On the other hand, if your institution, as well as the patrons who will be borrowing your films, only have standard 8-mm projection equipment, then you may be compelled to continue acquiring standard 8-mm film. Until recently, more film titles were available on standard 8 mm than on super 8 mm, but this is rapidly changing and the opposite is becoming true. It is possible that within a few years standard 8-mm film will become a collector's item as more and more super 8-mm films and equipment are manufactured.

One further consideration must be noted regarding 8-mm film. It was recommended that super 8-mm film be acquired for audience viewing (20–30 people). If there is a possibility that larger audiences might be viewing your films, then 16-mm film should be acquired—the observations made earlier about projected picture deterioration continue to hold true: A 16-mm film projected the same distance will produce a better quality image than a super 8-mm film. Many libraries acquire 16-mm films for audience viewing and super 8-mm films for small group or independent viewing. Incidentally, some film experts claim that super 8-mm can do the job of 16-mm film if good projectors are used and room darkening conditions are improved. Perhaps in the final analysis it would be best to conduct your own viewing experiment on super 8-mm and 16-mm film under conditions identical to those under which your patrons will be viewing your films. If super 8-mm films can be used, the cost of both film and equipment is substantially lower.

In regard to sound, super 8-mm film is available in both optical and magnetic sound tracks whereas standard 8-mm film is predominantly available in magnetic sound track only. At present, magnetic sound is more popular because 8-mm film appeals to nonprofessional photographers who want to make home movies with sound. Because magnetic sound tracks are more prevalent, more magnetic sound projectors are available, too. Actually, as has been noted previously, magnetic sound tracks produce much better sound fidelity than optical sound tracks and can be locally revised, narrated, or edited; but they are slightly more expensive and more susceptible to "accidental" erasure.

8-mm Film Containers

With 8-mm films, concern must be given to the type of container used to store the film. (See Figure 8.2.) The two most important considera-

Figure 8.2. 8-mm film containers. Left to right: open reel; Technicolor loop cartridge; Fairchild loop cartridge; Kodak cartridge.

tions are (1) How easy is it to use? (2) How well does it protect the film? When choosing between these two factors, it is sometimes necessary to make compromises.

The open reel is obviously the least complicated. The end of the film is slotted into the hub and wound on to the reel. But the film must be handled when it is threaded on a projector. Also, an open reel is more susceptible to collecting dust. (Note: All film, regardless of container, should be stored in a closed package.)

Technicolor and Fairchild containers are similar in that the film is housed in an almost closed container, the only opening being a small aperture through which the film comes in contact with the projector to drive the film and reproduce sound. The end of the film is spliced to the beginning, creating an endless loop. Both Technicolor and Fairchild containers are called loop cartridges. (Other companies make similar cartridges for use in their respective projectors.) The film in a loop cartridge receives no physical handling, but if you examine it carefully when it is in a projector, you will observe that the film loops rub against each other. Granted the film has a special lubricant to minimize friction, you nevertheless must be extremely careful to avoid dust because any dust that should collect on the film will act as an abrasive as the loops of film rub against each other. This highlights the need to keep the cartridge in a closed container when it is not in use to prevent dust entering the aperture. Both cartridges are sealed, and a special tool is required to open them if film repair becomes necessary.

The Kodak cartridge, which is not a loop, allows the user to load film easily. The cartridge actually houses a regular open reel enclosed without the need of special tools or skills. This cartridge has more open spaces than loop cartridges and is more susceptible to dust, but on the other hand, it does not have the friction problem of film loops rubbing against each other.

Assessing the pros and cons of 8-mm film containers, one finds that the open reel is least expensive but requires that the film be handled in threading and rewinding; it is also the most susceptible to dust. The loop cartridges are the easiest to use and have the smallest apertures for minimal dust exposure, but any dust entering will act as an abrasive; the film cannot be rewound (i.e., if the viewer does not wish to see the entire film, the film still must be projected in its entirety in order for the next viewer to see it from the beginning), and a special tool and skill are required to repair damaged film. The Kodak cartridge loads easily using an open reel, the film can be rewound at any time during viewing, and repairs are easily made; but it has a comparatively large opening to collect dust, and the machine on which it is used is slightly more complicated than a loop projector because the film must go through an automatic threading phase before it is ready for viewing.

8-mm Projection Equipment

When you are in the market for an 8-mm motion picture projector, your decision must be predicated on intelligent reasoning and fact finding, and not solely on the recommendation of a salesperson. This is not a criticism of sales people; actually they can be most helpful. But ultimately it has to be your decision, and once it is made, you have to live with it.

Before you even start thinking about equipment, you must first consider your patron, the user. Is your patron skilled (e.g., many institutions have trained projectionists available, and the viewer does not even touch the film), or is the patron a first time user; will the film be viewed in your building, or does your patron have to carry equipment (if the latter, portability is a concern); will the film be viewed by one person or a large group?

First consider ease of operation. Is the projector a manual threader or a self-threader; or as in the case of a loop cartridge, does it require no threading at all? With a manual threader, the threading path should be simple and easy and not a maze requiring that film be inserted into places accessible only to fingers shaped like tweezers. The requirements of self-threaders vary from nothing more than putting the cartridge loaded with film on to a feed spindle, to using an open reel requiring that the film be inserted into a slot in a special way and, after the film is threaded, slotted into the projector (and there is only one way to do it) before turning on the projector.

Examine the quality of the projected image. Be certain that (1) the image is stable and does not vibrate on the screen; (2) the image is bright enough under the conditions in which it will actually be used; (3) it is easy to focus and is in focus over the entire screen (some projectors have such critical focusing that if you move the lens just slightly the image is out of focus).

Some projectors come equipped as complete units with built-in rear projection screens. These projectors are designed for independent viewing. Note if the controls are conveniently accessible. Is there any glare on the screen from light in the room? The screen should not have any hot spots (i.e., one area of the screen brighter than another).

Next listen to the projector. Does it sound like a cement mixer, or is it smooth and almost noiseless? This is an important consideration if you have a half-dozen independent units being used in the same room at the same time. While listening to the projector in operation, look at it and see if there are any areas putting excessive wear on the film.

List any additional features the projector may have, being certain they are features you need or can use (remember, you are paying for them). Some additional features are stop motion, reverse, sound (magnetic or optical), high as well as low beam lamp, capability of projecting both standard 8-mm and super 8-mm films.

Other features to consider are (1) size or compactness (independent viewing unit should be as small as practicable); (2) weight (it should be easy to carry); (3) durability (a strong, lightweight metal will take more abuse than a thin brittle plastic); (4) cooling system (the fan should more than adequately—and quietly—disperse the heat generated by the lamp); (5) ease of maintenance (e.g., lamps should be easy to replace); (6) is a dealer available locally to service the unit; and (7) cost (it should be worth the price).

Keeping all these categories in mind, the best way to select a projector is to field test it with a side-by-side comparison. Any reputable dealer would be more than pleased to consent to this type of evaluation.

Criteria for Selecting 8-mm Films

A first consideration in selecting an 8-mm film is that it must be packaged in a container that is compatible with your equipment. If all you have is cartridge projectors and the film is only available on an open reel, then you must send your film to the company that makes the projector you own and have it packaged into a cartridge; this is obviously going to be an additional cost. Conversely, if your equipment is open reel and you buy a cartridge film, you must remove the film from the cartridge and wind it on an open reel, which of course means you paid for a cartridge you will never use. Fortunately, some 8-mm film producers package their films in all popular formats, but there are still many titles available in one format only.

You must consider how the film is to be used (i.e., is it primarily for independent viewing or is it for audience presentations?). Remember that if your audience is large, maybe you should acquire a 16-mm rather than an 8-mm film.) If intended for audience use, the film should be a complete entity requiring no supplementary materials. On the other hand, many films designed for independent viewing are complemented with supplementary materials.

When other materials are required, you must determine whether they are provided with the film or you will have to produce or acquire them. As an example, a study guide or script usually comes with the film, but consumable worksheets would require local production. Furthermore, some films for independent viewing that are not complete entities require follow-up activities involving some type of apparatus. If the film is to be truly meaningful, the apparatus must also be available.

There is a whole genre of 8-mm films called single concept films (caveat emptor!). These films average 4–8 minutes in length, but you must be careful in selecting them. Each must be previewed by someone knowledgeable on the topic. A true single concept film should only present one single concept. So-called single concept films have been made that present a half-dozen concepts and do more to confuse then inform.

With single concept films, another criteria to consider is whether the film is part of a series. If so, then is it necessary to purchase the entire series or is the particular concept you need complete in itself?

More silent motion picture films are available in 8 mm than in any other size. Although motion picture films stress picture primacy, i.e., the visual is more important than the sound, with a silent film you must determine that indeed sound is not required. The film may be accompanied by a detailed printed description that can be read prior to viewing. If a silent film meets your needs, you can realize tremendous savings because you do not have to pay the additional price for the sound track, nor do you need a more expensive sound projector to view it.

If you do select a sound film, be certain that it is compatible with your equipment. An optical sound track is worthless to you if all you have is equipment designed for utilizing film with magnetic sound tracks.

Eight-millimeter films have a place in the library. They are less expensive than 16-mm films; the projection equipment is less expensive than comparable 16-mm equipment; both the films and equipment require less storage space; and they are ideal for small audiences and independent viewing.

Selected Bibliography

Bell, G. *8mm Film for Adult Audiences.* New York: United Nations, Educational, Scientific, and Cultural Organization, United Nations, 1968.

Miller, E. E. *Single Concept Film Clip Project: Final Project Report, U.S.O.E. No. 4-16-030.* East Lansing: Michigan State University, 1967.

SELECTION AIDS

Books

Audiovisual Market Place. Annual. New York: R. R. Bowker.

Educator's Purchasing Master. Englewood, Colo.: Fisher Publishing Co., 3 West Princeton Ave., Vol. 1: *Instructional Materials.* Vol. 2: *Instructional Equipment.* Vol. 3. *Publishers.*

Kone, G. A., ed. *8mm Film Directory.* New York 10023: EFLA. Comprehensive Service Corp.; 250 W. 64th Street, Dept. 8., 1969-70.

Limbacher, J. L. *Feature Films on 8 mm and 16 mm.* New York: R. R. Bowker, 1971.

Multi-Media Reviews Index, 1970. Ann Arbor, Mich. 48108: Pierian Press, Box 1808.

New Educational Materials, 1970. New York 10035: Citation Press, Educators Service Div., Scholastic Magazines, Inc., 50 West 44th Street.

NICEM. *Index to 8 mm Educational Motion Cartridges.* Annual. New York: R. R. Bowker.

Westinghouse Learning Corp. *Learning Directory.* New York: Westinghouse Learning Corp., 100 Park Avenue, 10017.

Periodicals

Audience. Robert A. Wilson. Wilson Associates, New York, N.Y.

Audiovisual Instruction.

Business Screen. Bob Seymour Echter. Harcourt, Brace, Jovanovich Publishers, New York, N.Y.

Cine-Review. J. Van Cottam, editor. Cine-Review Publish, Brussels, Belgium.

Educational Product Report. New York: The Educational Products Information Exchange (EPIC) Institute, 385 Park Avenue South.

Educational Screen and Audiovisual Guide. Chicago: Educational Screen, Inc. 434 S. Wabash Avenue. *Blue Book Annual.*

Media and Methods.

Preview. Chris Wagner Echten. Bloomington: Indiana University.

9

Filmstrips and Slides

Filmstrips and Slides: Physical Characteristics

The fundamental difference between filmstrips and slides lies in the fact that filmstrips contain a *group* of still pictures on a continuous piece of transparent film whereas slides are individually mounted still visuals on separate pieces of transparent film. Both filmstrips and slides can be made in the same camera, use the same film, contain exactly the same information, and be used the same way; again, the difference being that a filmstrip is a series of still visuals on one physical piece of film while slides are cut and mounted to be used as individual still visuals.

When compared, filmstrips and slides have apparent advantages and disadvantages. A filmstrip is easier to control physically: All the visuals are placed on one continuous piece of film which is usually stored in a plastic or metal canister. When checking a filmstrip in or out of the library, the librarian can quickly and easily determine if it is complete and intact. Slides are more difficult to control—each visual is an entity and must be stored, labeled, and distributed separately. On the other hand, filmstrip visuals, because they are on continuous pieces of film, must be used in a prescribed order; slides can be arranged in any order deemed necessary by the user, and it is possible to shuffle, add, delete, and update a series of slides. In this sense, a slide presentation can be tailor-made to the needs of the individual user. In defense of fixed filmstrip sequences, they are photographed in a prescribed, logical sequence; and the user usually would never need or want to rearrange the sequence. Filmstrips are usually less expensive than slides because slides require the additional cost of materials and labor involved in having them individually mounted.

The bulk of both commercially produced and locally produced filmstrips are photographed on 35-mm film. Some producers have considered the feasibility of using 16-mm film, but to date very little has been produced. Sixteen-millimeter filmstrips are somewhat cheaper to produce and occupy less storage space. But they require 16-mm still projectors for viewing, and the fact that few libraries have such projectors is a main reason why the format has been very slow in gaining acceptance. Librarians should keep abreast of 16-mm filmstrip developments, however, for they could prove to be an economic boon. To return to 35-mm filmstrips, they are available in only two formats: single frame and double frame.

Single-frame filmstrips make up well over 99% of available 35-mm filmstrips. You will observe from Figure 9.1 that the visuals are photographed on a vertical plane and that the ratio of picture (or frame) height to width is approximately 3 to 4. The double-frame filmstrip is photographed on a horizontal plane, and the height–width ratio is 2 to 3. This

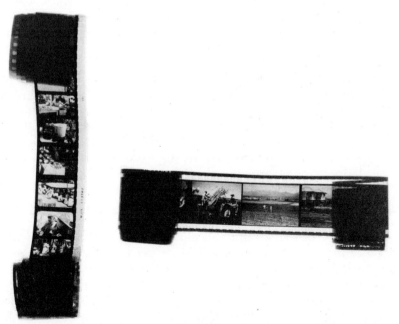

Figure 9.1. Single frame filmstrip (left); double frame filmstrip (right).

means that a librarian selecting a filmstrip projector must know what type(s) of filmstrips are to be projected. If the library has only single-frame filmstrips, there would be no need to purchase a projector capable of projecting double-frame filmstrips, and the additional capability obviously increases the cost of the projector. Conversely, if the library has only single-frame filmstrip projectors, it should not consider purchasing double-frame filmstrips. (Note: If information is available in double-frame format only and your institution does not have double-frame filmstrip projection equipment, the filmstrip can nevertheless be purchased and the visuals cut and mounted as individual slides. This procedure requires no special equipment or skill, and any local camera shop has cardboard mounts available.) Observe that the overall dimensions of 2 single frames are exactly equal to those of 1 double frame. This explains why they are called single frame and double frame; some librarians call them half-frame and full frame. But whichever way they are named, the ratio is still 1 : 2.

Slides are available in various sizes, the 2 × 2 inches being most prevalent. Its overall dimension, including the mount or frame, measures 2 inches wide by 2 inches high. The 2 × 2 inch mount can contain 35-mm half-(or single) frame film, 35-mm full (or double) frame film, or 127 size film (see Figure 9.2). Because of the same size mount, all three sizes can be viewed using the same type of viewing equipment. Other size mounts are the relatively new 110 size, the 2¼- × 2¼-inch mount used with 120 film size, and the 3¼- × 4-inch mount. Each of these sizes in turn requires viewing equipment adaptable to its respective size. As a result, commercial producers and libraries have adopted the 2- × 2-inch format as a standard. However, the librarian should keep abreast of new developments. The new 110 (1³/₁₆- × 1³/₁₆-inch) size is rapidly gaining in popularity. A further consideration is that technically the larger the film the better its quality of resolution and rendition when projected. As a result, many art, architecture, and medical visuals, which demand extreme clarity of detail, are photographed with larger size films. In fact, many commercially available visuals for art, architecture, and medicine are available on 35-mm full frame, 2- × 2-inch slides, or on 3¼- × 4-inch slides rather than the more common half-frame filmstrip.

A final type of transparent still film is the stereoscopic slide which projects a three-dimensional image. Most stereo equipment is intended for individual viewing. Because stereo slides require the simultaneous viewing of a pair of visuals or slides, they must be mounted in juxtaposition in order to give the three-dimensional effect. Some companies mount the visuals on cardboard wheels; other companies mount them on rectangular cardboards. Again, it is critical to know this when select-

Figure 9.2. Photographic slides. Top row: 2- × 2-inch slides, left to right—half-frame 35-mm film; Instamatic 126 film; full frame (standard size) 35-mm film; super slide 127 film. Bottom row: 2¼ × 2¼ inch 120 or 620 film; 3¼ × 4-inch sheet film.

ing stereoscopic visuals; each format (wheel or rectangular card) requires its own type of viewing equipment, and the two are in no way interchangeable.

Advantages of Filmstrips and Slides

If you want your patron to view graphic or pictorial information under conditions that show such visual information as brilliantly and realistically as possible, then you should use photographic film. A picture in a book communicates well, but a slide or filmstrip when projected adds a depth and vitality unobtainable from a paper print. Also, the slide or filmstrip, although it can be viewed by an individual using a slide or filmstrip viewer, can be projected on a large screen. This permits many people to view it at the same time, which is not possible with visuals in a book. Compared to large prints or photographs, slides and filmstrips cost much less, are easier to manage and store, and are less susceptible to damage. Still another consideration for using filmstrips and slides is that if the information to be viewed does not require motion, then a filmstrip or slide is far less expensive than a motion picture film.

Filmstrips and slides have a distinct advantage over motion pictures in that viewers can pace the viewing of information at their own rate of speed. They can have a visual projected for only a fraction of a second or leave it projected for as long as they want to look at it.

Used by a competent librarian for group presentations, filmstrips and slides can compel attention, generate discussion, and involve follow-up activity such as reading books for further information. When the librarian provides filmstrips and slides to children and young adults, the results are usually most gratifying. They tend to stimulate an interest in the library, and most filmstrips and slide sets can be viewed in one sitting, not requiring a long attention span. This makes them a great motivational device for the culturally deprived not inclined toward reading. It is quite probable that the reticent reader, after viewing a few filmstrips, will be less reluctant to attempt to read a book, feeling that if the library has good filmstrips it may also have some enjoyable books. For the good reader, accessibility to filmstrips and slides means that supplementary and enrichment materials are available to embellish the book. Actually, the task of the librarian is to select the right information, in the proper medium, to suit best the needs of the patron.

Many filmstrips contain visuals accompanied by captions. The librarian should know how best to use the captions in group presentations. If they are used with a young group, the librarian or different youngsters may read them aloud. It is suggested that when necessary captions be further discussed, for they usually give only basic information. When captions are used with literate adults, it is advisable as a rule of thumb that you read each caption silently to yourself twice then proceed with any necessary discussion or advance to the next visual. This type of pacing provides an opportunity for slower readers to read all the caption but does not bore fast readers with a slow, dragging presentation.

An ever increasing number of sound filmstrips and sound slide sets are being produced. They restrict the flexibility of viewing, because the visuals must be shown at the pace dictated by the sound commentary unless the sound source is stopped to allow for prolonged viewing; however, sound adds a new dimension to filmstrips and slides. The viewer can be given more information than would be feasible on a caption; and the use of music, real sounds, and sound effects greatly enhances communication of the visual information. The sound is provided on either a disc record or an audio tape. The addition of sound gives filmstrips and slides the scope of a sound motion picture film, and when motion is not essential, a sound filmstrip or sound–slide set can do the job just as well at a fraction of the cost.

A librarian should spend some time perusing filmstrip and slide selection aids to get an idea of the extremely wide range of information available. With a comparatively small expenditure of funds, a good collection can be acquired. The librarian can investigate an infinitely wide range of titles, concentrate on a particular topic, or even consider the acquisition of a series. Incidentally, series acquisitions give a continuity to the filmstrip or slide program, as many patrons will want to view more than one filmstrip or slide set of a particular series.

Filmstrips and slides enhance the viewing quality of a visual, can be viewed individually or in groups, are more economical than motion picture films, and are easy to manage. Each visual can be viewed for as long as desired, further stimulating interest. They are either captioned or accompanied with sound, and a breadth as well as an in-depth range of titles and topics is available.

Local Production of Filmstrips and Slides

Because cameras are fairly inexpensive and do not require professional photographic training to use, librarians can produce their own filmstrips and slides. Oftentimes, there is information of local interest that is not available on a commercially produced filmstrip that can be easily photographed by the librarian. If the information is nonexistent in a filmstrip or slide format or must be uniquely photographed or arranged, or if your patrons have a particular need, then local production is justified. Local production can never be justified on the basis of economy, for you will immediately find that even if you work for $1 per hour, the eventual cost in time expended will usually far exceed the cost of purchasing a commercially produced filmstrip or slide set of comparable quality.

Examples of filmstrips or slide sets locally produced include those that, for example: provide the viewer with instruction on how to use your particular facility; supply information regarding local library programs; offer promotional packages advertising the library and its services for purpose of informing or encouraging patrons to use the library; request additional funds; or provide a community service. Libraries also produce filmstrips and slide sets as an in-service training device. Local production provides an opportunity to photograph information that the viewer can readily identify. Another ideal locally produced filmstrip or slide set would involve a field trip to a community resource. The viewer can learn and observe specifics prior to the field trip, or perhaps the need for the field trip can be eliminated. If the field trip is taken, then it becomes more meaningful, and the filmstrip or slide set can be viewed later as a follow-up activity if needed.

There are several basic considerations to be resolved when producing a filmstrip or slide set. Assuming that the necessary equipment is available for both photographing and projecting the information, it must first be determined if the end product is to be a filmstrip or a slide set. Filmstrips, as explained earlier, are less expensive and easier to manage than slides. They require a little bit more technical skill in producing than do slides. It is strongly advised that a half-frame camera be used to produce a filmstrip as this is overwhelmingly the prevalent format. The visuals for a filmstrip must be photographed in a prescribed sequence. Although a filmstrip can be spliced—which means visuals (frames) can be added, deleted, or rearranged—this is not recommended. Filmstrip splices have a tendency to jam in a projector, and they are usually a weak link in the physical durability of a filmstrip. This means that if upon processing a roll of film some of the visuals are not satisfactory and must be rephotographed, it is best to reshoot the entire filmstrip.

In photographing slides, the problems are not so acute. The visuals can be photographed in any sequence that is convenient, unsatisfactory shots can be deleted and replaced with more satisfactory shots, and the finished slides can be arranged or rearranged whenever or however desired. The end result, be it filmstrip or slides, will be same, it is just that filmstrips allow less margin for production error.

When you have decided whether you will be making a filmstrip or a slide set, your next consideration is the type of material to be photographed. If the material can be photographed with a hand-held camera or a camera mounted on a tripod, there is no problem. However, if material is to be copied from a book or is comparatively small, then a copystand must be employed. This is not an insurmountable difficulty—a copystand like the Kodak Visualmaker allows slides to be made by those having no photographic skills whatever, and complex cameras with interchangeable lenses or lens attachments allow you to photograph extremely small objects. If you want to make a copy of a slide, you will need a slide copier, which according to your ability and equipment can be either a simple camera accessory or a copy camera like the Repronar. In fact, if copying slides is not a frequent occurrence, it would be best to have it done at your local camera shop.

Because making them is rather difficult and time consuming, captions are hardly ever used in local production of filmstrips and slides, which leads to the next consideration: Do you want to produce a sound filmstrip or sound slide set? If yes, you must prepare a script and record the sound with a tape recorder. If the finished product is to be viewed independently, the tape must be cued. If you have equipment that automatically advances the filmstrip or slide on electronic cue or signal, then you must put the electronic cues on the tape. If automatic equipment is not available, then audible cues must be put on the tape. The problem with audible cues is to make them sound pleasant and not distracting. Some people use bells, clickers, or "cricket" devices; others strike water glasses or create other sounds. (Note: The author's experience has been that a device that produces a C# tone is best and can be purchased in a music store [e.g., a child's xylophone]; also good for generating a tone is a code practice oscillator with variable volume and tone control and can be purchased in an electronic equipment store.) Unfortunately, the end result is oftentimes far from what is desired and can turn an otherwise fine production into a fiasco. If the package is to be used only for group presentations, do not use any audible cues; instead, provide the projectionist with a printed script, and let him advance the projector while listening to the tape and reading the cues from the script.

When you become adept at producing filmstrips and slide sets, you might want to consider a multiimage, multimage, or multiscreen presentation. The foregoing terms are synonomous and simply mean a presentation using more than one projector simultaneously. Although it requires more work, patience, and perhaps just a little bit more skill, the results can be gratifying. Again, depending on your skill, production time, and equipment, your multimage presentation can range from a simple affair using 2 manually operated projectors all the way to a complex automated, computerized production using 30 or more projectors.

Another consideration is that of making multiple copies of your production. If additional copies are required, special equipment is required, e.g., a Repronar copy camera. However, most libraries in need of multiple copies can have them made by the local camera shop for a nominal fee. One word of caution, the quality of the copy will never be as good as that of the original; something is always lost in the succeeding generation (e.g., realism of color, sharpness, etc.); therefore, examine each copy carefully to insure that it meets your minimum standard of quality.

Somewhat related to the consideration of multiple copies is that of copyright. Legally, when you copy information out of a book or anything else that is copyrighted, you must have permission from the rightful owner to do so. Ignorance of this law is not an excuse; and as a professional, you (or your institution) are responsible for any violations of copyright.

These considerations are basic to the actual local production of a filmstrip or slide set. There are others of a more technical nature which are beyond the scope of this text. The purpose here is to inform you about what is basically involved in producing a filmstrip or slide set. It can be done, it is not difficult, and it can be rewarding because it provides your library with material unobtainable from any other source.

Assessing Filmstrip and Slide Projection Equipment

A recurring theme in this textbook with respect to audiovisual equipment is that it is of value only if it is being used. Is it truly worth the price paid for it, and does it do everything you expect it to do and do it to your expected level of performance? These concerns serve as primary guidelines in assessing filmstrip and slide projection equipment.

When selecting filmstrip and slide projection equipment, you must first ascertain what size collection of filmstrips and slides you have and how it is being used. The size of the collection will help you determine how many pieces of equipment are needed. Of course, there are libraries with large collections that receive little use so that little viewing equipment is needed. Where this is true, it indicates an extremely poor system—a large collection not being used is a sure indication of poor selection procedures. If the collection is extensively used, an analysis must be then made to determine how many patrons use it (e.g., number patrons during peak utilization periods). This will give an indication of the number of projectors needed. You then determine how the patrons are using the equipment, i.e., large group, small group, individual viewing, and where it is used, i.e., in the library or in a remote location that would require it to be light and portable. Having determined equipment use patterns, how the patron will be using the equipment, and your budget, you can calculate how much you should allocate to purchasing any particular type of equipment. You may find that you can afford something better than you originally intended to purchase or you may have to make compromises in order to satisfy your needs. Bear in mind that equipment can range from simple, hand-held, manually operated viewing equipment for individual use all the way to automated electronic equipment for large group use. With such a wide range of selections and prices, it is essential that the equipment receive its intended use.

If sufficient equipment use can be justified, then it would be best to select equipment designed for a specific type of use; if not, then equipment with greater versatility should be selected. As an example, if your patrons individually view filmstrips in the library extensively, then a small air-cooled projector with its own rear projection screen built into the cabinetry of a viewing carrel should be considered; but if both portability and in-library use is expected, then a lightweight portable unit with a self-contained viewing screen should be selected. If the same piece of equipment has to be used for both individual and small group use, then a still different set of selecting criteria will have to be considered. There is no one piece of viewing equipment that can satisfy all needs. A host of questions for each type of use must be answered when selecting filmstrip and slide equipment.

Individual Use

Depending on your particular type of library, you may want to select filmstrip or slide projection equipment that is permanently installed into a learning carrel, as well as portable equipment capable of being used both in and out of the library. With permanently installed equipment, thievery problems are eliminated since it is virtually impossible to steal a projector when it is built into a large piece of furniture. But this can present problems, too: If your projector needs repair, it will have to be removed from the furniture it is built into; if repair is to take some time, a replacement unit should be installed in its place. Built-in equipment has the dual advantage of not cluttering a working area and being esthetically more attractive.

A prime concern for filmstrip and slide viewing equipment for individual use is ease of operation. The equipment should be simple enough to operate that even a school-age child can use it with little or no instruction. If the patron has to load and unload the projector, it should not have a difficult and complex loading or threading mechanism. If the equipment is permanently loaded, it should have a procedure for cycling or rewinding in order for every patron to view the presentation without the difficulty of finding the beginning.

If the equipment has audio capabilities, audio cassettes are strongly recommended because they are easier to operate and are more compact than either open audio reels or disc records. Also, with audio combination systems, attention should be given to headsets; they should be acoustically good, comfortable to wear, and hygienically safe. If your library can afford it, it is recommended that equipment which automatically responds to inaudible electronic cues be purchased in preference to manually operated equipment because it eliminates the task of having to advance the filmstrip or slides, thereby freeing the user to enjoy and concentrate on the information presented.

Because projection equipment for individual use does not require a large projection lamp, many projectors do not require fans to cool the lamps. If possible, select such a projector, as this eliminates any noise a fan would generate, uses less electricity, and is one less thing in need of maintenance. However, before an air cooled projector is purchased, it should be tested under conditions exactly like those under which it will be used by your library. Leave the lamp on and the projector loaded with a filmstrip or slides for an extended period of time (several hours if necessary); observe whether any damage is done to the filmstrip or slides and that the projector does not become too hot to be handled safely or a potential fire hazard.

The viewing surface or screen should be large enough to provide sufficient magnification for even the smallest caption to be read without eyestrain. The screen should be evenly illuminated and not have any bright (hot) spots. It is very uncomfortable to view a projected image that is blindingly bright in the center and rapidly falls off to a dark, shadowy image toward the edges.

Small Group Use

For purpose of definition, a small group would consist of from 2 to about 10 people. If your group will rarely exceed 2 or 3 people, consider selecting equipment that is intended for individual use but has a large enough viewing screen to be used by a group of 3 as well. If the group is going to be larger (4–10 people), a first consideration will have to be room darkening if the equipment is for front projection (front projection occurs when a projector at rear of room projects an image on the *front* surface of the screen). Presently there are some excellent rear projection screens for small group viewing that can be used in a normally light room (rear projection occurs when a projector, usually using a front surface mirror, is placed behind a translucent screen and the image is projected on the *rear* of the screen). In either case, the image should be of adequate size and quality to be properly viewed by everyone in the group. As regards seating arrangements, the person closest to the screen should ideally be no closer than the equivalent of 2 screen widths from the screen, and the furthest person ideally no more than 6 screen widths away.

It is recommended that equipment have some type of remote control device that permits a member of the group to advance or stop the presentation without actually being at the projector. Oftentimes small groups become involved in discussion as the presentation proceeds. Although small group equipment tends to be larger than individually used equipment (i.e., projector, screen, sound system), concern should still be given to portability and ease of assembly and dismantling.

Table 9.1. Lens and Screen Selection Chart

Width of screen	40 inches	50 inches	60 inches	70 inches	84 inches	8 feet	9 feet	10 feet	12 feet
Lens focal length (inches)		Projector-to-screen distance (feet)							
				2- by 2-inch slides					
3	7	9	11	13	16	18	20	22	27
4	10	12	15	17	21	24	27	30	36
5	12	16	19	22	26	30	34	37	45
6	15	19	22	26	31	36	40	45	54
				35-mm single-frame filmstrips					
3	11	14	17	19	23	27	30	33	40
4	15	19	22	26	31	36	40	44	53
5	19	23	28	32	39	44	50	56	67
6	22	28	33	39	47	53	60	67	30
7	26	32	39	49	55	62	70	78	93

Large Group Use

A prime concern in selecting projection equipment for large group use is adequate lamp wattage to illuminate the screen properly. The best way to determine this is actually to try out the projector under the severest conditions under which it will be used. The equipment should be relatively quiet, but there need be less concern about complexity of operation because in large group presentations a qualified person usually operates the equipment. Lenses should be properly selected for the size of the screens to be used and the distance the projector is to be located from the screen (see Table 9.1). For a multiplicity of projection situations, e.g., large screen–small room ranging to small screen–large room, a zoom lens with a variation of lens sizes should be acquired.

Combination Projection Equipment

For a library with a limited budget or equipment that will receive limited use, combination equipment should be considered. Some projectors project both filmstrips and slides, can be used for both front and rear projection, (individually as well as by a large group, and with or without sound), and have detachable sound systems to be used independently (either with or without headsets and manual, remote, or automatic operation).

Storage Equipment

Although not a part of utilization, storage of filmstrips and slides warrant consideration. Storage equipment should be compact and not waste space, designed for modular addition or expansion, and impervious to light, dust, and humidity. Slide storage should require minimal handling of slides, provide proper separation so slides do not rub together, and allow for accession numbering. As an added feature, some slide storage cabinets permit viewing of slides in great numbers without physical handling or removal from the cabinet. This is expedient when the librarian has to select each slide from a large collection.

Selecting and Evaluating Filmstrips and Slides

There is no one universal form for selecting and evaluating filmstrips and slides. Depending on its purpose, a library could perhaps have need of more than one type of filmstrip and slide evaluation form. The criteria used to evaluate are pretty much standard, the variation arises in determining how many criteria you want to use; the degree or depth to which the criteria will be examined; who is doing the evaluating as regards knowledge, interest, and amount of time that can be devoted to the task; and the purpose for selecting and evaluating, e.g., acquisition, deletion, special programs, abstracts, etc.

Use the following standard criteria as a guide in constructing a filmstrip and slide evaluation form. Each criterion is provided with a basic definition in the form of a question and should be developed (contracted, expanded, combined, deleted) to the degree that it fulfills its intended function for your particular library.

1. *Proper medium:* Is the topic or subject applicable to the filmstrip or slide medium?
2. *Content:* Is it accurate, truthful, up to date, authentic, and complete, applicable to more than one subject or topic area? Is it an overview or an in-depth investigation?
3. *Bias:* Does it contain unfavorable propaganda, extreme points of view? Is it partial?
4. *Appropriateness:* Is the method in which the information presented appropriate for intended patron?
5. *Organization:* Are components integrated, is there continuity of information, serious gaps or omissions, overcondensation?
6. *Photography:* Is the quality of exposure good? The quality of color, composition of photographs, quality of art work and graphics? Do visuals effectively communicate intended message? Are orientation devices included when needed?
7. *Captions:* Do captions provide sufficient information? Are they easy to read, succinct? Are attention getting devices used, e.g., italics, underlining, capitalization of key words, color? Is vocabulary suitable?
8. *Sound:* Is the fidelity good, does it relate to and enhance the visuals, are interesting sound techniques used, e.g., music, sound effects, background sound, fades, dissolves, etc.? Is sound necessary, does it heighten interest?
9. *Special features:* Does it contain numbered frames, introductory frame, summary frame? Are guides or supplementary materials available?
10. *Series:* Is the filmstrip or slide presentation part of a series, and if so, can each one be viewed as an entity, can they be viewed in random order, or must they be viewed in a prescribed sequence?

11. *Patron reaction:* Will the patron identify with the material, is it
    challenging and compatable with intelligence of the viewer, does
    it promote discussion or further investigation?
12. *Related materials:* Can it be used to complement other materials,
    e.g., books, motion picture films, etc.

Again, the preceding criteria should be developed to the needs of your
particular library. The arrangement, style, and detail of your evaluation
form will depend on how much information you need and the skill of
the people using the form. As a cardinal point, do not ask for information you do not intend to use. The evaluation form can either be subjective, i.e., respondent writes in own comments to questions, or objective,
i.e., respondent makes check marks in appropriate places. The preceding criteria can be incorporated into an evaluation form in the following
suggested arrangement:

1. *Vital statistics:* Bibliographic information (title, producer, cost,
   number of frames, color or black and white, series, sound, price)
2. *Precis:* Short description of what material is about
3. *Content information:* Criteria 1, 2, 3, 4, and 5
4. *Technical quality:* Criteria 6, 7, 8, and 9
5. *Possible uses:* Criteria 10 and 12
6. *User:* Criteria 4 and 11
7. *Evaluator:* Name and credentials of evaluator
8. *Summary:* Overall yes–no statement or reaction to material

A final consideration in developing criteria for evaluating filmstrips
and slides is the time factor. Any evaluation of filmstrips or slides should
be done efficiently. It is rather foolish to spend an hour evaluating a
30-frame filmstrip when you consider how many filmstrips would be
previewed by a library building a collection. The evaluation criteria and
corresponding evaluation form should contain only the information you
seek and present it quickly in terms of both filling it out and retrieving
information from it.

Selected Bibliography

Audio-Visual Equipment Directory. Evanston, Ill.: National Audio-Visual Associa-
    tion, 1975.
Audiovisual Market Place: A Multimedia Guide. Annual. New York: R. P. Bowker.
Blue Book of Audiovisual Materials. (Annual in December issue of *AV Guide.*)
Cox, C. T. "Filmstrips: Selection, Evaluation, Cataloging, Processing." *Wilson
    Library Bulletin* 38(Oct. 1963):178–182.

Eastman Kodak Company. *Kodak Annual Notebook.* Annual. Rochester: Eastman Kodak Company. (Insets on slides.)

Eastman Kodak Company. *Some Sources of 2 × 2 Inch Color Slides.* Kodak pamphlet No. S-2. Rochester: Eastman Kodak Company, 1972.

Educational Sound Filmstrip Directory. 4th ed. St. Charles, Ill.: DuKane Corporation, n.d.

Educator's Guide to Free Filmstrips. Randolph, Wisc.: Educators Progress Service, 1975.

Educator's Purchasing Master. 3rd ed. vol. 1 *Instructional Materials;* vol. 2; *Equipment.* Englewood, Colo.: Fisher Publishing Company, 3 West Princeton Avenue, 1971.

Ellis, S. "Thousand Words about the Slide." *ALA Bulletin* 53(June 1959):529–532.

Filmstrip Guide. New York: H. W. Wilson, 1962.

Guide to Government Loan Filmstrips, Slides and Audio Tapes. Alexandria, Va. 22305: Serina Press, 70 Kennedy St. (331 slides, slide sets available for purchase from Government agencies; slides available on free loan.)

Gunther, A. "Slides in Documentation." *UNESCO Bulletin for Libraries,* 17(May 1963):157–162.

Lennox, T. "Evaluation of Purchase Sources for 35 mm Art History Slides." *Picturescope* 19(Spring, 1971):10–49.

Lennox, T. "Slide Acquisitions: A Media Librarian's Problem." *LJ/SLJ Previews* (Nov. 1972):5–11. (A selected list of a multidiscipline collection of slides [see module].)

National Information Center for Educational Media (NICEM). *Index to 35 mm Filmstrips.* 2d ed. New York: R. R. Bowker, 1970.

Rufsvold, M. *Guides to Educational Media.* 3d ed. Chicago: American Library Association, 1971.

Selected List of Catalogs for Short Films and Filmstrips. New York: UNESCO, 1965.

Simons, W. W., and Tansey, L. C. *A Slide Classification System for the Organization and Automatic Indexing of Interdisciplinary Collections of Slides and Pictures.* Santa Cruz: University of California, Santa Cruz, 1969.

Sources for Motion Pictures and Filmstrips, Rochester: Eastman Kodak Co., n.d.

U.S. Library of Congress, *Library of Congress Catalog—Motion Pictures and Filmstrips.* Washington, D.C.: U.S. Library of Congress, 1967.

U.S. Library of Congress, *Motion Pictures, Filmstrips and Other Projected Images a MARC Format.* Washington, D.C.: U.S. Library of Congress, 1970.

Westinghouse Learning Corporation, *Learning Directory.* New York: Westinghouse Learning Corporation, 1971.

10

Audio Recordings

Advantages of Audio Discs

Audio recordings are one of the first nonprint media to be incorporated into the library's repertoire of information services. Undoubtedly the growth of the audio recording industry has been parallelled by a similar growth in library record collections. Libraries have been quick to respond to new developments in audio recording technology. It is quite common to visit all types of libraries and see vast arrays of audio software and hardware. Oftentimes, entire rooms are allocated to audio listening stations where patrons can listen to disc or tape recordings either independently or in groups.

The reason for the popularity of audio recordings is quite obvious. There is a whole body of information that can best be appreciated or acquired only in an audio form. The information most characteristically preserved by audio recording is music. Although there are films and videotapes on music, the patron will ultimately request an audio recording: It is a convenient medium, and even more important, the fidelity of the reproduction is invariably far superior.

Perhaps the predominant audio form is the disc recording. Older collections may still contain 78-rpm recordings, which are no longer produced. The sound quality of 78-rpm records at best can be considered adequate. The newer and more prevalent 33⅓- and 45-rpm disc records use a much smaller record groove (.001 inches for 33⅓- and 45-rpm records versus .003 inches for 78-rpm records) and reproduce sound of much higher fidelity. A further advantage of 33⅓- and 45-rpm disc records is their availability in monaural (one track), stereophonic (two track) or quadraphonic (four track) sound with sounds being reproduced that closely simulate the original live performance.

When selecting disc recordings, it is essential to make sure that they are compatible with the equipment on which they are to be used. It makes little sense to acquire stereophonic recordings if the equipment is only capable of playing monaural recordings. Most libraries, because they have maintained pace with technological developments in audio recordings, will in all probability have a variety of equipment capable of handling all available recording formats. At present, the 33⅓-rpm stereo disc recording (10–12 inches in diameter) is the most popular with record libraries. It is a long-playing record and often contains a musical composition of lasting value. The smaller 45-rpm disc recording (7 inches in diameter) plays only for approximately 3 to 5 minutes and usually contains popular music of a more temporary value.

Although most people think of disc recording only in terms of musical compositions, there is a wide range of spoken records available as well. The librarian should become familiar with the several audio selection aids cited at the end of this chapter which list a wealth of available audio recordings. Primarily, when you select a spoken (i.e., nonmusical) recording, it is essential to consider who is the performing artist. A recording of Robert Frost actually reading his poems is a treasure that will grow in value over the years. Hearing two professional performers engage in the Lincoln–Douglas debates engenders a feeling in the listener of actually being there and reliving a historical event.

A disadvantage of audio disc recordings are their susceptibility to scratching and surface damage. Although not fragile, they can nevertheless be rapidly worn by worn out recording styluses, and even worse, they are easily scratched by abusive handling. Because many patrons have their own record players, disc recordings can be taken out of the library and used on the patrons' personal equipment, but patrons should be encouraged to use disc redordings under the best conditions possible, i.e., use a good stylus, avoid scratching, handle a record by its edge, and keep it as clean and dust free as possible.

The audio disc recording contains information in a convenient format that is readily accessible to patrons by virtue of the availability of equipment. When compared to other audiovisual forms (motion picture, videotape), they are much less expensive and have a wider range of selections. Because of the availability of such a wide range of recordings, the librarian can build a narrow and specific of collection, e.g., major emphasis on classical music, or encompass a wide range of audio forms, e.g., various types of music, famous speeches by the original presentor, reenactments of famous events, discussions of a plethora of topics. Audio recordings have their own unique characteristics and can be the best means of acquiring information that is intended to be heard. The disc recording can satisfy these requirements.

Differences in Disc Recording Formats

If there is any one piece of audiovisual equipment that most people are familiar with, it is the record player. At present, libraries lend more disc records than all other nonprint media combined. Still there are some additional fine points worth knowing about disc recordings that will help to preserve their physical quality.

Disc recordings are available in three playing speeds, 33⅓, 45, and 78 revolutions per minute (rpm). A speed of 16⅔ rpm, called a transcription, is also available, but these are not generally found in libraries. The 78-rpm recording is no longer being commercially produced, but many libraries still have extensive collections. Today, 33⅓ and 45 rpm are the only speeds of disc recordings being acquired by libraries.

Figure 10.1 charts the differences among records made at the three different speeds. Most of the data on the chart are just informational, but the data on stylus (needle) are of particular importance. You will note that the stylus used to play a 78-rpm record is .003 inches in diameter to fit a .003 inch record groove, whereas the stylus used to play a 33⅓- or 45-rpm record is .001 inches in diameter to fit a .001-inch record groove. This means when playing a disc recording the proper size needle must be used; practically all record players are equipped with both .001-inch and .003-inch styluses. In many cases, this can be unfortunate, because some people never have occasion to play 78-rpm records, and when their .001-inch styluses wear out, they use the .003-inch styluses. This is false economy! The 33⅓- and 45-rpm records will play, but the stylus is three times thicker than the groove, and it tends to gouge out the groove. After a few playings a record can be ruined—it would have been far less expensive to buy a new stylus for the 33⅓- and 45-rpm records.

The following practical pointers are also worthy of consideration:

1. It is not recommended that stereophonic records be played on a monaural record player, even though some of the newer monaural record players claim no ill effect.
2. Keep fingers off record grooves.
3. If a record needs cleaning, wipe the record groove gently with a

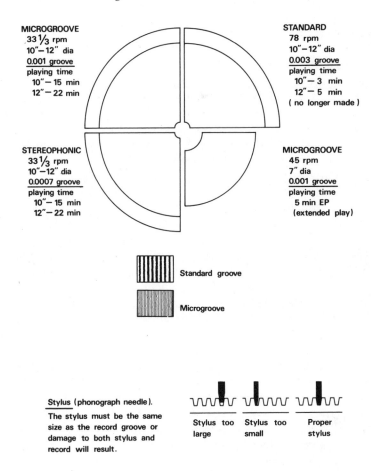

MICROGROOVE
33 1/3 rpm
10"–12" dia
0.001 groove
playing time
10" – 15 min
12" – 22 min

STANDARD
78 rpm
10"–12" dia
0.003 groove
playing time
10" – 3 min
12" – 5 min
(no longer made)

STEREOPHONIC
33 1/3 rpm
10"–12" dia
0.0007 groove
playing time
10" – 15 min
12" – 22 min

MICROGROOVE
45 rpm
7" dia
0.001 groove
playing time
5 min EP
(extended play)

Standard groove

Microgroove

Stylus (phonograph needle).

The stylus must be the same size as the record groove or damage to both stylus and record will result.

Stylus too large

Stylus too small

Proper stylus

Figure 10.1. Disc recording formats.

soft cloth that has been dipped in cool water and wrung dry (record stores sell special cloths and brushes for this purpose).

4. Never allow a stylus to sweep across the face of a record.
5. Never push down on the tone arm or force a stylus down into a record groove.
6. Know and keep record of the recommended playing life of a stylus, and replace it when that time has expired regardless of how good records sound when played.
7. Store records on edge, in dust jackets and away from sunlight or direct heat.

Audiotapes

Another audio information form is the magnetic audiotape. It has the same capability of storing and playing back as the disc recording, but it has several unique advantages. Listening to an audiotape does not require the use of a stylus, i.e., phonograph needle, hence there is no physical wearing of the tape. Audiotape can store a far greater amount of information in considerably less space. Because of this compactness, the equipment needed to listen to an audiotape can be much smaller than an audio disc record player, and many tape recorders are portable, battery-operated models.

Although the range of titles available on audiotape is not as large as that available on audio disc recordings, it is still quite extensive and growing daily. Whereas a 33⅓- audio disc can play for approximately 22 minutes, an audiotape can play without interruption for 1 or more hours depending on the length of the tape and the speed at which it is played. When you select audio tape, concern must be given to the formats available: open reel, cassette, and cartridge. The open reel was the first format available, but it is gradually being replaced by the cassette and cartridge which eliminate the need for physically handling of the tape and, being automatic, not have to be manually threaded on to a tape deck. Like audio discs, audiotapes are available in various playing speeds and recording formats (monaural, stereophonic, and quadraphonic) as well as various tracking configurations, the librarian selecting audio tapes needs to pay particular attention to those factors in order to insure that the audio tape selected is compatible with the equipment used in the library or by the patron at home. A brief knowledge of audio tape characteristics is beneficial when considering their selection.

Differences in Audiotape Formats

Tapes are made of plastic and coated with a layer of iron oxide or chromium oxide. The plastic is either an acetate or a polyester. Some people prefer acetate tape because it does not stretch and cause sound to be distorted, others prefer polyester tape because acetate tape breaks too easily and the tensile strength of polyester tape makes it very difficult to break. Concern of stretching is minimal because a tape recorder usually does not have enough power to stretch a tape seriously even when it is malfunctioning. In addition, polyester tape can be made thinner than acetate tape, which means a reel can hold more. The standard thicknesses of tapes are 1.5 mil, 1 mil, and .5 mil (1 mil = one-thousandth of an inch), 1.5-mil tape usually being acetate, and 1 and .5-mil tape being polyester. A 7-inch reel will hold 1200 feet of 1.5-mil tape, 1800 feet of 1-mil tape, and 2400 feet of .5-mil tape (bear in mind that the thinner the tape the more easily it will stretch).

Tape reels are available in the following popular sizes: 3, 4, 5, and 7 inches in diameter, each subsequent size capable of holding twice as much tape, i.e., a 3-inch reel will hold 150 feet of 1.5-mil tape, a 4-inch reel 300 feet, a 5-inch reel 600 feet, and a 7-inch reel 1200 feet. All reels accommodate a tape that is 1/4 inch wide.

Cassettes are of two basic types: reel-to-reel cassettes and loop cassettes (usually called cartridges). Both cassette and cartridge are designed to eliminate the need for threading. You simply insert them into the tape recorder and they are ready to be played. The cassette tape is approximately 5/32 inch wide while the cartridge tape is 1/4 inch wide. The cassette is reel to reel in design, which permits tape to be advanced or rewound at high speed, whereas the cartridge, being a loop, operates only in one direction and at one speed. Cassettes are labeled with a capital letter C followed by a number, e.g., C15, C30, C45, C60, C90, C120. This indicates total playing time, i.e., a C90 cassette will hold a maximum of 90 minutes of playing time. Even though cassettes vary in playing time, they are all housed in the same size cassette. This is achieved by using thinner tape on the longer playing cassettes. As a note of caution, it is not generally wise to use a C90 or C120 cassette unless it is absolutely necessary; the thinner tape has a greater tendency to jam in the cassette, and once this occurs, it is difficult, if not impossible, to rectify.

All these preceding variables are important when selecting or producing tapes. You will know what length of tape to purchase, what size reel or cassette (and if cassette, which type), the proper thickness of tape. Bear in mind that whatever tape you choose, it must be compatible with the machine you use.

Electromechanical Characteristics of Tape Recorders

The types of tape recorders discussed in this section are those available to the general public. Although you may come across a tape recorder with features other than those described, this would be an exception rather than the rule.

Reel-to-reel tape recorders operate with the tape placed on the left spindle, threaded through the record and playback mechanism, and

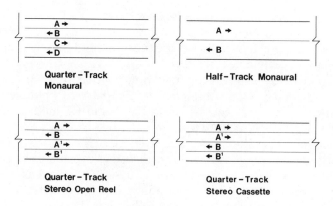

Figure 10.2. Tape recorder track patterns.

wound on to a take-up reel, both reels rotating in a counterclockwise direction. As the tape is played, it first passes an erase head then a record and playback head. When the tape is played for listening, the erase head is inactive. When information is being recorded on a tape, the erase head is activated and erases any existing information from the tape; then, when the tape passes the record head, new information is put on to the tape. In this way, a tape can be used time and time again. When information is no longer needed, it can be erased and new information recorded.

Tape recorders vary in their tracking abilities. (See Figure 10.2.) A full-track tape recorder records and plays back information on the full width of the tape; a half-track tape recorder uses only one-half the width of the tape. Then, when the tape is completely played through and wound on the take-up reel, the reel is flipped over and placed on the feed reel. The tape is then threaded through the recorder and the other half is recorded upon or listened to. If a tape recorded on a full-track tape recorder will last 1 hour; a similar tape recorded on a half-track recorder will last 2 hours. There is also a quarter-track tape recorder with which, by manipulating a switch, one can record information on four separate tracks.

It is important to know tracking when purchasing commercially produced tapes. The format (i.e., tracking) with which the tape was recorded must be identical to that of the machine on which it is played. For example, if a full track recording is played on a half-track machine, it will sound shallow and be of poor fidelity because the half-track recorder is picking up information from only one-half the width of the tape. Conversely, if a half-track recording is played on a full track recorder, you will hear both tracks simultaneously, one played forward and the other backward, resulting in a garbled sound. Bear in mind that the variable is not in the tape but in the machine; it is all the same tape, the machine is what makes the difference.

Another variable in equipment is whether it is monaural or stereophonic. During recording, a monaural tape records information using one microphone; a stereo tape requires two microphones. This means that a stereo tape recorder records information on two tracks at the same time, one track for each microphone. (See Figure 10.2.) If recorded using two microphones, then a stereo tape must be played back on a stereo tape recorder with two speakers, one for each track. A stereophonic tape can be played on a monaural tape recorder, but the separation of sound that is uniquely stereo is lost.

Still another variable is playing speed. The popular speeds are $1\frac{7}{8}$, $3\frac{3}{4}$, and $7\frac{1}{2}$ inches per second (ips). A tape must be played at the speed at which it was recorded. If you purchase a tape recorded at $1\frac{7}{8}$ ips and your equipment plays at $3\frac{3}{4}$ ips, the tape will be played at twice the speed at which it was recorded, and voices will sound like a high-pitched, fast talking Donald Duck. Conversely, $3\frac{3}{4}$-ips tape played at $1\frac{7}{8}$ ips will sound bassy, extremely slow, and slurry.

Cassette recorders are usually of either half-track monaural or quarter-track stereo format. Both a monaural and stereo cassette recorder will record on one half the width of the tape, then the cassette can be flipped over and recorded on the other half of the tape. A C60 cassette records 30 minutes on one half-track in monaural or on two quarter-tracks in stereo, then the cassette can be flipped over and recorded for an additional 30 minutes of monaural or stereo information for a total of 60 minutes.

Cartridge recorders are mostly of the 8-track stereo type. Remember that stereo requires two tracks to record information, so in fact an 8-track stereo has four channels of information, and the tape (being a continuous loop) will automatically advance the tape to the succeeding two tracks when the tape has played through the entire loop. The machine is also equipped with a channel selector allowing manual change to any of the four channels.

Selecting and Evaluating a Tape Recorder

"You only get what you pay for." If ever this adage were true, it is true of purchasing a tape recorder. Therefore, when selecting and evaluating a tape recorder, decide how it is to be used and how much you can afford to pay.

If the recorder is to be used by an individual to listen to speaking voices, then a 3-watt amplifier will be more than adequate. On the other hand, if the recorder is to be used in a large room, you may need an amplifier in excess of 25 watts and a minimum of a 10-inch speaker. Again, the best criterion in selecting a tape recorder is actually to try it out under the conditions under which it will be used, making sure it has adequate power and tone quality.

A present trend in selecting tape recorders favors cassette units. They tend to be more compact, they are definitely easier to operate, and commercially prepared tapes are becoming more and more available in the cassette format.

If portability is a concern, you may want to consider a battery-operated tape recorder. If this be the case, it would be best to select a unit that operates on AC or DC, electrical current, i.e., can either be operated by batteries or plugged into an electrical wall receptacle. The transformer that allows the unit to use AC should be built into the unit; when designed as a separate unit, it is just one more thing to misplace. As a note of caution, if a battery-driven unit is to go for long periods without use, it is strongly recommended that the batteries be removed; even the best batteries are subject to corrosion which can ruin the electrical terminals of a tape recorder.

Is the tape recorder to be used for listening to music? Because most musical recordings are produced in stereo, it will be necessary to have a stereo tape recorder in order to realize the full potential of the tape. Otherwise, if your tapes are primarily recordings of speaking voices, a monaural tape recorder is more than adequate. Besides deciding whether the unit is to be monaural or stereo, when selecting a reel-to-reel tape recorder, a decision must be made about tracking. Is it to be full track, half-track, or quarter-track? Half-track monaural and quarter-track stereo units are the most prevalent, but to be absolutely certain, investigate the catalogs of the producers with whom you do business and see what formats they provide.

Many institutions acquire tape recorders when in reality they never actually record any tapes and use their equipment solely to listen to tapes. In such cases, only a playback unit is needed. When a tape recorder is purchased, it includes a microphone (two microphones if it is a stereo unit), as well as the erase/record electronics, all of which obviously increase the cost of the unit. If they are never to be used, a playback only unit should be purchased at a lower cost. As an added advantage, with a playback-only unit, because it does not have erase and record capabilities, it is impossible for a user accidentally to erase information from a tape.

Although it has nothing to do with selecting a tape recorder per se, listening to many tape recorders in designated areas of a library requires the use of headsets. If this be the case, headsets must also be evaluated, for they become part of the unit. The headset should be light, durable, adjustable, and comfortable; above all it should reproduce quality sound. An added consideration is hygiene; it is not recommended that headsets that are inserted into the ears be used unless provisions are made for sterilizing them after each use. Ideally, a headset with a large plastic-covered cushion pad is best; they do not go into the ear, are easy to keep clean, are comfortable, and tend to block out room noise that could disturb a person listening to a tape.

All these criteria are basic. Obviously there are others unique to particular institutions, for example: if an institution has many patrons listening to the same tape at the same time, it may need a single playback unit with many headsets; if a patron needs to have information but cannot conveniently get to the library, a dial access system is needed; a patron learning a foreign language may need a tape recorder with which he can listen to a native voice, record his own voice, then play the tape back to hear both the native voice and his own for comparison. In any case, the state of the art of tape recorders is such that with judicious evaluation the librarian can select the right kinds of tape recorders for the particular ways in which they will be used.

Making a Tape Recording

Many libraries produce their own audiotapes. Libraries are becoming involved with talking books, which are entire books recorded on audiotape for the benefit of people with visual handicaps.

In making an audiotape, a professionally trained voice will lend polish to the recording, but it is not essential. A pleasant sounding voice of a person who can read in a natural way with natural expression is all the talent that is needed. A word-by-word reader or a voice with artificial expression is deadly. Incidentally, the voice does not have to be perfect. An occasional stammer or speech mistake is human, and if it does not detract from the material being read, it could perhaps be beneficial, for it tells the listener that the speaker is human. Of course, speech impediments or unusual accents should be avoided.

While making the tape, the performers should be made as comfortable as possible in pleasant surroundings and neither in a room that is acoustically dead, i.e., in which the voice loses its vibrance and resonance, nor in a room that produces echoes or unwanted overtones.

The microphone should be placed approximately 6–8 inches away from the speaker's mouth but not in a direct line with the speaker's breathing. This placement prevents the sound of breathing from being recorded but puts the microphone close enough to the sound source to keep it from picking up ambient or extraneous sound, e.g., the hum of an air conditioner. On the tape recorder, there is some type of level device (a flashing light or a gauge) that indicates the best volume range for recording. If the voice stays within this range, the recording should be technically perfect within the limits of the tape recorder. If a mistake or an undesirable sound is recorded, all that has to be done is to stop the tape recorder, rewind it, and re-record the correct information. It is advisable when re-recording to commence after a logical speech pause like the end of a sentence or paragraph. A long recording that cannot be completed comfortably in one session should be terminated in a logical place, preferably the end of a chapter or at the end of the reel of tape. It is amazing how a voice can subtly change from one day to the next, and the difference can be distinguished when listening to a tape.

Making a copy of an existing tape is easier. (By the way, if the material is copyrighted, you need the owner's permission to duplicate an audiotape.) The best way to duplicate is to use a patch (connecting) cord directly from the tape recorder which will play the original tape to the recorder that will duplicate it. A patch cord (usually provided with the recorder when it is purchased) is an insulated wire connecting the output of the master recorder directly to the input of the duplicating recorder. When a tape is duplicated by this method, there is no concern for room noise because there is no microphone to pick up extraneous sounds. A patch cord also ensures that the duplicate tape will sound as close to the original as is electronically possible.

Audiotape recorders allow the librarian to produce audiotapes. There is always the possibility a particular library needs something in audio form that is not commercially available. This being the situation, the tape can be produced locally. If the only information recorded consists of spoken voices, audiotapes of respectable quality can be produced. However, attempts to record musical compositions will only result in audiotapes that are only adequate in quality at best. Properly recording music requires a proper acoustical environment and a professional audio engineer. One of the more frequent applications in which libraries produce audiotape recordings is the making of talking books for patrons with visual handicaps or other reading problems. Whenever readers are selected to make talking books, it is essential that their voices be pleasant and their speech delivery clear and free of impediments or displeasing accents or intonations. As a point of information, when producing audiotapes, the librarian needs to be aware of copyright infringement. If the information on the tape is created by the library, copyright violation is not a concern. However, recording a book on audiotape could be in violation of copyright, and the librarian should check the book to determine whether it contains any statement that expressly forbids duplication. More often than not, there is no objection to transferring information to another medium, i.e., print to audio. When libraries make copies of existing audio recordings, however, there is a flagrant violation of copyright.

Speech Compression

Talking books provide a valuable service to patrons with reading handicaps, but listening to a talking book introduces the problem of speed of comprehension. Normal speech is delivered at about 120 words per minute, and a maximum speed of about 170 words per minute is possible. Speaking faster than this results in poor enunciation and pronunciation. However, psychologists have reason to believe that the brain can comfortably think at 400 words per minute. Actually, the human voice, by virtue of its slow speed, is an inefficient way to communicate.

A speech compressor is an electronic device that literally compresses information on an audiotape. By using such a device, one can play an audiotape much faster than it was recorded. It is no longer necessary for a person to plod along, listening to a tape at normal speaking speed, when by adjusting the speed he can listen as fast as he can assimilate. This is a boon for people with visual handicaps who must use their ears to "read." The compression of sound is achieved without any loss of tonal quality. Although it is not advised that audio compression be used to listen to music or poetry, where timing is essential for meaning and appreciation, it is of great help if the listening is only for acquiring information as efficiently as possible.

As an added option, some electronic speech compressors are also capable of expanding speech. This is especially useful with mentally handicapped people who have difficulty in comprehending a voice at normal speaking speed.

Selecting Professionally Prepared
Audio Recordings

Before selecting any audio recording, the librarian must first formulate a policy about the type of audio service the library will provide. Decisions must be made regarding how and where recordings will be used, what types of collections will be acquired, and what services will be provided.

How and where recordings will be used indicates the equipment needed. If the bulk of the collection is to be used by patrons at home, disc recordings are the best selection because more homes have record players than have tape recorders. However, your library may have a large collection of speeches available primarily on audiotape cassettes, and an inexpensive lightweight playback unit can be checked out by the patrons. Of course, any recording selected must be compatible with the equipment in your library.

Type of collection is predicated on the needs you want to serve. Special collections serve unique needs. If the special collection is educational, then within this category there are areas of specialization. A collection of foreign language recordings, for example, should use native speakers, make provision for the learner to make overt responses, and have an organization with a method of progression that permits the learner either to acquire more skill with each succeeding recording or to select a recording comparable to his entry level skill. A history collection, whenever possible, should record the actual speaker or event. It should provide a perspective that is unattainable from the printed word.

Music collections, which are most popular, can and perhaps should be both educational and entertaining. The librarian selecting musical recordings should be especially aware not only of what kind of music to acquire but also of the best performing artists. it is even feasible to have the same music recorded by several different artists.

Ideally, in considering types of collections it would be best to make selections that serve a multiplicity of needs. The following questions are worthy of consideration:

1. What range of patrons will the collection serve, e.g., age, interest, ability, needs?
2. What percentage of the collection should be devoted to each topic?
3. Does collection have cross-applicability, i.e., is it educational, entertaining, multidisciplinary?
4. Is it the type of collection that has high audio primacy, i.e., is audio recording the best format in which to have this information?

5. Are supplementary materials essential to the collection, e.g., musical scores, guidebooks, printed scripts, etc.?
6. Should the collection or particular recordings, be monaural, stereophonic, or quadraphonic?

Selecting audio recordings is an important function of the librarian. Too often it is slighted because many people feel that in our current television era people are no longer interested in audio only information. It must be kept in mind, as indicated earlier in this chapter, that there have been and continue to be tremendous technological strides in the development of the audio only media form. Commensurate with them is the growth in material available. There are recording companies whose sole purpose is to commit great books, plays, poems, and other printed works to an audio form. The quality of many of these recordings is truly remarkable. Through the use of professionally trained talent, the audio recording brings a living quality to the printed word. There is a slight problem, however, in acquiring materials from recording companies in that they are usually reluctant to provide material for preview. The reasons for this are quite obvious: The unethical librarian can easily copy the material; even more important, when previewed material is returned, there is no way for the record company to know its physical condition, and it may not be reusable. The librarian dealing with a recording company for the first time should request a "sampler" audio recording indicative of the company's product. Many companies produce samplers containing representative excerpts of their audio line for promotional purposes and welcome requests for them. In this way, the librarian can assess a particular recording company's product and have some assurance that any recordings selected will be of comparable quality. If neither preview recordings nor samplers are available, the librarian will have to gamble on the company's reputation. But because audio recordings are not expensive when compared to other media forms, such a gamble will not be too risky—the majority of company's have respectable products.

Still another consideration in selecting recordings ties in with the services provided by the library. Recordings for handicapped people should attend to their handicaps. A recording for the blind should be made at a speed (assuming you do not have a speech compressor) that is efficient for a blind person; on the other hand, aging people may need information recorded at a slower speed. If the library has story hours, recordings should be selected that require a minimum of introduction but offer a great deal of opportunity for follow-up discussion. Although this is not part of the actual recording, if a library provides promotional programs as a service, a recording is more appealing when it is packaged in an attractive dust jacket containing well-written information.

Audio Recording Selection Aids

Audio recording selection cannot be accomplished by one universal selection aid. Therefore, a variety of selection aids should be available to the librarian selecting audio recordings.

Selection aids should provide basic bibliographic information (title, artist, producer, playing time, format, date, cost, annotation). In addition, selection aids should be available that provide the following information.

1. Current listings and recent releases
2. Listings of producers and distributors as well as the types of recordings they sell
3. Listings of recordings by discrete categories, e.g., American opera, political speeches, shorthand dictation, etc.
4. Recordings made in foreign countries
5. Recording evaluations and reviews
6. Trends in library collections and programs
7. Listings by titles which includes all the renditions of a particular recording by various artists and groups
8. Listings by artists and groups detailing the recordings they have produced
9. New technology that may affect the format of recording selected
10. Sources of free and inexpensive recordings
11. Library's proprietary rights on recordings in its collection, i.e., duplicating, cost of multiple or replacement copies, broadcast, editing, etc.

Obviously, it requires several different kinds of selection aids to provide the essential information needed when acquiring recordings. Along with standard indexes, the librarian should subscribe to periodicals and be on the mailing lists of recording companies. Invariably it will be in the catalogs of recording companies (distributors' catalogs) that the most detailed information is available. Obviously, these catalogs will be promoting only one company's collection, but this should not be a problem. As indicated earlier, practically all recording companies have high standards of quality. The differences in recording companies is in the particular genre of recordings they distribute, the writers and performing artists they have under contract. By having a variety of producers' catalogs and cataloging them with regard to types of recordings, the librarian will have access to perhaps more audio recording selection aid material than could possibly be needed. In fact, because audio recordings are relatively inexpensive and the general public spends hundreds of millions of dollars purchasing them, it is not uncommon for libraries to make their collections of audio recording selection aids available to patrons for perusal and in so doing provide still another service to their patrons.

Selected Bibliography

Burstein, H. *Questions and Answers about Audio Tape Recordings.* Blue Ridge Summit, Pa.: Tab Books, 1974.

Cabeceiras, J. *Auto-Tutorial Audio Unit.* San Diego: Technological Applications Projects, 1974.

Crowhurst, N. *ABC's of Tape Recording.* New York: Bobbs-Merrill, 1972.

Hanna, E. F. "First Steps toward a Record Collection in Kujoth." *Readings in Non-Book Librarianship.* Metuchen, N.J.: Scarecrow Press, 1968.

Hellyer, W. H. *How to Choose and Use the Tape Recorder.* New York: Morgan and Morgan, 1970.

Jargensen, F. *Handbook to Magnetic Recording.* Blue Ridge Summit, Pa.: Tab Books, 1970.

SELECTION AIDS

Information Sources

Center for Cassette Studies, Inc., 8110 Webb Ave., N. Hollywood, Calif. 91605.

Educational Record Sales, 157 Chamber St., New York, N.Y. 10007.

International Teaching Tapes, Inc., Educational Development Corporation Building, P.O. Drawer 865, Lakeland, Fla. 33803.

National Center for Audio Tapes (NCAT), Room 320, Stadium Building, University of Colorado, Boulder, Colo. 80302.

Pacifica Tape Library, 2217 Shattuck Ave., Berkeley, Calif. 94704.

Wible Language Institute, 24 South 8th St., Allantown, Pa. 18105.

Wollensak Teaching Tapes, Mincom Division, 3M Center, St. Paul, Minn. 55101.

Xerox University Microfilms, 300 North Zeeb Rd., Ann Arbor, Mich., 48106.

Catalogs

Educator's Guide to Free Tapes, Scripts and Transcriptions. Randolph, Wisc.: Educator's Progress Service.

Harrison Catalog. Bimonthly. New York: M. & N. Harrison, Inc., 274 Madison Ave., Record and Radio-Phonograph Research, Inc.

Library of Congress Catalog. *Music and Phonorecords: A Cumulative List of Works*

Represented by the Library of Congress Printed Cards. 1953 to date. Washington, D.C.: U.S. Government Printing Office, 1953–.

Music Index: The Key to Current Music Periodical Literature. Monthly and annual. Detroit, Michigan: Information Service, 1949–.

National Information Center for Educational Media (NICEM). *Index to Educational Records.* New York: R. R. Bowker, 1972.

———. *Index to Educational Audio Tapes.* New York: R. R. Bowker, 1970.

Pearson, M. D. *Recordings in the Public Library.* Chicago: American Library Association, 1963.

Records in Review. 1955 to date. New York: Charles Scribner's Sons, 1955–.

Roach, H. *Spoken Records.* 3rd ed. Metuchen, N.J.: Scarecrow Press, 1970.

Schwann Record and Tape Guide. Monthly. W. Schwann Inc., Boston, Mass. (Available in record shops but not by individual subscription.)

Periodicals

American Record Guide. James Lyens, editor and publisher. New York. N.Y.

Audio. Gene Pitts, editor. North American Publishing Co., Philadelphia, Pa.

Crawdaddy. Raianne Rubenstein, editor. Crawdaddy Publishing Co., New York, N.Y.

High Fidelity and Musical America. Leonard Mareus, editor. Billboard Publications, New York, N.Y.

Previews. (Nonprint software and hardware news and reviews.)

Rolling Stone. Jann Wenner, editor. Straight Arrow Publishers, San Francisco, Calif.

Stereo Review. William Anderson, editor. Ziff-Davis Publishing Co., New York, N.Y.

11

Television

Impact of the Television Medium

When you stop to reflect that there are more television sets than bathtubs in the United States, you will realize this does not imply that we are becoming a less clean society but that we spend much more time watching television then we do bathing. In fact, the average American between his second and sixty-fifth years spends approximately 3000 entire days (almost 9 years of his life) watching television. The growth of television has been phenomenal: In 1946 there were only 6 television stations and 8000 receivers (television sets) in the United States; just 20 years later, in 1966, the number had grown to 699 stations and over 70 million receivers. Presently, over 96% of the total United States population have television in their homes (60 million of these sets are color receivers). A startling illustration of the impact of television can be found in an examination of the viewing habits of the 6- to 11-year-old group, which amounts to over 24 million people. This group spends an average of 3 hours a day watching television. Considering that each child is awake about 15 hours a day, this means that television is consuming one-fifth of his waking time. These data are quite astonishing, especially when you add that by the time they reach the age of 14 these children will have seen some 18,000 murders on television, and by the time they reach 17, viewed over 350,000 commercials. The viewing habits of the overall population lean overwhelmingly toward commercial television in preference to educational television, or what should more properly be called the Public Broadcast System (PBS). Regardless of a person's socioeconomic status, after a busy day he or she seeks the entertainment offered by commercial television. A PBS television program is considered an astounding success when it captures 12% of the viewing audience. A program with such a rating would never survive on prime time commercial television. However, Wilbur Schramm *et al.*, in their 1961 study, *Television in the Lives of Our Children*, did find that families with highly educated parents watch television less than families where the parents have more modest educations and that families that believe in the middle-class social norm of work and self-betterment watch less television than families that do not subscribe to the middle-class norm. Schramm *et al.* also found that when children with average or above average intelligence reach the 10–13 age range they have a shift in viewing habits and begin to watch less television and do more reading.

The preceding information is presented to give a brief idea of how television affects the public. The library cannot be considered a sacred tabernacle of information that the public must, or wants, to visit. Rather, the librarian should be aware of the impact of the television medium, as it too is a dispenser of information, and work with it by providing needed information services not obtainable from television.

Bearing in mind that television is a visual medium, perhaps the librarian should consider having more visual material to assist the television-oriented patron in making the transition from television to print media. The library's film collection should contain films of a genre not available on television. A good film program is an excellent lure to get the patron from the television set to the library. Books that complement television offerings should be considered. The mid-1970s was the era of the detective and policeman on television; books on these topics should also tend to be popular. Books that can fill a need not met by television should also be considered; the patron may want to escape from television to something more stimulating. But having films and books that complement television, as well as offering material that allows an escape from the medium, will have little impact to an unaware public. The library must advertise. It should have a daily or weekly review presented in the local newspapers, on radio, and yes even on television, informing the public of what is happening at the library. Maybe a criterion in selecting material should be "How would it appeal to the television viewing patron?" The library provides an important function, it is not a sanctuary for people escaping television, rather it can serve the unique, varied, and *individual* needs of a society that is affected by the mass communication medium of television. The library can be human and personal, which is something quite difficult for television genuinely to achieve.

Library Trends in Television Utilization

In a few short years, television has had a pervasive effect on our society; to say it will not be an integral part of a library's program is ludicrous and a denial of reality. Rather, the issue is when to incorporate television into the program (in many libraries it has already occurred), to what degree, and what services to provide. This is quite a challenge, and librarians will have to become more knowledgeable about the medium and its scope, limitations, and alternatives.

The library can be both a producer and a distributor of televised information. A library desiring to produce television information is taking a giant step that should be attempted only with considerable consultation with television production experts and maybe ultimately with the addition of television producers and technicians to the staff. Too often an institution proceeds on the premise that all that is needed to produce television is the necessary equipment, and the end result is usually that thousands of dollars worth of equipment receives little or no use. The library should know why it wants to produce its own televised information, what and how much it wants to produce, and finally the staff and equipment needed to achieve the objective. Once the decision has been made to produce television information, each program should have a uniqueness that precludes obtaining a comparable program from a commercial source that would be far less expensive.

The library producing its own television information can provide a tremendous service to the community, but only if the information it produces is unavailable from any other source and reflects what the community wants or needs. A few examples of televised information could be interviews with authors or interesting community people, book talks and reviews, story hours for children, puppet shows, discussion groups, community events (e.g., social events, community government meetings), dramatic performances, art shows, programs as hobbies and vocational skills, continuing education, etc. The productions could be televised live or recorded for future use. Again, it is for each library to determine the degree to which it wants to, or can, get involved with local television production.

If a library decides that its role is limited to that of distributor of televised information, it can still provide a tremendous service. It can build a video recorded collection of significant historical events; serve as a depositry for locally videotaped events and productions; and acquire commercially produced programs. It is predicted that video formats will eventually replace 16-mm films in libraries because videotape is cheaper and does not require a projector to be viewed. Remember from the

preceding section that over 96% of the population has television receivers: Eventually these sets will be either replaced or adapted with the
necessary electronics to view recorded, nonbroadcast programs. The
patron will obtain the video recorded program from the library and play
it back at home through his own television set whenever convenient.
Although this is currently a projected trend, it is predicted that within 10
or 15 years time there will be millions of home television receivers with
this capability. The wise librarian had better know the technological
trends in television and be ready to provide the type of library service
that will be demanded by its patrons.

Legal Implications of Making Video Recordings

A library can install television receivers for patron use, but once it
records a program for future use it could become involved in an infringement of copyright. For over a decade the federal government has been
wrestling with the copyright issue, realizing that modern technology can
locally and relatively inexpensively copy or reproduce virtually any format of information. However, there is a fair use clause which, though
still nebulous, can be interpreted to mean that a commercial television
program can be recorded and played back only once at a future time,
assuming that the time at which the program was originally broadcast
was not convenient for viewing. Schools may record an evening television program to play back once during school hours on the premise that
the evening broadcast time was not convenient for scheduling a class.

Actually, the 1909 law governing the copying from copyrighted works
(e.g., books, periodicals, recordings) left the "fair use" clause to the
courts for interpretation, which meant that any librarian copying
copyrighted material was risking a lawsuit. Fortunately, the United
States Congress late in 1976 passed the much needed Copyright Revision Law, and the law is now more applicable to the technology of the
1970s that makes copying information such an easy process.

The guidelines of the Copyright Revision Law give a minimum, not a
maximum, standard—which means that any type of copying not covered by the new law may still be permitted under the old law's "fair use"
clause. It is now legal to copy (a) a chapter from a book, (b) an article
from a periodical or newspaper, (c) a short story, short essay, or short
poem, whether or not from a collective work, and (d) a chart, graph,
diagram, drawing, cartoon, or picture from a book, periodical, or newspaper. It is assumed that these criteria can be paralleled and applied to
the television medium as well. Also in the new law is a provision for

brevity and spontaneity. Brevity allows the copying of a part of an entire work. With printed material, this means that, depending on the size of the work, up to 10% of it can be duplicated. Spontaneity refers to the need for use arising so quickly that it would be unreasonable to expect a reply to a request for permission in time for it to be useful. The new copyright law is not intended to allow the copying of information in lieu of purchasing it, the replacement or production of complete multiple copies, or the sale of copies for profit. The new law is a major improvement with regard to what the librarian can legally copy.

However, the issue of copyright remains very tenuous. It would be best for a library to obtain written permission from the producer if it plans to make extensive use of a copied broadcast television program.

As regards videotaping of a library's own produced programs, the library should develop an explicit policy with the help of legal counsel. Any performer appearing before the camera, as well as producers, directors, and script writers should be informed of library policy; any necessary clearances should be signed prior to production. It is only fair that everyone involved know of his rights and be properly protected.

Because copyright laws are still in flux and generating great deal of controversy as regards rights to information in any format, it would be extremely wise for the librarian who is duplicating information continually to keep abreast of federal copyright legislation.

Video Recording Formats

When your library begins to build a video recording collection, it will face the dilemma of which recording format to acquire. Perhaps there may be a need to select video recordings in more than one format. The library that restricts the use of video recordings to in-library use only can perhaps settle on one format, but the library that will be charging video recordings out will have to survey the library community to determine what kinds of playback equipment are owned by its patrons.

The main considerations in selecting video recordings for in-library use would be (1) availability of commercial offerings in particular formats; (2) complicity of use, i.e., if a video recording is to be set up by a staff person, complicity is no problem, but if the patron must operate the equipment, then simplicity is essential; (3) use of locally produced video recordings, which currently require open reel videotapes or videocassettes; (4) quality of sound and visual image; (5) cost and durability of both video recording and playback equipment. An additional consideration for charging video recordings out of the library would be

Figure 11.1. Prevalent videotape formats. Left to right: ¾-inch U-matic videocassette; ½-inch Videotape; 1-inch videotape; 2-inch videotape.

selecting video recording formats compatible with the playback equipment owned by patrons.

The librarian should bear in mind that any decisions made regarding video recordings should not be final. New technology is continually being invented, and in all probability decisions on video recordings made today will have to be modified with the advent of new technology; but conversely, anyone who decides to wait for the final technological development so as to avoid obsolescence will indeed be obsolescent by not having a video recording collection. It is strongly advisable to seek technical assistance regarding the projected state of the video recording art, then make a selection decision that can serve your patrons' needs for several years regardless of technological developments. What is needed is a 5-year program for selecting videotapes, after which an update assessment is made of the state of television trends and technology, followed by another 5-year program. A look at the current state of video recording formats will give a perspective on the magnitude of this problem and provide an idea of what the librarian should be considering for his or her particular library.

Figure 11.2. Videocassette playback unit.

Open Reel Video Tape

Video tapes are available in ¼, ½, 1, and 2 inch widths. (See Figure 11.1.) Two-inch videotape is used for broadcasting, and there is little likelihood that libraries would be involved with this size. One-inch videotape is used mostly for studio production. Half-inch videotape is presently the most popular open reel format for localized viewing (localized viewing is done from a recording hooked directly to a monitor or via closed circuit television [CCTV]). Quarter-inch tape is presently in an early stage of development; as a result, it is being stringently compared with half-inch videotape quality. If these tapes are acceptable, the cost of quarter-inch videotapes is obviously lower than that of half-inch videotapes containing a comparable amount of information.

Most studios record on 1- or 2-inch formats and duplicate onto ½- and ¼-inch formats for marketing.

Videocassette

Videocassettes containing ½- and ¾-inch videotape are presently realizing tremendous growth (see Figure 11.1). It requires no special skill to operate videocassette playback equipment, which means the patron can do little or no wrong when using it. (See Figure 11.2.) However, the threading mechanism of a videocassette playback unit is extremely complicated, and it is advisable to be quite careful when moving the equipment. A distinct advantage of the ¾-inch videocassette is that it adheres to the EIAJ standard, which means that each videocassette is generally playable on any ¾-inch videocassette machine regardless of brand. (Note: Compatibility has been a major problem in the video recording industry. Many videotapes can be played only on the brand of machine on which they were recorded. The Electronics Industry Association of Japan [EIAJ] has decided on a standardized, wholly compatible format for the ¾-inch videocassette system.)

Videodisc

In all probability, it will ultimately be the videodisc that libraries will use as a standard for acquiring commercially prepared materials. At present, videodiscs are being field tested; of all video recorded formats, they appear to be most economical in terms of both equipment and the cost of recordings. Several companies have developed videodiscs, and each is trying to get its videodisc form accepted as the standard for the industry. RCA, Teldec, and MCA/Philips at this time are the strongest competitors in the videodisc market. Bear in mind that these competitors are developing products that are incompatible with each other's systems. The possibility exists that all three formats could receive wide domestic use, and the librarian will then have to know what kind of system patrons are buying in order to select videodiscs in the proper format. In some instances, libraries may have to purchase all formats; only time will tell.

Videodiscs have a promising future for commercial video recording. They can be duplicated faster than videotapes; the materials are cheaper than those of videocassettes; and the equipment is easier to operate than videotape equipment and less sophisticated and less expensive than videocassette equipment. Videodiscs will be able to store as much information as any videotape format.

The videodisc itself is similar in shape to an audio record but has the magnetic properties of videotape. One system uses laser electronics that do not require a stylus or sensing mechanism to come in physical contact with the videodisc. This means there is absolutely no wear on the videodisc, and theoretically it could last indefinitely. At present, videodiscs are limited to commercial production only, and any local production must still rely on videotape, videocassettes, or super 8-mm film. A library could conceivably utilize two basic formats, videodisc for commercially required materials and videotape for locally produced materials.

Super 8-mm Films

The Eastman Kodak Company has developed a system that allows super 8-mm films to be played through a television set. This allows both commercially produced and home movies to be played through the television set.

Other Systems

Other systems in various stages of development and marketing are the CBS Electronic Video Recording (EVR) System, which uses a silver halide film and the NBC Selectavision that puts a hologram on a mylar film; other videodisc systems are being developed by Zenith Radio and Thomson CSF.

There are many formats and systems from which the librarian must choose. The problem is analagous to the Gordian Knot, but by relying on qualified technical consultants, keeping abreast of technological developments in the television industry, and assessing the needs of the patrons the library serves, you can embark upon a program that will keep pace with developments in television and be a valuable asset to the library.

Selecting Video Equipment

In selecting video equipment, the librarian must think in terms of systems. There are various video formats available, and each format has its own unique characteristics, advantages, and disadvantages. Even more important is the fact that no two video formats are compatible with each other. Depending on the format(s) chosen, all the video equipment selected must be chosen to complement it. It must be known to what degree the library wants to be involved with the television medium, the size of the budget allocation for television, the kinds of information to be acquired (or produced), and the types of distribution. If the library is to be involved in television production, it must set minimum standards of acceptable quality and provide for the necessary staff, equipment, and facilities to produce it. The library must contend with the basic decision of whether it wants solely to distribute information in a television format or to produce television programs as well. Therefore, video equipment can generally be categorized either as production or as distribution equipment.

Production equipment requires space for producing videotapes and can even include a studio for recording elaborate productions. The most basic setup would be a single videotape recorder to record programs from broadcast television (be careful of copyright violations). Next would be a portable single-camera videotape recording unit for televising and recording live productions. An expansion of the single camera unit would include the use of two videotape recorders with editing capabilities, which makes a tremendous improvement in the quality of the finished videotape. Finally would come the multiple camera studio which would, depending on the extent of commitment, include two, three, or even four video cameras, control equipment (switchers, special effect generators, audio mixers, lighting control), and equipment for editing and duplicating videotapes. Regardless of the degree of television production involvement, whenever television cameras are used, attention must be given to lighting, editing, audio control, and special effects.

Distribution equipment would include video playback units and television monitors and receivers. There is a difference between a receiver and a monitor, technically the terms are not synonomous. A television receiver, which is what we are most familiar with and what is found in homes, works on a RF (radio frequency) signal. The RF signal transmits both the audio and video signals through the air. A monitor receives the audio and video signals separately and by wire or cable. Some playback units do not transmit a RF signal, and a monitor is therefore required for viewing. Television sets are made that are both monitors and receivers, which obviously cost more than those that are just monitors or just receivers.

The following criteria give an idea of the scope of the problems that must be considered in order to select video equipment intelligently. The criteria do not explore minute areas but rather highlight main concerns which must be considered in determining to what degree your library will be involved with the television medium.

Compatability

Consider television as an electronic system. Each component must be perfectly compatible with every other component, or the system will not function properly. If you produce 2-inch video tapes and the playback equipment is in ½-inch format, you have a compatability problem that must be resolved by a recorder that can make ½-inch copies from a 2-inch tape. If the library community will be charging out videotapes, the tapes produced or acquired by the library must be compatable with the patrons' equipment (or vice versa). If ½-inch tapes are produced, they cannot be broadcast over network television because they are not compatable with network (FCC) specifications (although they are acceptable for cable [CATV] transmission). All the pieces must fit perfectly, or else the library has a system that will not be able to perform to expectations.

Black and White versus Color

The library will have to make a decision for black and white or color television. Tied in with compatability, if the library has a black and white production facility, there is no need to purchase color television monitors. If color is not essential, the librarian should not even consider color equipment, as it is considerably more expensive than black and white. The trend however, is definitely toward color equipment.

Portability

Studio production console equipment need not be portable. Playback equipment and receiver–monitors can be portable, thereby permitting them to be moved around the library or even charged out. Stationary built-in equipment is much more attractive and again would be nice if the library can afford it. If the library is going to produce on-location videotapes, it will need to have portable, battery-operated video recording equipment.

Wiring

Adequate AC electrical wiring must be accessible to the equipment. If a large quantity of equipment will be used simultaneously, it is essential to be careful that the equipment will not blow fuses or cut out circuit breakers. Along with wiring, battery operated equipment should be considered; although the batteries must be charged, they allow the most portability possible, for they can be operated away from an AC electrical source. Equipment layouts must be planned for along with electrical wiring; television wiring (coaxial cable, audio patch cords, etc.) have to be used to connect cameras to recorders and recorders and cameras to monitor–receivers. All electrical wiring should include a ground wire (i.e., contain a 3-prong polarized plug) to eliminate the possibility of electrical shocks.

Service

When television equipment is acquired, the warranty should be carefully read. Also, quality of maintenance and repair service should definitely be investigated. Equipment is of little use if it takes weeks to have a unit repaired when it malfunctions. Bear in mind that television equipment is extremely complicated and some of it quite delicate; therefore, select equipment that has a reputation for being sturdy and backed by reliable service.

Monitors and Receivers

Determine whether the library needs monitors or receivers, and in black and white or color. Know how large a group will be viewing a monitor or receiver at any given time. Ideal viewing requirements are as follows: viewer not be seated any nearer the set than 5 times the picture width, nor further away than 15 times the picture width (although children at home usually viewer at a distance of 3¾ times the picture width).

Expansion

A basic video system may be all the library needs. Any expansion would involve acquiring a second basic system, and so on. However, the librarian should also consider the possibility of acquiring a system initially large enough for current needs but able to be expanded later. For example, it may be practical to start with one video camera with later plans for adding a second camera. If so, the original camera should be of a type that can be synchronized with multiple cameras. With viewing monitors, if more than one will be used from the same video recorder, it should have what is called looping (i.e., connected in series); it is necessary to determine how many loops or monitors a half-inch video recorder can drive (some manufacturers state that their equipment is limited to handling a maximum of four monitors).

Purpose

Know exactly the purpose or intended use in selecting a particular piece of equipment. To purchase a video camera with just one normal lens could be a waste of money when perhaps a zoom lens was originally needed. In the same way, libraries purchase videotape recorders when indeed all they need is a video playback unit because they have no intention of ever using the unit to record video information. Why buy battery equipment when it will always be used with relatively close access to AC electricity?

These criteria will serve as guidelines when your library considers becoming involved in selecting equipment. Remember, always seek the assistance of an expert consultant when making decisions.

Impact of Cable Television on the Library

Cable television, also known as Community Antenna Television (CATV) is a service, usually privately owned, that sets up a master antenna and from it distributes television signals by means of a wire (coaxial cable) to customers in a licensed geographical area who subscribe to the service. Although the subscriber must pay for cable television service, he no longer needs to erect an antenna on the roof of his home; he receives a high-quality signal from both local and distant sources and has access to a greater number of television channels. Some televised information accessible to the community is available only via cable television. This restricted access is where the library becomes involved.

The librarian should become familiar with cable television policy as prescribed by law. The potential impact of cable television on the library is tremendous: It could provide a whole new concept in information dissemination. Being a community service, the library is entitled by law to transmit information via cable television. Libraries acquiring television equipment should consider how it complies with their current or projected cable television utilization plans. As an example, 2-inch videotape is the accepted standard for open broadcast television, but cable television will distribute information recorded on ½-inch videotape. Knowing this might eliminate any plans a library might have for acquiring 2-inch videotape equipment. Another example involves studio production. The cable television operator must maintain a minimal production facility and make it available at a reasonable charge. This means that a library planning to produce television programs can do so without having to construct its own studio; because television studios must receive considerable use to justify their existence, the existence of a cable television studio facility could result in great savings for libraries involved in limited television production.

Video recordings that patrons visit the library to view or charge out for use on their home video playback units can also be transmitted via cable television. The library could eventually develop a full program that would utilize cable television for several hours a day. It could present library reports to the community, motion pictures, story hours for children, live puppet shows, and book talks, and conduct discussions, in-service education, art and crafts programs, etc. Actually the library, via cable television, could fill a huge void that presently exists in television as regards a community's cultural and educational needs. If enough people want to take a college course offered at a distant campus, they might arrange for the library to obtain video recordings of the course to be transmitted via cable. The library would also have the necessary reference and resource materials (books, periodicals, etc.) for patrons to take the course as efficiently as if they had actually taken it at the distant college campus.

To project into the more distant future, the library will eventually provide individualized home library service through cable television. The technology currently being developed is exciting in regard to how it can affect the library. Envision a patron wanting to read a particular book who calls the library to have an ultrafiche microform of the book projected on his home receiver. He proceeds to transfer it to his own piece of photographic microform, to be read at leisure on his own microform reader. All this would take place without the patron ever leaving his home. Such capability is not destined to wait for the distant future. Bear in mind that there are companies currently experimenting with the transmission of information for individual use via television.

Cable television is here now. It is going to continue to grow in the number of subscribers it will serve, as well as the types of services it will provide. It will be the wise librarian who keeps abreast of cable television progress and uses it to provide more and better library services.

Selecting and Evaluating Commercially Produced Video Recordings

In many ways, television is similar to motion pictures, and many of the criteria used for evaluating motion pictures are applicable to television (see Chapters 7 and 8). However, television does differ from motion pictures in that it is usually viewed at home on a small screen. Granted that much of current television presents movies produced for theater use, it is exactly in this area that a distinction must be made in evaluating commercially produced videotapes. As an example, a scene in the film

War and Peace depicts armies preparing for battle, and thousands of movie extras are staged on a large field. The tremendous impact of viewing so many people on a large theater screen is really felt by the viewer, but when the same scene is projected on a 21-inch television tube, it loses most of its impact. Along with the criteria used to evaluate films, it is necessary to distinguish those criteria that are unique to television. An added consideration would be to acquire videotapes not available to the patron from other sources. The following criteria are what makes television unique in its ability to communicate effectively.

Close-Up Shots

Television makes extensive use of people close up. Tight, full-length shots or medium close-up shots of people are quite effective. It has been found that this aspect of television gets the viewer more emotionally involved than wide-angle shots showing a panorama of scenery. Close-ups require careful transition from scene to scene in order to eliminate a jumpy production.

One-to-One Shots

The close-up shot gets the viewer emotionally involved; the one-to-one shot gets him personally involved. Television has been called a one-to-one medium: When the performer looks directly into the television camera, the home viewer gets the feeling that the performer is looking him directly in the eye and talking to him personally on a one-to-one basis. Videotapes that use this one-to-one technique will have great viewer impact. The librarian should be aware of it occurring and evaluate how well it achieves its intended purpose. A variation of the one-to-one technique occurs when the performer looks slightly off camera as if talking to another person in the studio. This makes the viewer feel that although the performer is not speaking directly to him, he is nevertheless involved in the conversation.

Lighted Room

Television is viewed in a lighted room and not in a darkened theater. Besides a small screen, the viewer has many things in the room competing for his attention. The videotape should be done well enough to command the viewer's attention. If a scene does not have enough motion or is held too long, then the viewer's attention is likely to drift away from the television receiver as he becomes more interested in the other features of the lighted room. Videotapes that make extensive use of a close up of a person lecturing are deadly. Television requires continual motion, freshness, and a pace of action that holds the viewer's attention.

Special Effects

The electronics of television, by use of a special effects generator (SEG), can create a wide variety of visual effects. Information from a second video camera can appear on the monitor as a wipe from left to right or as a small square of information which can be expanded or contrasted on different parts of the viewing surface. Information can appear in the various shapes (diamond, rectangle, circle, etc.); images can be multiplied; and many other special effects can be generated. You should beware of these special effects, for if they heighten the interest of the information presented, they are well used; but if their only purpose is to show trick camera work and they cause the viewer to be distracted, confused, or annoyed, then you should evaluate the videotape downward.

These four criteria are uniquely relevant to television, and when they are combined with selected criteria used for evaluating motion picture films, the result will be a complete intensive evaluation of videotapes. Perhaps the only other factors that can be considered when evaluating and selecting commercially produced videotapes have to do with the fact that television has other unique traits. Television (as well as radio), has the highest multiplication factor of any communication medium: It is possible for millions of people to receive the same information at the same time. Television can also be a live medium in that what is being televised is actually occurring as it is broadcast and can be viewed many thousands of miles away. Coupled with live television is the capability for instant replay, which again is unique to television. These additional traits, although not necessarily germane to selecting videotapes, do, however, illustrate the uniqueness of the television medium. The librarian needs to be aware of the full potential of the medium.

Selected Bibliography

Anderson, C. *The Electronic Journalist: An Instoduction to Video.* New York: Praeger Publishing, 1973.

Barnouw, E. *Tube of Plenty: The Evolution of American Television.* New York: Oxford University Press, 1975.

Bogart, L. *Age of Television: A Study of the Viewing Habits and the Impact of Television on American Life.* 3rd ed. New York: Frederick Ungar Publishing Co., 1970.

Bower, R. *Television and the Public.* New York: Holt, Rinehart, and Winston, 1973.

Buchsbaum, W. *Fundamentals of Television.* 2d ed. Rochelle Park, N.Y.: Hayden Book Co., 1974.

Carlson, R. A. *Educational Television in Its Cultural and Public Affairs Dimension: A Selected Literature Review of Public Television As an Issue in Adult Education.* Syracuse, N.Y.: Syracuse University Press, 1973.

Dinsdale, A. *First Principles of Television.* New York: Arno Press, 1971.

Frost, J. M., ed. *World Radio, TV Handbook: A Complete Directory of International Radio and Television.* Cincinnati: Watson-Guptill Publishing, 1975.

Gattegno, G. *Toward a Visual Culture: Educating through Television.* New York: Ed Solutions, 1969.

Groombridge, B. *Television and the People.* Baltimore: Penguin Books, 1975.

Halloran, J. D., and Elliott, P. R. *Television for Children and Young People.* New York: International Publications Service, 1970.

Hawker, J. P. *Radio and Television: Principles and Application.* New York: Hart Publishing, 1970.

Kennel, L. *Ecology of the Airwaves: A Popular Study of TV and the Influence It Has on the Coming Generation.* Scottdale, Pa.: Herald Press, 1971.

Knecht, K. *Designing and Maintaining the CATV and Small TV Studio.* Blue Ridge Summit, Pa.: TAB Books, 1972.

Kuhns, W. *Exploring Television.* Chicago: Coyote University Press, 1974.

Liebert, R. M. *et al. The Early Window: Effects of Television on Children and Youth.* Elsford, N.Y.: Pergamon Press, 1973.

Mayer, M. *About Television.* New York: Harper & Row, 1972.

Millerson, G. *Technique of Television Production.* 9th rev. ed. New York: Hastings House Publishing, 1972.

Minus, J. *et al. Film-TV Law (Your Introduction to Film)—TV Copyright, Contracts and Other Law.* Hollywood: Seven Arts Press, 1973.

Rayner, R. *The Story of Television.* Chicago: Rand McNally, 1972.

Schramm, W., ed. *Quality in Instructional Television.* Honolulu: University Press of Hawaii, 1973.

Schramm, W. *et al. Television in the Lives of Our Children.* Stanford, Calif.: Stanford University Press, 1961.

Stasheff, E., and Bretz, R. *Television Program: Its Direction and Production.* rev. ed. New York: Hill and Wang, 1968.

Stavins, R., ed. *Television Today: The End of Communications and the Death of Community.* Washington, D.C.: Gryphen House, 1971.

Williams, R. *Television: Technology and Cultural Form.* New York: Schocken Books, 1975.

Zettl, H. *Television Production Handbook.* 2d ed. Belmont, Calif.: Wadsworth Publishing Co., 1968.

12

Globes, Maps, Models, Realia, Games, and Simulations

Properties and Characteristics of Maps

By definition globes and maps are symbolic replicas of the earth's features or characteristics. The librarian should have a basic knowledge of globe and map properties and characteristics in order to select from the various types available those that best serve the needs of the library. Globes and maps vary in the amount of detail they contain and in the accuracy with which they are intended to represent a portion of the earth. When they are intended for the novice or young person, globes and maps may limit the amount of information they contain, whereas when made for the expert they may contain highly specialized information in great detail. But whether the globe or map is intended for novice or expert, it is important that it be accurate in presenting the information it was designed to show.

The earth, being a sphere, is best represented by a sphere or globe. In this way the globe, or replica of the earth, is accurately replicated in miniaturized detail. For ease in translating, earth and globe are measured in like units which are then expressed as a ratio. The earth has been found to have a diameter at the equator of approximately 500-million inches, therefore, a globe 50-inches in diameter will have a ratio of 50:500,000,000. This ratio, reduced to 1:10,000,000, would be printed somewhere on the globe as a fractional scale, or representative fraction (RF), e.g., 1/10,000,000 or 1 : 10,000,000, the same distance on a 50-inch globe. Once one has determined the representative fraction, scales in other units can easily be transposed (e.g., miles, kilometers). A 50-inch globe tends to be rather large for the library. The prevalent diameters of commercially produced globes range from 8 to 24 inches, 12- to 16-inch globes being most popular. Regardless of size, it is important to examine the accuracy of detail and legibility of information.

A globe has a unique advantage over maps in that it can be used to measure true distances in any direction using only one scale. However, globes have several inherent disadvantages: (1) no more than one-half of a globe can be seen at any time; (2) globes tend to be bulky and unwieldly and occupy valuable space; (3) they are difficult to store; (4) it is difficult to make measurements on a curved surface; (5) they are expensive to reproduce and require the use of expensive materials (when compared to maps); (6) a globe contains the whole earth, and in most cases a patron is interested in examining only a portion of it. Unless globes are needed for particular courses of study, libraries tend to have very few of them in their collections. Usually one large earth globe suffices as an accurate replica of the earth which can be used as an orienting referent whenever a patron wants a precise representation of the earth unavailable from any map. The librarian may also consider having globes of the universe, the planets of the solar system, and the moon. These globes would also be used in conjunction with their map counterparts.

Because the earth is a globe, it is impossible to replicate it accurately in its entirety on a flat surface such as a map. Therefore, cartographers, in their efforts to represent the earth as accurately as possible, have to make some sacrifices in distance, shape, or form. Most of the properties of map projections are the result of scale relationships which are either maintained or altered in the process of transforming spherical data to a flat surface. Map projections are limited in their kinds of accuracy. They may (1) accurately represent true angles around any point of the map, (2) show direction correctly, (3) show distances between points correctly, or (4) replicate shapes or sizes of area precisely enough that all parts of the map are in proper relation to each other. The map, or flat projection, can achieve any of the four preceding characteristics either singly or in combination, but it cannot achieve all four at the same time. Usually maps that attempt to achieve accuracy on all four characteristics are difficult for the novice to read and comprehend. The Mercator map projection is especially popular with novices, and although it distorts areas and distances, it is true along parallels and represents shapes quite well within small limits anywhere on the map. Bear in mind that although the problems of maintaining the accuracy of the four preceding characteristics are evident when mapping large areas of the earth, they virtually disappear when mapping small geographic areas.

When you select a map, there are basically four fundamental matters applicable to all maps: (1) map scale, or the size of the map area represented compared with that part of the actual earth it represents; (2) type of projection used; (3) types of information represented on the map and the various methods or symbols used to illustrate them; and (4) quantity and quality of detail.

Map Scale

Map scale is determined in the same method used for globe scale, i.e., as a ratio of the actual distance it represents on earth. The size of the area being mapped and the actual physical size of the map will determine the scale to be used. Obviously, the smaller the ratio, or representative factor, the more detail can be included, e.g., a map of a city can include more detail than a map of a state. It is recommended that the map scale be in a ratio that is amenable to easy application and measurement. With certain type map projections, several scales may be required to be used on different areas of the map. Usually maps requiring several scales are not intended to be used for measuring distances; and when distances are needed, a key or table is usually provided indicating distances between major points.

Map Projection

A map projection involves a grid of intersecting lines (longitudes and latitudes) upon which the earth or a portion of it is plotted. As stated earlier, it is impossible for a map projection to be accurate in all aspects (distance, shape, area, direction). The cartographer selects the projection which best depicts a partial feature or aspect of the earth. This also means that map projections are truer in some areas of the grid than in other areas. It is for the librarian to select the map projection that provides the best and truest means of displaying information for a particular need. If accuracy of polar areas is important, a map projection that is best and truest for these areas will probably achieve its purpose at the expense of distorting equatorial areas. Compromises in map projections are purposely done to maintain accuracies in some aspects at the sacrifice of other aspects. It is also important for the librarian to bear in mind that a map with the most accurate replication of a particular aspect may indeed be a disadvantage if it is in the type of projection difficult for the user to comprehend, especially if he or she is a novice. It is important to have a variety of map projections in the map collection of varying degrees of complexity. A good map collection ranges from maps that are used to learn the reading of maps all the way to maps that are read to learn. Figure 12.1 illustrates the more popular types of map projections and their respective properties, uses, and limitations.

Information Represented

Maps illustrate the areal distribution of many things that are on the face of the earth. This information is represented by the use of a vast array of symbols, codes, and colors that attempt to communicate such features as shape, size, outline, pattern arrangements, land relief or elevation, and the distribution of statistical values of an actual or relative quantity. When these are presented effectively, the map user has the graphic means which make it easy and efficient to recognize, compare, and examine patterns, relationships, surface features, locational data, scientific data, places, ocean currents, geological formations, climate, weather, demographic distributions, political boundaries, economic data, agricultural capabilities, industrial production, military disbursement, etc.

The symbols and codes should be easy to understand and interpret and should appear in the legend. The legend is the key to the map, and it should clearly and succinctly define the codes and symbols used. Color greatly enhances a map. It is used for identifying such features as land, water, political units, elevation, rainfall, and vegetation. Various shades of blue usually indicate water areas and their respective depths; white is used for polar regions, green for lowlands; and yellow, red, orange, brown for progressively higher elevations or lower rainfall. The important criterion when examining the use of color in maps is that its symbolic meaning be easily and readily understood.

Quantity and Quality of Detail

Again it is important for the librarian to be aware that one map cannot accurately provide all kinds of information. If a map becomes too cluttered with information, it does so by obscuring other equally important details; even worse, it will repulse the reader from using it. It would be far better to have several maps of a particular area each revealing a particular characteristic than to have one map do it all. This is clearly illustrated in Figure 12.2. With regard to quality of detail, it must be realized that distortions are often necessary for the sake of conveying information. An example of this could perhaps be an exaggeration of the

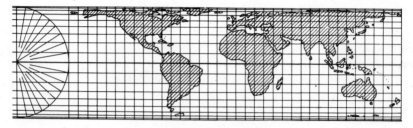

A. Cylindrical equal area projection

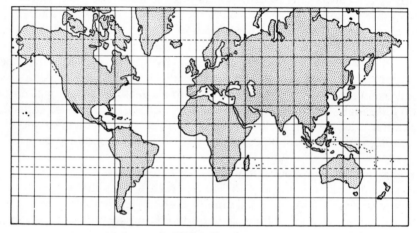

B. Mercator projection

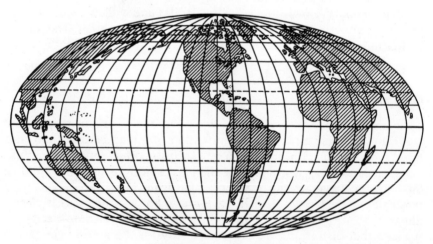

C. Mollweide (oval) projection

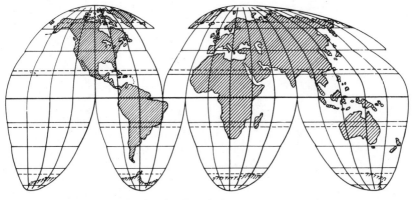

D. Goode's homosoline projection

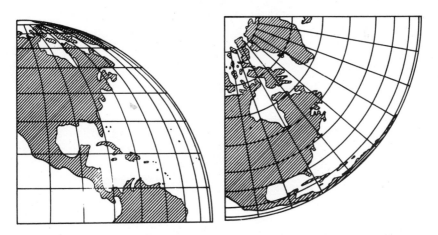

E. Orthographic projections

Figure 12.1. Various map projections. (A) Cylindrical equal area projection. Use: Illustrates problems of projecting a globe onto a flat surface. Properties: Higher latitudes are stretched out. (B) Mercator projection. Use: Navigation, compass location. Properties: Land distortion in higher latitudes. (C) Mollweide (Oval) projection. Use: Equal areas. Properties: Best in central middle latitudes, polar axis is one-half the length of the equatorial axis. (D) Goode's homosoline projection (interrupted). Use: Equality of area, fairly good shape. Properties: Interruption in overall continuity, fairly accurate in shape and area. (E) Orthographic projection. Left: Centered on equator. Right; Centered on north pole. Uses: Gives a rounded three-dimensional perspective. Properties: Distortion increases from center, cannot project entire globe.

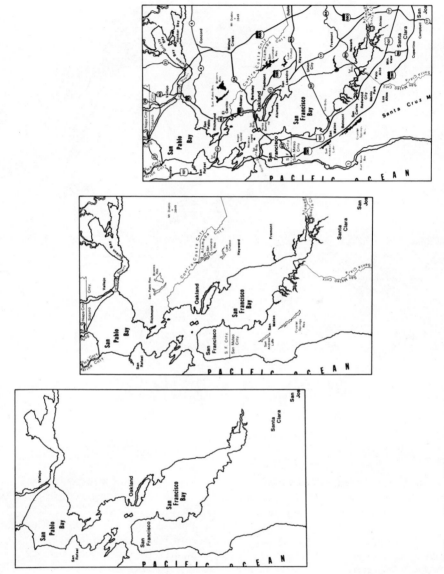

Figure 12.2.　Three maps of the same area providing various amounts of detail and information.

size of the Nile River Delta in an attempt to portray its shape and mean-derings; however, if this is properly done, the reader will readily understand the distortions as a means to communicate particular aspects of the Nile River Delta.

Perhaps the most accurate maps available are those made by aerial photography. Libraries can now acquire maps based on photographs taken from airplanes and manmade satellites. Many aerial maps are reproduced at a scale of 3 inches to the mile (1 : 20,000). Cartographers in the United States use aerial photography as an aid in making accurate maps. The standard United States topographic maps made by the U.S. Geological Survey, containing a quadrangle of 0°15′ latitude and longitude, are available in ratios of 1 : 62,5000 (1 inch = 1 mile) or 1 : 24,000 (2½ inches = 1 mile).

Knowing the essentials involved in map making is important in selecting the right maps for the library collection. It is equally important for the librarian to know something of the material characteristics of various maps as well as some of their advantages. Consider the following:

1. *Atlas:* Atlases are books of maps; they are available in many dimensions. They are intended for individual use.
2. *Wall maps:* Wall maps are considered as entities, meaning they are unbound. They are usually 40–65 inches wide. It is important to know the map scale as it will determine how far away from the map a person can stand and still be able to read it. Wall maps are intended for display and group use. They can be folded, mounted on spring rollers, or attached to dowels for hand rolling.
3. *Bound wall maps:* Bound wall maps are designed to be attached to a tripod or stand permitting them to be flipped over.
4. *Overhead transparencies:* Maps on overhead transparencies are designed to be used expressly on an overhead projector. Information can be added by the use of overlays or can be written on to transparencies with water-soluble ink (which can be erased).
5. *Slides and filmstrips:* Maps photographed on to slides and filmstrips are intended to be projected on a screen in a darkened room.
6. *Relief maps:* Relief maps provide a three-dimensional perspective of the earth's surface. The relief, to be at all effective, must be grossly exaggerated in some of its proportions. For example, if a relief map of the world 72-inches square were to depict Mount Everest accurately (5+ miles high) in relief, it would be less than 1/60 of an inch high.

A final consideration is the physical durability of the map. Folded maps usually wear out at the folds or creases. Maps with cloth backing, printed on heavy durable paper stock will last longest. Add to this a plastic lamination on the front surface, and the map can be written upon with washable inks and crayons and protected from dust, dirt, and tearing. It is for the librarian to know when selecting maps how they will be used, under what conditions, and for what purposes.

Models and Their Characteristics

A model is a replica or representation of a real object. Often, when the real object is inconvenient to examine and observe, a model is used to facilitate its investigation. Although an abstraction of the real thing, a model provides a three-dimensional representation of the original and thereby permits a highly concrete learning experience. When the printed word or a visual communicates inadequately, a model can perhaps successfully fill the gap. In the preceding section, globes were discussed, which are models of the earth. Looking at globes, it becomes obvious that it is impossible to observe the real thing in its entirety; and printed words or visuals cannot communicate or describe the physical appearance of the earth as well as a globe.

By being replicas of real things, models provide a means of minute examination and investigation. Perhaps models are able to satisfy people's inquisitiveness about the world around them. Models on display in libraries always seem to draw attention, and patrons are not only fascinated by them but find that they learn from them as well. The librarian should not overlook the facts that not only do models communicate extremely well by virtue of being replicas of real things but also that people are extremely familiar with them. Children grow up, mature, and learn with toys which indeed are models taken from real life, e.g., dolls, dollhouses, toy cars and trucks, stuffed animals. Upon growing up, adults become involved with model trains, boats, or automobiles; practically every home is beautified and decorated with a model of some type, e.g., ships, statuettes, and miniatures. In essence, models do not require the use of special skills in order to be understood or appreciated. What may be difficult to comprehend in written form becomes immediately lucid in a model.

When selecting models, the librarian needs to be critically aware of their characteristics and attributes. With regard to the accuracy of a model, its intended use will determine the degree of accuracy required. To use the globe as an example, if some of the rivers that appear on the globe were accurately replicated as to size and shape, it would require a magnifying glass to see them. This is a case where accuracy can be sacrificed for the sake of more essential information such as location, direction, and generalized shape. It has been found that when people examine models they are more concerned with the functionally significant parts. Both adults and children seem to prefer models that are less complex than the original things, in which the emphasis is on the major concept, function, or operation of the things represented. This fact gives positive indication that models do not have to be exact replicas in every detail. The accuracy with which the model represents the original should be dependent upon its intended use. With the transparent model of a man, where the internal organs and structure of the human body can be observed, it is not necessary to have a liquid representing blood, which would only obscure the viewing of the internal organs and structure. Indeed, this is a case where too much attention to detail would distract or confuse the viewer who is primarily interested in significant organic structure.

Models are made because it is difficult or even impossible to view real objects. Generally, models are reproduced in three relative sizes: the same size as the original; an enlarged or blown-up replica; or a reduced or miniaturized reproduction. Exact-size models are used chiefly as substitutes for the original which could be dangerous, expensive, rare, fragile, perishable, odoriferous, or difficult to maintain in a library. Enlarged models are extremely helpful in examining very small things. It would require the workings of an electron microscope to view the invisible molecular world, but a representative model of a molecule vividly portrays its structure in three dimensions. Conversely, a miniaturized model affords the opportunity to view the immensity of a large object in its entirety, e.g., a globe of the earth. Because of various size alterations in the relation of models to the things they represent, the model should always be labelled with regard to its scale. It is significant to know what degree in size the model is a replica of the real thing. This is especially important when models are close to the exact size of the original. The degree of scale exactness provides needful information in order to prevent misconceptions in learning. If a replica of a cross-section of a human torso is slightly enlarged or reduced, a misconception can be acquired with regard to unfamiliar body parts. However, the librarian should always consider the possibility that a slightly enlarged or reduced model of any object may be easier to view, handle, maintain, or store and might even be less expensive to purchase. Regardless of the intent of acquisition, information concerning scale should be conveniently available to the user.

Various types of models are available, and the librarian needs to be familiar with such terms as exact model, simplified model, static model, working model, mockup, cutaway, transparent model, cross-section, and diorama. An exact model is one that except for being enlarged or reduced is exact in *every* detail and can even be a working replica. An example of an exact model would be a model airplane where every part is included at exact scale. When selecting working models, it may be necessary, in a pure sense, to distinguish between a model and a miniature. If the model is made of the same material and can do the same thing as a larger version, it should be called a *miniature* rather than a model. As an example, it is possible to purchase an electric motor that can fit in the palm of the hand (e.g., the motor of an electric shaver); this then is not a model of a motor, rather it is a real working motor. If the motor needs outside mechanism in order to function, i.e., cannot operate in and of itself, then it is a model. An exact model essentially is one that is authentically enlarged or reduced for easier examination.

A static model is one that has no moving parts, even though it is quite possible that the original item it replicates does have moving parts. The purpose of a static model is basically to show what the original looks like and not what it does. A working model shows how the original operates and functions, and unlike the static model, it does not necessarily have to show what the original looks like, but rather what it does. This leads to the next type of model, which is a mockup. A mockup is a symbolic version of the real thing designed to show how it works even though it does not resemble it in many aspects. Although it would be difficult and complex to show the operation of an actual hydraulic system, a mockup would demonstrate the primary functions of its various components, and the use of liquid would illustrate how the system functions. A mockup is used to illustrate the principles involved in the function or purpose of a real thing.

The next type of model is a cutaway. A cutaway, as the term indicates, is a model with a surface that has been removed or cut away revealing the inner working, function, or structure of the real thing. A cutaway can be extraordinarily revealing and informative whenever the interior of the real thing cannot be seen. Models of the human torso are available with the flesh and bone cutaway revealing inner organs. Similar to cutaways are transparent models in which the outer surface is made of a clear plastic and the interior parts are clearly visible. Both the cutaway and transparent models have distinct advantages. The cutaway, although part of the exterior surface has been removed, provides physical access to interior parts, whereas with the transparent model, although none of the exterior surface has been removed, the actual color of the real thing is lost and the interior is not physically accessible. These are the general characteristics of cutaways and transparent models; however there are commercially made models that combine the best attributes of both, having see-through capability and removable or cutaway surfaces.

Similar to a cutaway is a cross-sectional model. Rather than having a portion of the surface removed, a cross-sectional model is literally a slicing of the model revealing the interior arrangement, location, and function of the real thing. A cross-section of a model automobile engine is an excellent device for showing how it is constructed.

A diorama is a three-dimensional scene with a painted background. Objects are arranged to depict an actual setting; to add a greater sense of realism, the scene is enclosed with an appropriate background. A homemade diorama utilizing the appropriately painted and decorated insides of a shoebox is easy to make and enjoyable to look at. Libraries make extensive use of dioramas by constructing them inside glass display cases. A diorama can contain real objects, like flora and fauna, and range in size from a small diorama using the inside of an eggshell for a scenic background all the way to a large room-size display of the kind found in museums. Not as prevalent as dioramas are cycloramas, which differ from dioramas in that instead of being viewed from the outside they are made to be viewed from within a large circle. A planetarium is a form of cyclorama. Perhaps the most famous cyclorama is one housed in its own building near Atlanta. It depicts the Battle of Atlanta fought on July 22, 1864. It combines real objects, models, and a background painting 50-feet high, 400 feet in circumference, and weighing 9 tons. It is considered to be the largest painting in the world.

The terms used to describe the various types of models indicate their predominant features. Many models contain several characteristic features: It is possible to have a cutaway, cross-sectional, mockup, simplified, working model of a real object. Again, it is for the librarian in selecting a model to determine which features are desirable and best communicate the objectives for which the model is selected.

There must be a reason for selecting a model. It should contribute information on a subject that cannot be communicated by other media as well or as economically. It should replicate the original and provide better information than the original for the reasons cited earlier. Some models are intended to be handled and thereby to provide tactile experience. When you select a model, it should be evaluated in regard to how well it can comply with the following criteria:

1. The original item would not be feasible as part of the library collection.
2. It provides a service better than, or a service not provided by, other media.

3. The scale is properly represented, and all related parts are of the same scale.
4. It is accurate, or any simplification at the expense of accuracy is wholly justifiable.
5. It does not misinform; and if inaccuracies are evident, they are for a purpose and will not confuse.
6. If it is to be handled, it must be of durable construction.
7. The cost must be justified. (Because models tend to be relatively expensive, their purchase should be justified in terms of use, efficiency in providing information, and perhaps esthetic value.)

Selecting and Obtaining Realia

As described in the preceding section, a model is a representation of the real thing to be used when it is not feasible to house the real thing in the library collection. However, there are a great many real things the library can acquire in order to provide the patron with first-hand experiences. Real items, specimens, relics, and real materials are collectively classified as *realia*. It cannot be disputed that the more real the thing being viewed, the more concrete and permanent will be the learning experience. By virtue of being the real thing, it has the virtue of having a natural, built-in, intrinsic interest. After all, why view or learn about a thing via substitute communication means (e.g., models, films, books) when the real thing is available for examination? Realia are capable of providing substance to a study.

It is practically impossible, and certainly extremely dangerous, for a library patron to go off in search of a rattlesnake, but a stuffed rattlesnake can conveniently and safely be examined in the library. The library patron is now practically afforded a first hand sensory experience. The rattlesnake is not viewed in its natural habitat, but that can be simulated by displaying the snake in a diorama.

Realia can be quite costly, and in order to justify their expense, it is recommended that their use be incorporated into a systematized approach. Too often libraries regard the realia in their collections as nothing more than dust-collecting junk, when indeed they can provide valuable information and enjoyment. Realia should be displayed or used with other materials. In the case of the rattlesnake, it can be prominently displayed in a diorama, study prints can be put on a display board, and relevant motion picture films and books can be shown or made available with it. In this way, a total sensory approach is provided: the patron sees, and perhaps even handles, a real rattlesnake, studies various pictures of it, views a film of it living and functioning in its natural habitat, and finally does further extensive and intensive reading about it. The total systematized approach affords the library patron with either the opportunity to examine a rattlesnake via a multitude of sensory and media channels or the option to select the media channel he or she deems most appropriate. But regardless of how the patron decides to investigate rattlesnakes, it is practically a foregone certainty that he or she will not bypass the opportunity to examine the real thing.

In pursuing the systems approach when utilizing realia, the librarian should strongly consider the acquisition or locally fabricated realia kits. A realia kit is a collection of real things, near-real things (models), and other supporting media (films, books, art prints, charts, audio tapes, etc.) that give a saturated study of a real thing. The realia kit has three distinct advantages: (1) it contains the elements of a complete multisensory, multimedia study of a real thing; (2) practically everything the patron needs is assembled in one package from which he or she can select whatever is wanted, thereby eliminating the need to search all over the library for materials; and (3) the realia kit contains all the materials for constructing a display or exhibit. Realia kits do have the disadvantage of tying up a lot of material, and when they are used or checked out by a patron, all the items in them are taken even if they are not all needed. When charged to a single patron, they obviously cannot all be used simultaneously.

When dealing with realia, the librarian can also consider a realia exhibit, which is essentially a collection of related materials. The acquisition of realia to be used in exhibits can be justified in terms of having displays in the library that are both esthetically pleasing and of educational value and interest. If the librarian wishes to have realia exhibits, it is important that they be displayed dynamically, with purpose and meaning. Too often, exhibits are static and uninspiring—and left on display well beyond their period of importance. Realia exhibits are not intended merely to take up space in the library, rather they are meant to entice the viewer to investigate them, perhaps learn more about and even develop an interest in them. If realia exhibits do not motivate patrons, they cannot be justified. An effective realia exhibit should communicate the purposes, functions, and structures of the realia as well as their relationship to one another and to the viewer as well.

Another category of realia is that of the *specimen,* which by definition is part of a real thing or one unit of a thing that is representative of a class, genus, or whole. As an example, a particular species of bird may be representative of birds of a particular region, e.g., predators. And it would not be necessary to collect several species of predators of that region. Perhaps when selecting a particular bird, it would be beneficial to include a specimen of that bird's skeleton—which would provide information regarding its internal structure. The selection of specimens is a complicated process, and the librarian should consult a person with expertise in order to insure that the right specimen is selected and that it provides the best means of informing the patron.

When selecting realia, the librarian needs to consider whether or not they will be handled by patrons. If a particular specimen is particularly delicate, it may be best to put it in a display case. If it can be encased in clear plastic, it can be picked up and examined but not damaged. Ideally, it is best if realia can be handled by patrons because this affords a kinesthetic experience unobtainable by other means. A final consideration when selecting fauna specimens is the possibility of having living animals. Many libraries have been extremely successful in providing patrons with live animals which indeed provide about as real and concrete an experience that a patron can have. Of course, live animals create a host of unique problems, e.g., care, feeding, handling, the safety of the animal, and the safety of the patron. Many librarians feel that having real animals available is well beyond the scope of the library's mandate to serve the community, but libraries involved with live animals are gratified by the requests for them from patrons. It is up to each library to decide to what extent it is to be involved with realia, with regard to scope, specimens, kits, exhibits, handling, and whether living specimens are to be considered as part of the library's service to its community.

When it comes to the actual selection of realia, the librarian will be amazed at all the various resources available. There are companies like Ward's Scientific Co. that provide scientific realia to libraries and educational institutions. The library's immediate community usually has a superabundant wealth of realia, which upon solicitation can be either loaned or donated to the library. The hobbyist, amateur and professional, is gratified to have the opportunity to display his or her collection in the library and will often serve as a resource person as well. To avoid a proliferation of realia beyond the needs of the library, it would be best to classify areas of realia and then determine what types are essential to the library program. Once realia are classified, it becomes apparent what types from each of the classifications would be beneficial to the library and should be considered as bona fide informational realia.

General classifications include:

1. *Applied sciences and arts:* Realia related to industry, home, health and medicine, military science, and recreation
2. *Humanities and the arts:* Realia related to art, music, drama, and humanities

3. *Science:* Realia related to biology, chemistry, geology, natural science, physics, meteorology, ecology, and environment
4. *Social sciences:* Realia related to anthropology, geography, ethnic studies, geography, history, psychology, and philosophy

Having set up a classification of realia, the librarian can then determine the types of materials needed to enhance the library collection and decide whether such materials need to be purchased outright or can be obtained from the community either on a loaned or donated basis. It is extremely gratifying to locate really fine realia in the community that can be made available to the library at no cost. It is a good idea to start a community realia resource file listing locations for obtaining stamp collections, rare and foreign coins, rock collections, flora and fauna (both live and preserved), artifacts or relics of significant social value, and mementos of important events. Such relia certainly enhance the library's collection and make it a more stimulating place to visit. It is even possible that a room or space in the library can be set aside as a museum area where library patrons have an opportunity of gaining a direct and purposeful experience by seeing and perhaps even handling realia. When obtaining realia from the community, via either solicitation or donation, it is important to develop a form to be signed by the contributor explicitly stating the library's obligation in accepting any materials. The form should indicate specificly how the realia are intended to be used, the responsibility for their maintenance, who is to assume the cost for replacing damaged or lost items, the dollar value, permission to modify the realia in any form, period of time for disposal if and when they are no longer needed by the library, and any acknowledgments to be accorded to the contributor. If a procedure is followed whereby both the contributor and the library sign a form stating the terms under which the library accepts the realia (or any other material for that matter), there is no ambiguity of proprietorship and certainly no later occasion for dispute if problems do indeed arise.

The capability of realia in enhancing the library's program should not be overlooked. They provide concrete learning experiences, and they are useful in clarifying principles, functions, and classifications. Realia can also provide an esthetic experience by bringing the real world into the library. The library patron will gain and appreciate a powerful experience.

Defining and Selecting Games and Simulations

In an attempt to provide the patron with a wide variety of media alternatives from which to choose, the library can offer games and simulations as still another means for acquiring information. Games and simulations furnish an experience in which the patron is actively involved in the learning process rather than playing a passive, observing role as in the case of viewing a film or reading a book. By being actively involved, the patron experiences a greater psychological impact than he or she could possibly be afforded by observing. Also, games and simulations produce an enjoyable experience oftentimes involving group interaction, which is difficult to obtain from other types of media.

Games and simulations are structured activities with specific rules and parameters designed for the purpose of actively involving the participant(s) in exploring, investigating, or experiencing certain aspects of a contrived procedure, event, or situation, the control and outcome of which is affected, directly or indirectly, by the skill and behavior of the participant(s). When you are assessing and selecting games and simulations, it is important to bear in mind that the terms *games* and *simulations* are not dichotomous. For the purposes of identification, it would be best to place the terms at either end of a continuum, as an activity very often has elements of both. It is indeed very rare that a pure game or pure simulation is created; each almost always contains elements of the other. Actually, the term *simulation,* as used in this context, was adopted by the military during World War II in the training of pilots. As part of a pilot's training, he was required to fly blind and know how to land an aircraft in conditions of poor or zero visibility such as bad weather or darkness. Actually to practice or fly under such adverse conditions is extremely dangerous, with an inherent high risk of losing both the pilot and his aircraft. To eliminate this danger, the military used the Link trainer, which gave the student pilot most of the conditions and sensations of flying in situations of zero visibility without leaving the ground. The student pilot could make a "bad landing," but without the resultant risk to himself or his aircraft. Hence the Link trainer produced a simulation of a real activity that had the student pilot actively involved with and in control of the eventual outcome. A similar type of simulator familiar to many high school students is a driving simulation trainer. Again the student is actively involved in learning, is in control of the outcome, and experiences many of the sensations of driving an automobile without risk to student or to a real automobile. Many other games and simulations are commercially available to the library, and the librarian should seriously consider their inclusion in the library program as a service to patrons.

Games and simulations are generally chosen to make available a structured activity in which knowledge, information, or learning experiences can be acquired. Although the fun aspect is often an inherent factor of games and simulations, it is not the prime reason for selecting them. Rather they are selected as one means, perhaps even the best means, of achieving a learning experience. Therefore, it becomes critical for the librarian to know exactly what are the stated objectives of the games or simulations and if indeed they provide the best means of achieving them.

In order to assess games and simulations intelligently, it is necessary to have an understanding of their elementary characteristics and the functions they are intended to serve. In assessing the characteristics of games and simulations, it is beneficial to place games at one end of a continuum and simulations at the other, bearing in mind that although a characteristic is *usually* associated with either a game or simulation, it is not exclusive to it. The following list is helpful in identifying the characteristics of games and simulations.

1. Games usually involve the element of chance. This is achieved through the use of dice, spinners, counters, cards, etc. The participant, regardless of skill, has no control over the chance element. If he or she is unlucky to have a poor roll of the dice, a bad spin, or to pick a poor card, it will affect game performance and very possibly the outcome of the game.

2. Simulations usually emphasize participant behavior. The skill and ability the participant brings to the simulation will directly affect the progress of the simulation and influence the eventual outcome. This aspect of simulations should be carefully scrutinized, as it pertains to the active involvement of the participant, which is one of the prime reasons for selecting a simulation.

3. Games usually involve a win–lose situation. The game reaches a climax and a conclusion when the winners and losers are identified. This also suggests that games have definite points of termination, i.e., when someone wins or loses.

4. A simulation is usually based on a real-life situation. Hence, it has no finite ending other than that imposed upon it by the participants, i.e., the simulation lasts as long as the participants wish to participate. The simulation involves a "slice of life," whereby the participants act out an event and, as previously stated in Characteristic 2, they are in control and their behavior affects the outcome. The simulation can use such devices as scenarios, role playing, and recreated environments. It is quite common in a simulation for a participant to play the role of another person. In a play or drama, the role-player cannot affect the scripted outcome; but in a simulation, the outcome is predicated on the skill of the participant. The simulation focuses on the interaction of people en-

gaged in verbal discourse or performing with equipment (e.g., flight trainer).

5. Games are usually used to *learn* subject matter, data, or concepts. The game, while being a pleasurable activity, provides the participant with a means to learn, develop, and master skills.

6. Simulations are usually used to *apply* skills. Once a skill is learned, the simulation provides the context wherein the skill can be tried out, giving the participants an opportunity to experience an event within the partial framework of a real-life situation.

Functioning within the foregoing characteristics, games and simulations are intended to achieve the following goals.

1. *Motivate and increase enthusiasm for learning:* Because the participant is actively involved in the process and contributes to the outcome, he or she has a personal interest or stake in the activity. Also, most games and simulations incorporate an element of play that tends to make them enjoyable.

2. *Stimulate more sophisticated and relevant inquiry:* The participant is not passively acquiring information but is using personal skills to effect outcomes; therefore knowledge is being not only acquired but also applied. Because they allow participants to apply knowledge, games and simulations offer the added features of meaning and relevance.

3. *Improve decision-making, communicating, and learning skills:* It is one thing to know something, but it requires more ability to apply knowledge. Games and simulations afford participants an opportunity to exercise and apply learning in a controlled situation. Many simulations are designed to involve human interaction, whereby one participant must communicate with other participants and persuade them to accept other viewpoints. Being able to persuade another person to accept a particular point of view involves a much higher order of skill than just holding and accepting it oneself.

4. *Helps to interpret information:* The participant must use newly acquired information and apply it in a real-life social context. The information now has much greater meaning, and the degree to which it is used in various simulated situations will enhance its applicability to a host of broader, real-life situations.

5. *Provides an opportunity to examine the rational and emotional components of the process:* Because the participant is competing with or being influenced by other participants, personal outcomes of the game or simulation are always in doubt; and joys as well as frustrations can be experienced. Such a challenge, whereby a participant is actively involved in the process, has to make him or her aware of the rational and emotional components.

6. *Makes learning real:* Whether flying an aircraft in a Link trainer or buying Atlantic City real estate while playing Monopoly, the experience requires far more involvement than just reading about it or viewing a film on the subject. Perhaps for a brief moment the participant is able to escape from his or her own real world and into the fantasied world of games and simulations to learn, experience, feel, and apply new knowledge in a controlled situation unattainable by any other means.

Considering these goals of games and simulations, it becomes apparent that they can replicate certain aspects of the real world in an environment upon which some controls can be exercised, that will not put the participant in any real danger but at the same time provide a learning-by-experiencing situation with emotional involvement.

The librarian's task of selecting games and simulations involves several considerations including purpose, objective, patron, type of use, and management.

1. *Purpose:* It must be ascertained whether the game or simulation is a discrete entity or is to be specifically incorporated for use with other types of informational media. Also to be considered is whether the game or simulation is designed for the purpose of introducing, exploring, or investigating information and if this is to be achieved in a cursory or in-depth fashion.

2. *Objective:* The goals and objectives of the game or simulation should be clearly and concisely stated. The expected behavior or knowledge to be acquired by the participant needs to be known. Although the game or simulation is not intended solely for the purpose of fun, it should nevertheless be an enjoyable and rewarding experience for the participants. In the case of psuedogames and simulations like tinkertoys, the librarian will need to conceive activities and objectives for their use that are in keeping with the characteristics and goals stated previously in this section.

3. *Patron:* Something needs to be known of the patron who is expected to use the library's games and simulations. The supposedly wisest selection is of no value if it is never used. A good example of selecting games and simulations with the patron in mind can be made of the game of Monopoly. If the community the library serves is the type where most of its patrons own their own games of Monopoly, then obviously they will not be going to the library to request it. Conversely, if the library's community has no need for or interest in the game of Monopoly, again there will be no requests for its use.

4. *Type of use:* Basically there are two places where games and simulations will be used: in the library and outside it. If they are to be used in the library, an activity area must be allocated for this purpose. Because

games and simulations often involve verbal interaction, spaces used should have audio privacy so that participants neither disturb other patrons nor are intruded upon. When games and simulations are used outside the library, concern for their conscientious use by the patron becomes paramount as they are no longer under the control or supervision of the librarian. Because games and simulations are often boxed items containing many individual pieces, the patron needs to be encouraged to return them in a respectable condition for further use by other patrons.

5. *Management:* Because games and simulations contain many individual pieces, they can be difficult to manage. It would be absurd for the librarian to have to check in each individual item, for example, in a game of Monopoly. It would be equally foolish to assume that none of the pieces will eventually become lost. All the parts of a game or simulation will be used and can be expected to wear. It is for the librarian to project some type of life expectancy for a game or simulation, predicated not on a time period but on number of uses. Again using Monopoly as an example, if a librarian considers that after 25 uses the game will have received sufficient wear and enough pieces could be lost or destroyed that its use is impaired, the librarian should inform the administration that after 25 uses a request for a replacement is justified. The actual figure for the number of uses will be based on experience, and eventually a revised number of uses will be more in line with the actual need for replacement. The point here is that unlike a book which is far easier to control and does not receive the same kind of punishing wear, a game or simulation requires a use-line life expectancy and not a time-line life expectancy.

Introducing and using games and simulations in the library can be a welcome and valuable service. They are an interesting and exciting way to learn information and acquire new skills. They do have a place in the library, and their value as tools of communication and knowledge should not be underestimated. The bibliography at the end of this chapter contains valuable resources and references for the librarian needing to know more about the use of games and simulations as well as sources for obtaining them.

Selected Bibliography

Globes and Maps

Deetz, C. H., and Adams, O. S. *Elements of Map Projection with Applications to Map and Chart Construction.* 5th ed. Westport, Conn.: Greenwood Press, 1945.

Drazniowsky, R. *Map Librarianship: Readings.* Metuchen, N.J.: Scarecrow Press, 1975.

Geography and Map Division SLA. *Recent Practices in Map Libraries.* New York: Special Libraries Association, 1971.

Jennings, J. H. *Elementary Map Interpretation.* New Rochelle, New York: Cambridge University Press, 1960.

Moxon, J. *Tutor to Astronomy and Geography.* 3d ed. New York: Burt Franklin Publishing, 1968.

Richards, P., and Adler, R. K. *Map Projections: An Introduction.* New York: American Elsevier, 1972.

Steers, J. A. *Introduction to the Study of Map Projections.* Mystic, Conn.: Lawrence Verry, 1970.

Stevenson, E. L. *Terrestrial and Celestial Globes: Their History and Construction, Including a Consideration of Their Value As Aids in the Study of Geography and Astronomy.* 2 vols. New York: Johnson Reprint Corp., 1971.

Woodward, D., ed. *Five Centuries of Map Printing.* Chicago: University of Chicago Press, 1925.

Selection Aids

American Geographical Society—Map Department. *Index to Maps in Books and Periodicals.* First Supplement. Boston: G. K. Hall, 1971.

Bancroft Library, University of California, Berkeley. *Index to Printed Maps.* First Supplement. Boston: G. K. Hall, 1975.

Carrington, D. K., ed. *Map Collections in the United States and Canada: A Directory.* 2d rev. ed. New York: Special Libraries Association, 1970.

Dickinson, G. C. *Maps and Air Photographs.* New York: Crane-Russak Co., 1969.

Hammond Incorporated, eds. *Ambassador World Atlas.* Maplewood, New Jersey: Hammond, 1974.

U.S. Library of Congress, Map Division. *A List of Maps of America in the Library of Congress.* 2 vols. New York: Burt Franklin, 1967.

Models

Alt, W. E. *Modelmaking and Workshop Projects.* Westwood, Mass.: F. W. Faxon, 1969.

Cassin-Scott, J. *Models in the Making.* New York: International Publications Service, 1974.

Hopwood, R. R. *Science Model Making.* New York: Macmillan, 1963.

Nassiet, C. *World of Models.* New York: Drake, 1973.

Wylam, W. *Scale Models.* Boston: Herman, 1975.

Games and Simulations

Abt, C. C. *Serious Games.* New York: Viking Press, 1970.

Aredon, E. M., and Sutton-Smith, B. *Study of Games.* New York: John Wiley, 1971.

Babcock, S. S., and Schild, E. O., eds., *Simulation Games in Learning.* Beverly Hills, Calif.: Sage Publications, 1968.

Barton, R. *Primer on Simulation and Gaming.* Englewood Cliffs, N.J.: Prentice-Hall, n.d.

Carlson, E. *Learning through Games.* Washington, D.C.: Public Affairs Press, 1969.

Gillispie, P. H. *Learning through Simulation Games.* Paramus, N.J.: Paulist-Newman Press, 1974.

Greenblatt, C., and Duke, R. eds., *Gaming Simulation: Rationale Design and Applications,* New York: Halsted, 1975.

Huizinga, J. *Homo Ludens, A Study of the Play Element in Culture,* Boston: Beacon, 1961.

Kleitsch, R. G. *An Introduction to Learning Games and Instructional Simulations: A Curriculum Guideline.* St. Paul, Minn.: Instructional Simulations, 1969.

Nesbitt, W., ed. *Simulation Games for the Social Studies Classroom.* New York: Foreign Policy Association, 1968.

Pfeiffer, J. W., and Jones, J. E. *A Handbook of Structured Experiences for Human Relations Training.* Iowa City: University Associates Press, 1969.

Raser, J. R. *Simulation and Society; An Exploration of Scientific Gaming,* Boston: Allyn and Bacon, 1969.

Selection Aid

Kleitsch, R. G., and Wiegman, F. B. *Directory of Educational Simulations, Learning Games and Didactic Units.* Macalester, Minn.: Macalester College Press, 1969.

13

Programmed Instruction

Programmed Instruction: A Definition

Programmed instruction is called a process, and before a definition can be constructed it is necessary to define *process*. As it relates to programmed instruction, a process is a controlled sequence of events leading to a desired outcome. As long as there is a control of a sequence of events, then there is more certainty that the goal will be achieved. As a brief example, if you wanted to change a tire on your automobile, you would first read the handbook on tire changing for your car, after which you would change the tire. It is to be hoped that you succeed; but if the instructions for changing a tire are in a controlled sequence, whereby you receive a bit of information, perform the necessary act, and then, upon successful completion of that act, you are given a further segment of instruction with its inherent probability of success, then it would be safe to assume that the presentation of the information about changing a tire in a controlled sequence would in all probability lead to more success in tire changing than just reading the handbook and changing the tire.

By definition, programmed instruction is a process that involves a sequence of events leading to the acquisition of a set of desired learning objectives. The learner is given some information, then challenged on how well he knows the information by being required to make a response to a statement or question. Upon completion of the response, the learner is provided with a correct response so he knows immediately whether or not his response is correct.

Psychological Principle of Programmed Instruction

In preparing activities utilizing programmed instruction, knowledge of the learner's behavior is essential. Programmed instruction ascribes to the characteristics of behavioristic psychology. Attention is given to stimulus, response, reinforcement, or what is called the S–R–R theory. The procedure is quite simple. (See Figure 13.1.) The learner is given some information, this is the stimulus, and he is required to provide an answer, which is the response, he is given the correct answer immediately, which is the reinforcement. All these elements, stimulus, response, reinforcement, are essential; and to assure any degree of success, the reinforcement should occur immediately after the student makes his response. Any lag in time between response and reinforcement destroys the purpose of programmed instruction because in essence the reinforcement is a reward, and if it occurs immediately, the probability that learning is taking place greatly increases.

Linear and Branching Programs

Information in programmed instruction is usually presented in one of two formats called a linear and branching programs. In Figure 13.2, Diagram 1 (proceeding from left to right) at No. 1 a learner is given some information to which he responds, and his response is immediately reinforced. He then proceeds to No. 2 for more information to which he responds, and his response is immediately reinforced, and then on to No. 3, etc. As you can observe, the learner schematically proceeds along a straight line or linear path. The learner determines his own speed, and a more intelligent learner will proceed through the program at a faster pace than a slower or less intelligent learner. This, in a sense, provides for individual difference in students' rates of learning.

Diagram 2 of Figure 13.2 is a schematic of a branching type program. In a branching program, the learner is again given some information (the stimulus), but for his response he is given a choice of alternatives. Let's call these alternatives A, B, and C, with B being the proper response. If the learner answers B, he proceeds to No. 2 for more information. If he answers A, which is incorrect, he is branched off to receive information

Figure 13.1. Psychological principle of programmed instruction.

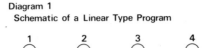

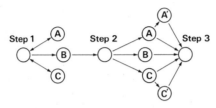

Figure 13.2. Linear and branching formats.

as to why his answer is incorrect and given additional information to assist him in making the correct response. He is then returned to the original piece of information (No. 1) and given another opportunity to respond. The same procedure would follow if the learner answered C. The difference between A and C is that in both cases the learner is given remedial information, but because answers A and C are not identical, he must be given different types of remedial information for each particular answer.

A variation of the branching program is illustrated in Diagram 2, Step 2. Here, if a student answers incorrectly, he is branched to A, given remedial information, and challenged. If he answers correctly, he is directed to new information at Step 3 and is back into the mainstream of the program. If he answers incorrectly, he is given further remedial information at Point A'; when he finally answers correctly, he returns to the mainstream of the program, Step 3. This type of procedure is usually found in programs utilizing a computer.

Major Developments

An understanding of the development of programmed instruction is beneficial to the librarian in selecting materials. Being aware of where material originated, as well as copyright date, will give information regarding the type of program, its applicability to different types of learning, and perhaps even its level of sophistication. Although many people have been involved in the programmed instruction movement, the names of Pressey, Skinner, and Crowder parallel major developments.

In 1926, Sydney Pressey developed one of the first instruments of what is now called a teaching machine. Using the behavioral principle of Stimulus, Response, Reinforcement (S-R-R), Pressey's machine gave the learner a bit of information to which he was required to respond. The response was in the form of multiple choices. If the student made the correct response by pressing the proper switch, the machine would advance and present new information. An incorrect response was not rewarded: The machine would not advance to new information. This basic machine principle is still in use today. Because Pressey gave the learner an opportunity to make a choice, one being the correct answer, his program is called the recognition type—the learner recognizes the correct answer from multiple choices. Pressey's programs use the linear format for presenting information.

Pressey's teaching machine did not gain very wide acceptance, and it was not until the launching of Sputnik by the Soviet Union in 1957 that we find any substantial development in programmed instruction. American education immediately went into a crash program, especially in the sciences, in an effort to improve the rate of learning. Terms such as information explosion, knowledge explosion, independent studies, and individualized learning came into vogue. About this time, the name of B.F. Skinner came to the fore of programmed instruction. Skinner had been conducting extensive research on animal behavior involving the study of the S-R-R theory. The programmed instruction Skinner developed was essentially a linear type similar to that developed by Pressey, but instead of recognizing the correct response among several choices, the learner is required to construct an answer by filling in a blank with the correct response. Filling in the blank is a recall type of learning because the learner has to recall the answer rather than (as in the Pressey method) recognize it. After filling in the blank, the learner compares his answer with the correct response.

The third person, Norman Crowder, is noted for developing the branching type program which utilizes corrective assignments for incorrect answers. Of the three types of programs, Crowder's is considered by many to be best because it provides for individual differences by giving the student, when needed, a corrective assignment. However, advocates of the Pressey and Skinner linear formats claim their programs provide for individual differences by allowing the student to progress at his own pace.

Present developments of programmed instruction finds the use of computers providing what is called computer based instruction (CBI) or computer assisted instruction (CAI). (The emerging role of the computer in programmed instruction is discussed in detail later in this chapter.)

This brief history of programmed instruction is important for the librarian responsible for selecting programmed instructional materials. The crash program that followed Sputnik resulted in a proliferation of programmed instruction glutting the educational market. Much of it was produced by many people with little or no knowledge of the principles of programmed instruction and of questionable value because learners, for a multitude of reasons, did not learn. Today, we find programs being developed by teams of highly trained specialists. A team may consist of a psychologist, with knowledge of learning theory, an educational researcher, a curriculum specialist, and teachers. Programs are extensively developed and field tested before they are made available for purchase. It is essential to use caution in selecting any program produced prior to 1968, and for any program selected, examine the validation statement to know how it was field tested, by whom, and the results. In this way, you can ascertain that the program selected is best for your learners.

Textbooks versus Linear and Branching Programmed Instruction Books

A textbook is defined as a book that gives instructions on the principles of a subject of study or any book used as the basis or partial basis for a course of study. A major difference between a regular text and a programmed instruction text is that the author of a regular text is concerned with the presentation of content. He wants to be certain that he has provided the learner with enough information to acquire knowledge of the topic being studied. Stated in a different way, the author provides the necessary information, all the student has to do is read and study the information.

On the other hand, the author of a programmed instruction text is primarily concerned with learner behavior. He addresses himself to the questions, "How can I best present the information for the student to learn it? Does the program motivate the student? Does it challenge the student? Is the student successful with the program? What is the terminal behavior of the student?"

When one examines formats of programmed instruction books, several factors become evident. Linear programmed instruction textbooks usually have smaller frames than branching textbooks. (A frame is a unit of information containing presentation of information [stimulus]; provision for an answer [response]; and the correct answer [reinforcement]).

Because the frames are smaller, there can be several per page, and the answers are close to the response space (printed either on the page margin or on the following page). In a branching programmed instruction textbook, the frames tend to be larger, and one can possibly cover several pages. When asked to make a response, the learner is referred to a page that discusses the correctness of the response. If the response is correct, the learner proceeds with the program. If it is incorrect, he is given remedial information then returned to the page containing the original set of responses where he is given another opportunity to respond. By design, answers are located on various pages and not in any prescribed order. Actually, the arrangement of pages is somewhat scrambled, and such books are known by many as scrambled textbooks.

To summarize, the author of a regular textbook is concerned with the "what," while the author of a programmed instruction textbook is concerned with the "how." Linear programmed instruction texts have smaller frames in sequence, while branching programmed instruction textbooks tend to have larger frames with a scrambled reading arrangement of information.

Emerging Role of the Computer

The continuing refinement and sophistication of programmed instruction have inevitably led to the use of the computer. As indicated in the preceding section, programmed instruction authors are concerned with learner behavior. Actually, each individual approaches a learning situation with a unique personal set of learning behaviors, and providing for these individual differences can become quite a complex task, even using a branching programmed instruction textbook. Hence, a computer with an infinite number of branching capabilities can branch the learner to the exact bit (frame) of information he needs.

Other advantages are possible with the computer. It can keep track of learner progress, reenter him into the program at the exact point where he left it, keep him challenged at his optimum level of performance; if he should make a certain number of successive incorrect answers, the computer can interpret that he is not ready for the program he is using and inform him to exit from, or leave, the program and engage in some other type of activity. A computer can give the learner a printed report of his progress; it can even report the overall effectiveness of the program along with information on any phase of the program in need of revision (e.g., a common rule of thumb is that if 90% of the learners are not correctly responding to 90% of the frames, the program is either in need of revision or not suited to the learners who are using it).

Computers can handle programs with verbal or visual information; the learner can respond on a typewriter keyboard or use a light probe and point to the response on an illuminated screen. With this level of sophistication, the computer now can challenge authors to make programs of infinite variety with primary concern on the basic premise of programmed instruction, i.e., learner behavior.

Programmed instruction utilizing the computer is generally identified as falling into two broad categories—computer based instruction (CBI) and computer assisted instruction (CAI). Computer based instruction involves a program in which the computer is the base or prime contact for learning, and if needed, an instructor can provide assistance. In computer assisted instruction, the learner gets basic instruction from a teacher and uses the computer to facilitate learning. There can be an overlap of function, and a program could be used for both computer based and computer assisted instruction.

Actually, the computer is here now and ready to perform, but to be used properly for programmed instruction, a computer requires a program that can utilize the sophistication it can offer the learner. Such programs are extremely expensive and take considerable time to produce, but once they are made and properly field tested they offer the potential for a learner to go to a library and, possibly without human intervention (i.e., a teacher) acquires knowledge to the extent that is now available only in a formal classroom environment.

Selecting Software and Compatible Hardware

Oftentimes, in selecting programmed instruction packages, librarians have a desire to use programs that include hardware (equipment). Some hardware appears to be quite exotic, making a programmed instruction text by comparison appear like a dull enterprise for the learner. It is essential not to fall into this trap but to adhere to the architect's dictum, "form follows function." Ask yourself, "What is it that the hardware can do?" or better still, "What is it that you want the hardware to do?"

Many kinds of hardware are nothing more than "electronic page turners," with some kind of a cheatproof device that will not allow the learner to see the answer until he has first made a response. If this is a sole concern, there is quite a bit of inexpensive hardware that will meet this criterion. On the other hand, a thorough analysis of hardware

Figure 13.3. Computer terminal—branching program.

Figure 13.4. Programmed instruction equipment (teaching machines). Left to right: Cardboard scroll box—linear program; electromechanical machine projecting film on a rear projection screen—branching program; plastic hand operated machine—linear program.

capabilities will provide the necessary direction in selecting exactly the right piece of hardware, if needed, for a particular type of learner.

Hardware has a wide range of capability. It can provide, in various degrees, the following features:

Present information in a linear format
Present information in linear and branching formats
Present information in a branching format
Provide for write-in answers
Provide for multiple-choice answers
Electrical or mechanical device to advance program
Cheatproof device
Provide record of learner performance
Several learners on same program at same time
Provide audio information
Project films, slides, filmstrips, or videotapes
Contain automatic stop and start devices
Use information in page, paper roll, or microform formats
Use consumable or nonconsumable programs
Accept locally produced programs

With this wide range of capabilities available, it becomes necessary for the librarian to determine which combination is best suited for the patrons' needs. Obviously, the more elaborate the hardware the higher the cost. (See Figure 13.3.) Prices range from less than a dollar for a scroll device to hundreds of thousands of dollars for a highly sophisticated computerized system. (See Figure 13.4.) Much of the hardware being purchased is generally in the $25–$1500 range.

Once a decision is made as to the type of hardware needed, the checklist (Figure 13.5) can assist in evaluating it. The list in no way implies there is a best combination of features, as perhaps such a machine does not presently exist for your unique needs, but rather it is an aid to guide you in selecting the best machine with regard to cost, maintenance, durability, effectiveness, versatility, and ease of operation.

Criteria can be developed to analyze the software (programs), and perhaps this is more essential than the analysis of hardware, as the software contains the actual information to be learned and thus the analysis could tend to be more subjective and personal. With the criteria in Figure 13.6, an assessment can be made of a program's value to the library as well as to the patron.

A final consideration in analyzing the merits of hardware and software is, of course, to inquire of other institutions using it. The manu-

Name of Machine_____ Manufacturer_____ Cost_____

(Directions: Respond by checking or filling in appropriate boxes.)

					Other comments
1. Construction of machine	cardboard	wood	plastic	metal	
2. Method of operation	manual	mechanical	electric	electro-mechanical	
3. Ease of operation	simple	easy	complex	difficult	
4. Type of program used	linear	branching	linear-branching		
5. Kinds of programs	none	one	several	special or general	
6. Physical characteristics of program	printed page	roll of paper	slide or filmstrip	sound-motion-color	
7. Learner response	written	keyboard	press button, lever	light probe	

	elementary	junior high	senior high	college–adult
8. Intended type of learner				
9. Provision for correct response	manually activated	automatic		
10. Compares learner response with correct response	yes	no		
11. Tamperproof feature, e.g., able to change answer or see correct answer before responding	yes	no		
12. Feedback to librarian	tally counter	punch card	answers on separate paper	no
13. Consumable materials	yes	no		
14. Group use	yes	no		
15. Approximate weight				
16. Approximate dimensions				
17. Length of warranty				
18. Cost of maintenance service contract				
19. Location of nearest dealer or service office				
20. Overall rating	excellent	good	fair	poor

Figure 13.5. Programmed instruction hardware evaluation checklist.

195

Name of program_____ Producer_____
Copyright date_____ Cost_____

1. Authority (credentials of program designers and areas of expertise)

2. Validation studies (Who were subjects? Where? When? Results?)

3. Completeness (Each program an entity? Part of a series?)

4. Adjunct materials (Require use of materials outside of program?)

5. Different programs (Are other nonrelated programs available for the hardware?)

6. Communication orientation (print, visual, etc.)

7. Availability of pretest–posttest materials

8. Program length (approximate time; number of pages; etc.)

9. Objectives (Specifically what is being learned and how well is it achieved?)

Figure 13.6.   Criteria in selecting programmed instruction Software. This form should be used in conjunction with the Programmed Instruction Hardware Evaluation Checklist (Figure 13.5).

facturer, if he is reputable, will have no reservations in providing you with such information. A discreet inquiry to a current user could provide invaluable information in reaching a decision.

Selected Bibliography

Center for Programmed Instruction. *Programs: A Guide to Programmed Instructional Materials.* Washington, D.C.: U.S. Government Printing Office, 1962–.
Columbia University Center for Programmed Instruction Materials, 1964065. New York: Columbia University, 1965.
Hendershot, C. H. *Programmed Learning, A Bibliography of Programs and Presentation Devices.* 4th ed. 2 vols. 1967–1968 supplement. Bay City, Mich.: Hendershot Programmed Learning, 4114 Ridgewood Dr. 1967.
Limsdaine, Arthur A. *Teaching Machines and Programed Learning, II.* Washington, D.C.: National Education Association, 1965.
Northeastern University. *Programmed Instruction Guide,* 2d ed. Newburyport, Mass.: ENTELEK, Inc., 1968.

Ofiesh, G. *Programmed Instruction: A Guide for Management.* New York: American Management Association, 1965.

UNESCO. *Programmed Instruction: An International Directory,* 1967. New York: Columbia University Press, 1967.

14

Books

Fundamentals of Book Selection

Books are without question the largest part of the library collection, and book selection is a topic of study in an of itself. This chapter is a very basic general overview of accepted procedures, included to achieve completeness of coverage, for books remain an important part of the multimedia library. Although the library does have other media forms, and newer media forms are continually being introduced into the library, the printed book is still the mainstay of the library collection. It would be extremely naive for librarians, even those that are proponents of advanced modern technology of information dissemination, to assume that books belong to antiquity and in a short time will be rendered obsolete. Granted the library can use and has need for modern technology, the book has and will continue to occupy a place of prominence in the library. It is quite possible that book information by the year 2000 will be predominantly available in some electronic form, but regardless of form, the content will still be arranged in some type of book format. The librarian will still need to be an expert in book selection and have a professional working knowledge of the basic elements involved in book acquisition.

All book selection is predicated on the principle of supply and demand. Supply simply refers to the types, titles, and varieties of books available in the marketplace from which to choose. Demand, on the other hand, refers to the kind of books the patrons of a particular library will request or need. This is where the acquisition skills of the professional librarian come to the fore. The library should not acquire, and in all probability cannot afford, every book published. It is equally important to know which books to accept as well as which to reject. Considering that approximately 30,000 books are published each year (and fewer than 10,000 of them are reviewed), the task of selecting books is by no means easy. The librarian needs to formulate and expound upon the basic elements involved in selecting books for his or her library in order that selection procedures be promulgated on valid principles.

1. *Philosophy of the library:* Although many libraries claim to have a philosophy for selecting books, it is difficult to locate a written statement that can be used as a working guide. The philosophy for selecting books should include the purpose of the library and its goals for filling the needs of the community it is created to serve. In adopting a philosophy of book selecting, the librarian needs to consider the best, demand, and least-cost theories of book selection. (These three theories are investigated in the next section.)

2. *Nature of the community:* The librarian needs to know the nature of the community which the library is to serve. In the case of the academic or school librarian, the task of identification is relatively simple, as the curriculum perfunctorily describes the literature needs of students. The librarian of a public library has to develop means of ascertaining the reading needs of its community. Factors such as quality of employment, recreational needs, and unique social, political, cultural, geographical, and historical traits of the community need to be identified.

3. *Availability of books from other agencies:* It must be determined if other agencies in the community provide similar book services. As an example, textbooks are provided by schools, and the library should not be expected to acquire them. If school textbooks are expected to be included in the library collection, then in all probability they will be presented to the library by the school district. It is also possible that other libraries in the community can work out reciprocal agreements regarding the sharing of books and indeed which kinds of books each will acquire.

4. *Books available from governmental agencies:* It should be determined if state or federal agencies have books that they make available to the public, e.g., books for the blind. It is possible that the local library may want to include books from other governmental agencies in its collection, or it may refer the patron directly to the governmental agency circulating books.

5. *Sociological trends:* The librarian needs to be aware of sociological trends that may have a bearing on patrons' needs or demands for certain

types of books. The influence of movies and television on what people read cannot be underestimated. Cultural events, recreational activities, scientific milestones, and ethnic composition of a community are potent forces on what types of books should be on the library shelf.

6. *Booklists:* Booklists are invaluable guides in building library collections. They tend to narrow down the range of books that should be included in certain types of collections. But it is the librarian who makes the final decision as to what extent the books listed will be those needed for a particular library community.

7. *Budget.* The importance of budget cannot be overlooked. All book selection lists should be based on priority of need, and books should be purchased within the constraints of the existing budget. It very often happens that the best thought out list of books to be selected must undergo revision because of limited availability of funds; hence the need for selection priorities. Budget constraints should be approached with optimism and not considered as ugly ogres inhibiting the development of the library collection. In the final analysis, the library does not need every book published; and although the budget mandates how many books the library can afford to acquire, if book selection is done judiciously, as evidenced by the use of the library, expenditures can be well justified and increases in future budgets can be deserved and expected.

These seven basic fundamentals are not intended to be exhaustive but to serve as the basis for developing a sound book selection policy.

Best, Demand, and Least-Cost Theories of Book Selection

When selecting books, the librarian can subscribe, either singly or in combinations of varying degrees, to the best book theory, the demand book theory, or the least-cost book theory.[1]

The Best Book Theory

Adherents of the best book theory maintain that the true purpose of the library is to provide its patrons with the best books available. In absolute terms, this means that regardless of the needs or desires of patrons, only books identified as being the best in their particular class are chosen. Obviously, the term *best* contains some degree of subjectiv-

[1]Mary Duncan Carter, *et al., Building Library Collections,* 4th edition, Metuchen, N.Y.: Scarecrow Press, 1974, Chapter 1.

ity. In general, these books have become classics, been given extremely favorable reviews, or been rated best for the social and cultural needs of the patron. There is no dispute that the classics are best books, for they have obviously stood the test of time and made worthwhile contributions to mankind. Books receiving excellent reviews for their literary quality can also warrant high selection consideration. When books are selected because they are best for the social and cultural needs of the patron, it usually involves to some extent the *subjective evaluation* of the librarian; and this can possibly be considered an incursion of censorship. In the final analysis, who has the right to decide what is best for the patron? As a result, the best book theory implies the possibility of selecting books that run counter to what the patron will actually read. Of what value is it to have a library of best books if they receive little or no use? This concept will be further explored in the demand theory of book selection.

Still another aspect of the best book theory deals with the physical attributes of the book. If a choice is available, the librarian should consider the quality of binding and paper; readability of the print; and the clarity of artwork, graphics, illustrations, and photography. Again, if the best book theory is subscribed to, there is no question that the best physical quality should be obtained; however, such a decision must be objectively justified on the basis of durability, long life expectancy, use, and patrons' appreciation that the high quality is worth the additional cost.

The Demand Book Theory

Advocates of the demand book theory maintain that a book should be selected only if it can be determined that the patron will want it. Book use becomes the overriding criterion of selection. If this theory is carried to its extreme, the library might house a collection of literary trash, but this is justified by being what the patron demands. Perhaps the philosophy of the library should be to nurture the cultural needs of its patrons, and some criterion of censorship should be formulated to eliminate the possibility that the library could degenerate into a purveyor of inferior literature. Obviously, some flexibility is needed in selecting what is best versus what is demanded. The librarian must be astute to developments and trends in book publishing. Again, considering that over 30,000 new titles are published annually, there is a need for some sort of sliding scale when selecting best and demand type literature whenever best and demand are not one and the same. It is safe to assume that best books tend to have a lasting quality whereas demand books tend to serve a temporary interest. If this indeed is the case, then perhaps decisions can reside in the physical quality of the books selected, with best books being purchased in the best physical quality available and demand books being purchased in a less durable format, e.g., paperbacks.

The demand book theory of selection can always be justified in terms of use, but it should never be used to sacrifice the library's literary standards, which perhaps is a justification for the best book theory.

The Least-Cost Book Theory

Subscribers to the least-cost book theory maintain that both best and demand theories can be entertained if all books are selected with the prime consideration that the least expensive version of a book be purchased. It is contended that by adhering to this theory more titles can be purchased. Unfortunately, a total commitment to this theory could eventually result in a rather shabby book collection in both content and physical quality. Purchasing less expensive books written by lesser known (and perhaps less qualified) authors could well ensue in literature of less quality. A renowned author of great literary skill, using primary resources for his work, has to produce a work of immensely superior quality than an author with less literary talent using secondary resources. However, when a work by one author is available in different formats, the least-cost book theory can be validly entertained. There should be an awareness as to why a cost structure exists for the same literary work. Perhaps the least-cost editions are abridged, the esthetic quality of pictorial information has been modified, the physical quality of the book has been reduced, or perhaps it is a less prestigious second printing. Whatever the cause, if the librarian can tolerate sacrifices when obtaining a least-cost version, it should be sincerely considered.

Not a direct corollary to the least cost book theory but still related to cost is the rent-to-own means of book acquisition, which is worthy of mention at this point. Briefly, there are book jobbers who rent books to a library for 1-year periods, after which the librarian can either return them or buy them outright. This gives the librarian a year to determine if a book is worth owning and thus to return books not worthy of or needed in the collection. This, in a sense, is a variation of least cost, as books that do not prove themselves in the actual library will incur only a rental cost not a total ownership cost and will not become deadwood in the collection.

The three theories of book selection tend to form a triad of justification and consideration. They should be seriously entertained by the librarian, as they give the necessary guidance as to the general attributes of the library's collection and are essential when considering book selection policy.

Developing a Book Selection Policy

Having investigated the basic elements involved in the selection of books and formulated an awareness of the implication of the best, demand, and least-cost theories as they affect building a book collection, the librarian needs to develop a realistic, workable policy for book acquisition. Depending on the particular library and how many people are actually involved, it may be a sound principle to have the book selection policy in a written form detailing precisely how books are selected. By adhering to a well-defined, prescribed policy, the possibility of personal preferences and biases interfering with the soundness and quality of selection will be greatly minimized. This is not to imply that the personal opinions of the librarian are not to be entertained; after all the librarian is professionally prepared and should possess a respected expertise in book selection, but a documented book selection policy makes provisions for valid, qualitative book selection procedures.

The following suggested policy considerations are not listed in hierarchical order, but rather attempt to be comprehensive. Accompanying each policy item are questions to be considered when developing policy for a particular library book selection program. Some of the items may appear mundane; however, just such items, when taken for granted and not properly developed, could negate the quality of the book selection program.

1. *Purpose of the library:* The book should not be in conflict with the philosophical goals of the library.
   Questions: Does the book belong in the library? Does the service provided by the library warrant the inclusion of this type of book?
2. *Quality:* The book should be in keeping with the qualitative standards set by the library as regards contents respectability, and physical characteristics.
   Questions: Is the book judged to be of the highest quality available for selection? If the book is a translation, is it the most accurate available? If book quality is sacrificed, what is the justifiable reason?
3. *Reviews:* Reviews should be consulted to assist in the selection.
   Questions: How many reviews should be consulted in making a valid decision? What are the credentials of the reviewers?

4. *Patron:* The book should be suitable to the abilities, needs, and interests of patrons.
   Questions: Who are the patrons that are entitled to use the library? What is the range of reading skills of the patrons? Who will be using this particular book?

5. *Applicability:* The book should be analyzed with regard to its applicability to a broad or narrow audience and assessed accordingly.
   Questions: If broad applicability, will the book serve the needs of a sufficient cross-section of patron types? If narrow applicability, will the book serve informational needs unavailable by any other means?

6. *Usability:* A determination should be made as to minimum anticipated usage. A book may have a short usage expectancy and soon become obsolete; but if it receives a prescribed number of uses, its acquisition is justified. Conversely, a book may receive rather limited use but be of permanent value. A formula could be devised to analyze this problem.
   Questions: Will enough patrons read the book to justify its acquisition? Is this a book the patron wants or needs?

7. *Selection aids:* Selection aids should be consulted in order to assure that the book being considered is indeed the best for the library.
   Questions: How many selection aids need to be consulted? What type of quantitative and qualitative information should the selection aid provide?

8. *Affiliated resources:* A book should not be required if it is conveniently accessible, or should be more properly housed in the collection of another community agency.
   Questions: Should another agency purchase the book and, if so, should they be so informed? Can the library afford to duplicate information more properly available from another agency?

9. *Cultural influence:* The book should support the position of local cultural, political, ethnic, religious, or social groups. It is permissible to have a controversial book that informs the reader about a particular sect but it should not hurt, misrepresent, or in any way be unjustly harmful.
   Questions: By whom and for whom is this book recommended? What specific cultural contribution is the book purported to make?

10. *Censorship:* Policy regarding censorship should be developed by a committee representative of cross-sectional interests of library patrons. Granted that a workable censorship policy can be rather nebulous, it should nevertheless be a policy under which the li-

brarian can function. Any book selected which generates a negative reaction vis-à-vis censorship should be referred to a censorship committee comprised of impartial responsible members for review.

Questions: What genres of information warrant censorship concerns? Is the censorship policy up to date and in keeping with currently accepted mores and morals?

11. *Balance of the book collection:* Books selected should keep the library collection properly proportioned according to patron need and use.

   Questions: What are the proportions of books being allocated to the various parts of the collection? Is there a use or datedness variable that may be a justification for altering existing proportions?

12. *Selector objectivity:* Books should be selected to serve patron needs and not what the librarian personally perceives to be those needs.

   Questions: Are books being selected (or omitted) because of personal bias or prejudice? Is a professional attitude being maintained with regard to book selection?

13. *Alternative media:* The consideration of alternative media can greatly influence the direction a library will pursue with regard to the acquisition of print and nonprint media.

   Questions: Is the book the proper medium for the particular information it contains, or would some other form be more appropriate? If another media form is chosen instead of the book, do the library and the patron have the technology (if needed) to use it?

These criteria are not exhaustive, but they will generate thought on constructing a book selection policy. The books will be selected with the needs of the patron in mind and enhance the development and enrichment of the community the library serves.

To institute this book selection policy requires the disciplining of the librarian with regard to personal opinions on book selection and the use of standard procedures in making decisions. The librarian must perform with objectivity; be thoroughly familiar with various book selection aids; have an awareness of library association book standards; identify with the community served by the library; know the library patron with regard to ethnic, social, cultural, attitudinal, educational, vocational, political, and recreational needs; and work within the parameters of the library's philosophy, operation, and budget. In summary, when involved in selecting books, or any other media forms, the librarian needs to be both a competent professional capably contributing to the operation of the library and a humanist with an acute awareness of the library community's informational needs.

Selecting and Evaluating a Book

Assessing a particular book considered for acquisition requires an intelligent evaluation conducted by a skilled librarian. It is essential that the librarian have a broad knowledge of books and be efficient in performing the selection process. It is not expected, nor is it possible, for the librarian to read each book; however, there are certain key features that need to be examined in making a determination to accept or reject a particular book. The examination of a book should include (1) the title page and the author of the book; (2) publication date, copyright date, name of publisher; (3) the preface or introduction should always be read, as it gives an indication of the purpose of the book and something about the author's point of view; (4) chapter headings should be examined, as they give an idea as to how information is structured; (5) if time allows, read the first and last chapters, for they usually give an indication of how the information is treated, also randomly select another chapter, preferably one that may appear somewhat controversial, and see if the author is consistent in his or her style and if he or she has any fixed biases that either help or hinder the presentation; (6) if the book has an index, try it out for accuracy and completeness. Looking at these features in particular will give the librarian a rather complete picture as to a book's worth and indicate if it should be acquired for the library's collection. To conduct the evaluation properly, it is helpful for the librarian to use clearly defined criteria upon which to base a decision. The degree to which the book being examined meets the evaluative criteria will determine whether or not it merits selection. The following six criteria need to be understood thoroughly when evaluating books.

1. *Authority.* Something should be known about the author or editor of the book. The author's credentials should be examined, especially with regard to qualifications for writing a particular book and any experiences he or she may have had that contribute to the quality of the book. It would be wise to take into account the reputation of previous publications and whether the present book is on a topic comparable enough to warrant similar merit. Any biases the author may be known to possess should be particularly considered in terms of how they affect the book.

2. *Scope:* Find out how broadly or narrowly the book handles the topic and how deeply it is developed. Ascertain what limits were placed on the book with regard to content and information; even though it may

be adequate, decide whether it is partial or complete in its presentation. Determine if the book contains any serious omissions or, conversely, if any areas are overdeveloped to the degree that it may distort the reader's perspective. Another factor that would affect the scope is date of publication, which has an important influence on the datedness of the material. Some books may have more than one printing date, which is an indication of their popularity, while other books come out in new editions. In the case of a new edition, it is important to know the difference between it and its predecessor.

3. *Treatment:* Note how the content is treated. The style can be scholarly or entertaining, which incidentally is not meant to imply that one is better than the other, but that style should be in keeping with the content and the purpose of the author. Didactic presentations can be dull, but an inappropriate style can border on absurdity if applied to the wrong topic. Identify the level of the writing in order to learn what reading skill is required and if indeed the book has appeal to that level of reader. Consider whether the readability makes the book applicable to a broad or a narrow range of readers. Inherent in the treatment is the author's style, which is a reflection of his or her talent to write an interesting manuscript. The book, regardless of the topic, should have vitality and be interesting.

4. *Arrangement:* The book should have an orderly flow to it. Information should be properly sequenced and there should be no gaps or serious omissions. Also pertaining to arrangement is balance, and it is necessary to be aware of whether there is too much or too little information or topical development. The content should have an intended, methodical progression and not confuse or disorient the reader. If the content by nature tends to be piecemeal, then the pieces should result in a coherent mosaic of information.

5. *Format:* Format refers to the physical attributes of the book. This would include: the overall dimensions of the book; number of pages; size and quality of the print, quality of paper and binding; the use, quality, size, color, and arrangement of graphics; quality of the cover; and the overall general physical appeal of the book. In some cases, even the dustjacket should be examined for any appealing traits, e.g., interesting anecdotal information, exciting illustration or artwork, photograph and biographical sketch of the author. (It has been found in the marketing of paperbacks that the covers have quite an influence on enticing the reader to the book.)

6. *Bibliographies:* Although not generally applicable to works of fiction, bibliographies should be examined for quality, datedness, and completeness. They give an insight to the author's expertise in the topic as well as an indication of his or her use and knowledge of primary and

secondary resources. The bibliography could be limited to documenting footnoted information and listing suggested readings or preferably a combination of the two. If the book does contain bibliographic information, determine whether it is at the end of each chapter or grouped at the end of the text. See if the book contains any other reference features, e.g., any methods to further investigate the topic (this is sometimes handled in annotative and qualitative information regarding particular bibliographic entries).

Exercising these criteria when evaluating a book does not require that the librarian be a subject matter expert; however, broad knowledge and a lifetime exposure to all kinds of books are valuable prerequisites to good selection. The librarian has to enjoy working with books. Through adherence to the criteria developed in this section, a procedure can be followed that provides a methodical evaluation of any book and results in building an excellent library collection. An added feature of this procedure is it gives the librarian a professional knowledge of the content of the library collection which can be used to defend its merits. Even more important it will prove to be invaluable in assisting the librarian to meet the reading needs of patrons by knowing something about what is on the library shelves.

Reference Works

It is appropriate that this section immediately follow the section on evaluation because the six criteria listed there have their strongest applicability in the selection of reference works. Indeed, the librarian needs to be especially discriminating when selecting reference works; They become the tools of the librarian in locating requests for information; and when placed in the hands of the patron, they should provide information clearly, quickly, and concisely. By definition, reference book is essentially a fact finder used to locate precise information that is available either as an overview or a summary. A reference work is usually a good place to initiate a search for information in that it not only provides capsulized information for quick enrichment but also can refer the reader to other sources for further investigation. Still another feature of reference works is their ability to provide answers to specific questions and to confirm inquires for information efficiently and succinctly. Hence it is obvious that when selecting reference works particular attention needs to be given to authority, scope, treatment, arrangement, format, and bibliographies.

It is essential for any library to have a well-balanced collection of

	Acceptable	Not acceptable	Not applicable

A. Authority
   1. Author's credentials
   2. Author's biases
   3. Quality of previous publications
   4. Publisher's reputation			

B. Scope
   1. Achieves purpose in
      broadness of topics covered
   2. Achieves purpose in narrowness
      and specificity
   3. Restrictions and limitations
      imposed on book
   4. Omissions
   5. Completeness of information
      presented
   6. Accuracy
   7. Copyright date
   8. Quality of newer edition as
      compared to preceding
      edition(s)
   9. Datedness of information			

C. Treatment
   1. Scholastic quality
   2. Ease of reading, vitality of
      content (i.e., style)
   3. Level of reading as it pertains to
      intended users			

D. Arrangement
   1. Sequencing of information
   2. Gaps in information
   3. Overall coherencey
   4. Ease in locating information			

E. Format
   1. Convenience of size of the book
   2. Quality of paper and binding
   3. Size of print
   4. Number of volumes
   5. Quality and relevence of art-
      work, graphics, photography
   6. Quality of color
   7. Overall appearance			

Figure 14.1. Reference works evaluation checklist.

	Acceptable	Not acceptable	Not applicable

F. Indexing, bibliography, etc.
  1. Footnoting
  2. Quality of indexing
  3. Completeness of bibliograhic
     information
  4. Cross referencing
  5. Use of locating devices, e.g.,
     tabs, color coding, etc.			

G. Comparison to similar reference
    tools
  1. Complements existing collection
  2. Distinctiveness and uniqueness
  3. Comparison to other works
     considered for selection
Overall remarks:			

Figure 14.1. Continued.

reference works both to serve as informational search tools for the professional reference librarian and to accommodate patrons with a wide range of skills who need access to it as well. The basic types of reference works housed in the reference section are encyclopedias, dictionaries, indexes, bibliographies, yearbooks and almanacs, biographical dictionaries, information media selection aids, and special topic references, e.g., geographical references, financial references, etc. Within each of these types, there are many reference works from which to choose. It is for the librarian to ascertain what each reference tool has to offer with regard to types and amount of information contained, arrangement and ease of locating information, and the way information is treated. It is suggested that the Reference Works Evaluation Checklist (Figure 14.1) be used as a systematic means of analysis. It contains the procedure for conducting an orderly and complete evaluation of any reference work being considered for acquisition.

Evaluating Fiction

Fiction encompasses such a wide range of topics it is difficult to apply a basic set of criteria that will work well with all fiction types. Nevertheless, it is necessary to apply some basic criteria in order to make fiction selection a valid process, which in turn may make it beneficial to generate subsets of criteria for particular fiction types that will make selection more reliable. Content criteria developed expressly for science fiction may not be applicable to a work of fiction that deals with romance. Therefore, rather than have works of fiction be subjected to fixed basic criteria, it may be better to design criteria to fit each type of fiction. Developing subsets of criteria could be a time consuming task, the worth of which could be measured only by how well and consistently it serves the librarian. However, by adhering to a policy of using prescribed documented criteria, the librarian can avoid the pitfall of using ambiguous means for evaluating fiction. If the librarian develops, even if only mentally, a personal set of criteria for each work of fiction being evaluated, then it is quite possible that books could be selected on the "how I feel about the book" criterion rather than on well-developed, prescribed criteria.

First, it would be well to examine the basic criteria that are generally applicable for evaluating works of fiction and from them generate any subsets of criteria that can be uniquely adapted to any particular types of fiction. The following seven criteria can be considered basic to evaluating works of fiction. (Refer to the criteria developed earlier. The criteria described here further expound upon them with regard to assessing fiction.)

1. *Author:* Is there something about the author that warrants the acquisition of his work? It could be that the author is popular or represents a particular type of fiction that appeals to a particular type of reader. Perhaps the author is relatively new and has something fresh and stimulating to offer.

2. *Style:* Some factors to consider are: Is it easy to read? Does it challenge the reader? Is the narrative interestingly worded? Does the vocabulary enhance the work? Generally style is that facet which lends a uniqueness to a work of fiction; well done it not only makes the work enjoyable but also makes it stand out as a means of communication. It is in the author's style that literary merit comes to the fore.

3. *Theme:* The theme, although it does not necessarily have to be spelled out, is the message of the work. Here the evaluator must exercise discretion with regard to truthfulness, which, for example, in a fairytale could mean nothing more than acceptability or believability. Perhaps of greater importance is the moral, ethical, and social value of the theme. Here is where the evaluator begins to become involved in censorship by assigning a worth or value to the book as it pertains to the welfare of the patron. When this occurs, the evaluator must become purged of any

prejudicial biases that are not beneficial or in the best interest of the patron.

4. *Plot:* The plot is the fabric in which are woven the style, theme, characters, setting, and purpose of the book. The plot must interestingly hold these components together, and upon its ability to do so rests the success of the book.

5. *Setting:* To be effective, the information about setting should be conveyed subtly but conclusively. Specificity is essential, which incidentally should not be mistaken for a tight, narrow, detailed description of the setting, but rather be understood as a means of giving the reader the information necessary to understand when and where events are happening, as well as what influence it has upon the characters.

6. *Characters:* The characters should give the reader insight and information as to what the book is all about. The characters should be interesting in and of themselves and generate a sense of realness or believability. Above all, the characters should not be static but should develop as the entire book develops. The success of characterization depends not only on what the person is but on what he or she represents.

7. *Reviews:* Although not part of the book, reviews can provide guidance in selection. However, it is necessary to know something of the reviewer's credentials for criticizing a particular type of fiction.

From these seven basic criteria subsets of criteria can be evolved with which particular types of fiction can be evaluated. The subsets are in effect modifications of the basic criteria and serve as an attempt to make them more applicable to particular fiction types. To keep the development of subset criteria manageable, a matrix (Figure 14.2) can be devised to provide a consistent means of selection. On the vertical axis are listed the types of fiction, while on the horizontal the selection criteria. Assigning a value to each criterion (very low, low, medium, high, very high) gives an immediate indication as to what is important in evaluating a particular type of fiction. As an example, authenticity may be of very high value in selecting a historical novel but be of very low value in selecting a fairy tale. The matrix is not filled out because assigning values, even though they may vary only slightly, could produce enough variance over the entire matrix to invalidate its use for a particular library. Therefore, it is suggested that the reader assign values to the matrix that will be more in keeping with the needs of the particular library in which he or she works. The matrix is not the final word of judgment, it is a guide to the selection of fiction whose value is measured by its usefullness.

Mark in the particular box what you consider to be the importance of each criterion in evaluating works of fiction for your particular library. Score as follows: 1—very low; 2—low; 3—medium; 4—high; 5—very high.							
Criteria Types	Author	Style	Theme	Plot	Setting	Characters	Reviews
Adventure							
Biography							
Classic							
Domestic							
Fairy tale							
Foreign							
History							
Mystery							
Philosophy							
Political							
Romance							
Science							
Western							
Other							

Figure 14.2. Fiction subset criterion matrix.

With the criteria for evaluating works of fiction and, if necessary, the fiction subset criteria matrix, the fiction selection essentials are now available to be incorporated into a fiction evaluation form (Figure 14.3). As with all evaluation forms, it should be concise and easy to use and require only that information which will actually be used in making a selection decision. The fiction evaluation form appearing here is a suggestion of format.

Title: Author:
Publisher: Copyright date: Price:
Number of pages_____ available in _____ Hardbound _____ Paperback
Type of fiction:
Author: (Credentials)
Style: (Uniqueness)
Theme: (What work is about)

		low			high
	Truthfulness	1	2	3	4
	Believability	1	2	3	4
	Moral value	1	2	3	4
	Social value	1	2	3	4
	Ethnic value	1	2	3	4
Plot:	(How theme is developed)				
	Completeness	1	2	3	4
	Cohesiveness	1	2	3	4
	Interest	1	2	3	4
	Quality	1	2	3	4
Setting:	(When and where events are happening)				
	Specificity	1	2	3	4
	Descriptiveness	1	2	3	4
Characters:					
	Effectiveness of main characters	1	2	3	4
	Development of main characters	1	2	3	4
	Development of secondary characters	1	2	3	4
	Contribution of secondary characters	1	2	3	4
	Success of characters to the book	1	2	3	4
Reviews:	(Name of Publication)				
	Reviewer's credentials	1	2	3	4
	Reviewer's assessment of the book	1	2	3	4

Use information

1. Who can use book?
2. Book warrants acquisition because of

	low			high
a. Temporary value	1	2	3	4
b. Value over several years	1	2	3	4

3. Acquisition priority: 1 2 3 4
4. Summary comments:

Name of Evaluator: _____
Position: _____
Date: _____

Figure 14.3. Fiction evaluation form.

Evaluating Nonfiction

Oftentimes, when selecting a book of fiction or nonfiction, a decision is made by judging the book's popularity, the assumption being that if the book is popular it must therefore be good. Using popularity as the sole criterion may more often than not be safe for selecting fiction books of temporary value, but popularity should not be the major criterion in selecting a book of nonfiction. A work of nonfiction must have genuine intrinsic merit to justify its acquisition. It is necessary to do research to determine if a nonfiction book is of any value to the library collection. The research is predicated upon criteria that objectively analyze the worth of a book. Ideally, the appraisal of a nonfiction book that receives approval should result in it meeting all specified criteria; but because of the varied scope of nonfiction works, it may be possible to have a book meet one criterion with such a high degree of perfection that its acquisition is warranted. Conversely, it is also possible to have a nonfiction book fail so miserably on one criterion that it is rejected.

The criteria used for evaluating works of nonfiction need to emphasize authenticity and accuracy. The prime purpose of nonfiction is to present information in a well-organized, understandable fashion. If the book is also interesting and enjoyable, those become additional strengths to merit acquisition. The librarian needs to be especially alert in selecting works of nonfiction, for it is in such books that the legacy of mankind is recorded and made available to everyone. The librarian must determine who are the best writers of this legacy and by so doing select the works of nonfiction that preserve and embellish the culture of a society. The following criteria for selecting works of nonfiction should be carefully digested, for they not only present a means for objective selection but also alert the reader to philosophical considerations that should be of paramount concern in building a library collection. (Refer to the section on selection and evaluation developed earlier in this chapter; the criteria described here further expound upon them with regard to nonfiction.)

1. *Authenticity (authority):* The author should be an expert with demonstrated knowledge of the topic. If any information, or the interpretation of facts, is presented with a bias, the author should admit to it, either by expressly stating it in the preface, by informing the reader in the substance of the text, or by a proper footnote that information contrary to his or her biases is knowingly being altered or omitted because it is not in support of the premise of the book. Actually, it is a rare author who would admit to such tactics unless they enhance the writer's objectives; therefore, the evaluator must be particularly aware of purposeful

omissions and make certain that the book is genuinely authoritative, trustworthy, reliable, and complete.

2. *Accuracy (authority):* Closely related to authenticity is accuracy. Are the events being recorded the author's own experiences, or are they the results of investigating other resources? If other resources are being used, are they primary or secondary? If it is a scholarly work, information from primary and secondary resources should be properly footnoted, and a bibliography should be included to substantiate and document the accuracy of the content as well as provide the reader with information for further investigation. Accuracy is not to be taken lightly. When inaccuracies occur whether by intent, omission, or ignorance, they destroy the value of a nonfiction work.

3. *Scope:* Scope pertains to how the author handled the topic. It can best be evaluated by considering antonymous terms such as exhaustive–brief, superficial–in-depth, broad–narrow, covers many points–investigates a specific point, introductory–summary, exploratory–advanced. Using these terms when analysing nonfiction helps to identify the scope with which the content is treated and determine if a book is needed for the library collection.

4. *Organization of material (treatment, arrangement):* As nonfiction deals with what is true, real, and factual, it is the organization of material that gives it the necessary credibility. Supportive to organization is the style of writing, which can range from scholarly to popular. Whatever the writing style, a work of nonfiction should have vitality and be interesting reading. Information needs to be presented with clarity. The nonfiction book's chapters collectively encompass the overall purpose of the book, but each chapter should be complete in and of itself and be identified as a logical, cohesive entity. Indexing, if applicable, is an aid to organization, but it cannot redeem poor organization. A positive attribute of organization is that the reader can accumulate knowledge from the book. When a book is properly organized, knowledge obtained early in the text becomes a prerequisite to acquring still more knowledge later on in the book.

5. *Graphics (Format):* It is often vital to nonfiction works to support them with graphics, especially when they deal with technical data. Graphics help to clarify the content. Visuals should be of proper size, easy to read, help the reader to understand the text better, and convey meaning better than the printed word.

6. *Bibliographies:* Bibliographies are invaluable in documenting information. Perhaps their greatest value lies in expanding the usefulness of the book by guiding the reader both to resources used in preparing the book and to sources of additional information. Bibliographic entries

```
Title:                        Author:
Publisher:                    Copyright date:    Price:
Number of Pages:              Available in:
                                [   ] Hardcover    [   ] Paperback


1. Author's credentials:
2. Authenticity of book:
3. Annotation (scope of book):
4. Ease of reading (organzation):
5. Quality of graphics:
6. Supplementary features (appendixes, indexes, etc.):
7. Overall recommendation (value of the book, need for the library, possible uses):
8. This book ____ should ____ should not be purchased.


Name of evaluator:            Position:          Date:
```

Figure 14.4. Nonfiction evaluation form.

should be examined for completeness and amount of information offered. In some cases, imprint information will suffice, in other situations, annotations and excerpts greatly enhance the value of a nonfiction book. Appendixes are a bonus to a book; and although not part of the basic text, they save the reader the need to search in other books to locate essential information applicable to the topic.

Once you have used these six criteria in analyzing a nonfiction work, a determination can be made as to who can use the book and for what purpose. The book can apply to a broad or narrow readership with regard to ability, need, and interest. The book can also be categorized as scholarly, popular, entertaining, informational, introductory, advanced, partial, complete, etc. Once you have determined the use and purpose, a decision can be made as to whether or not a book should be acquired for the library collection.

A nonfiction evaluation form (Figure 14.4) has been designed to be subjective, unlike the fiction evaluation form, which is objective. Either form can be revised vis-à-vis objectivity–subjectivity.

Selecting Textbooks

Textbooks are found primarily in the domain of schools and school libraries. However, public libraries are becoming more involved with communities' ongoing educational needs and do have textbooks in their collections. Colleges are now offering external degrees, (i.e., student can enroll in courses without even setting foot on campus), and as a result the public library is quasi-involved in formal education. An individual library does not usually choose a particular textbook but decides only whether or not to have it in the collection. The actual selection of textbooks is done by government agencies, e.g., state school board. It is recommended that when selecting a textbook from a prescribed list, the librarian do it with the cooperation of local school officials, e.g., school curriculum textbook committee.

It is difficult to define the term *textbook* because there is no specific class of books that fits a definition. It would be better to describe what a textbook does in an effort to arrive at a classification. A textbook is any book used as an integral part of the study of a particular curriculum. If a novel by Ernest Hemingway is used as a text for the study of American literature, for all practical purposes it becomes a textbook for that course. In this case, the student reads a Hemingway novel not primarily for pleasure but to learn some specifics of American literature. This is a case where a book written as a novel, because of unique qualities, also serves as a textbook.

Many books are written solely for a particular curriculum or course of study, and it would be advantageous to use this type of book in generating a definition of a textbook, with the emphasis on what it does rather than on what it is. A textbook provides information for a course of study by organizing a body of information and presenting it in a prescribed sequence. The author states the parameters of the textbook and develops the content accordingly.

In selecting a textbook, there are several characteristics to be considered beyond those already discussed: (1) the table of contents should be detailed and well developed; supporting it should be an index that helps to locate specific information quickly; (2) vocabulary should be geared for a specific reading level; (3) layout should be arranged for easy reading (textbooks often divide a page into two columns); (4) chapters should deal with specific learning objectives and limit discussion solely of them; (5) there should be some type of linear progression and organization, e.g., easy–difficult, past–present–future, basic–advanced, generalities–specifics, theory–application. There are other features that enhance the quality of a textbook: (1) chapter summaries or reviews; (2) question and work assignments; (3) teachers' editions which include answers, methods for using the textbook, and suggested activities. (4) supplementary materials, e.g., testbook, workbook, overhead transparencies, ditto masters, laboratory manual; (5) appendixes to supplement the text; and (6) glossary of terms and definitions. (See Figure 14.5.)

Textbooks are generally intended for group use, and a good textbook can be used by an entire group. In general, the textbook tends to keep the group together with regard to material being covered at any particular time during the course of instruction. In the past, courses were taught using only one textbook; and indeed the textbook was the course. Today, there is a trend toward making the textbook a supplementary aid to the course and using a host of media in conjunction with it, e.g., other books, films, filmstrips, programmed instruction, etc. This trend reflects

		Excellent	OK	Poor	N.A.
Title: Author: Publisher: Copyright Date: Price: Number of pages: Available in: [ ] Hardcover [ ] Paperback For use in the study of: Grade level:					
Applicability to course of study					
Vocabulary					
Table of contents					
Index					
Appendix					
Glossary					
Graphics					
Clearly stated objectives					
Organization of information					
Chapter arrangement					
Chapter summaries					
Supplementary materials					
List 1.					
List 2.					
List 3.					
List 4.					
Physical quality (durability of binding, quality of paper, etc.)					
Overall evaluation					
Comments: Name of evaluator: Position: Date:					

Figure 14.5.   Textbook evaluation form.

the realization that there is no such thing as a homogeneous group in which everyone performs equally well with one textbook. Any group is made up of students with a range of individual differences that can be best administered to by having a variety of learning materials. This trend does not belittle the value of the textbook because a good textbook still eliminates the need to use parts of several books to acquire information on a particular topic. When a textbook is used in conjunction with other media, the curriculum is further enriched.

When evaluating a textbook, one should be aware of a few characteristics that oftentimes are readily apparent. Textbooks have a tendency to be conservative in that they only consider one opinion or entertain a particular point of view. Often there is little consideration for cultural or ethnic differences, the assumption being that all readers possess the ideals and educational goals of white, middle class America. Although the author tries to be accurate, it is impossible to get everything into a text; as a result, editoralizing must be done. A textbook can surreptitiously persuade the reader toward a particular philosophical ideal which can be ignorantly accepted because of the lack of complete information. The textbook, in its effort to provide information, can lead the reader to accept conclusions without ever discovering or testing his or her own conclusions. Perhaps an awareness of these shortcomings is further evidence that although a textbook is geared for a particular course of study and may be its mainline of information, other information sources need to be made available.

As stated at the beginning of this section, textbooks lie more in the realm of the school librarian, and a government agency is usually responsible for their selection. However, the local librarian is responsible for his or her library collection and, although not involved in the selection process, should be vitally involved in the rejection process by making only the best textbooks available for patrons.

Selecting Children's Books

Children's books also need to be assessed and withstand the critical scrutiny of the criteria outlined in the section on selection and evaluation developed earlier in this chapter. Beyond this, the librarian needs an awareness of some basic considerations that apply in the selection of children's books. Perhaps to the library novice it may appear convenient to classify a whole section of the library collection as being children's books and proceed on the premise that it contains low level, simple materials on topics suitable for children. Such a broad categorization does not take into account the extremely broad range of reading skills children have and the types of books that must cater to those skills. When it is considered that the bulk of popular adult reading material is written pretty much at the eighth-grade reading level and that only the more serious and scholarly polished books venture into the use of more sophisticated vocabulary, the selecting of adult books with regard to adult reading ability is not really that difficult a task. However, with children's books the reading level ranges from that of a tot unable to read a printed word all the way to that of a sixth-grade child capable of mastering eighth-grade reading material.

The librarian should be aware of the child's general disposition toward reading. At present, there are many criticisms that "Johnny can't read," and that society is creating a generation of nonreaders. Accusations have been leveled at television, for discouraging reading, and at schools for not giving enough attention to the problems of reading. It would be ridiculous to deny that there are any reading problems, especially when there are presently in the United States over 20 million adults classified as functionally illiterate (i.e., unable to read a classified ad or fill out a job application). But the solution to the reading problem resides not in placing blame but in seeking solutions. The children's librarian can make an invaluable contribution toward achieving the solution. First and foremost, the children's librarian should be aware that children possess an uninhibited and insatiable curiosity, they are yearning to investigate and explore their big, wonderful world. The children's library can do much to nourish this enthusiasm with fine literature. For the very young nonreader and for the child beginning to master the intricacies of reading, there is enjoyment in having someone read them stories. Story telling is an art, that with practice can be easily mastered and will hold a child spellbound. The library needs a wide collection of books that can be read to children and initiate them to the adventures of reading. In addition to books read to children, there are books young readers can "read" for themselves. This type of book needs to be well illustrated and contain some of the basic vocabulary the child has already mastered aurally and is eager to master visually. The visuals help the child make the transition from nonreader to reader. Visuals need to have clarity of communication by almost spelling out pictorially what they are saying. The book collection should contain a gradient of picture books, with books having many illustrations and few words and gradually inverting the proportion to many words and few illustrations. The objective is to challenge and motivate the child to want to learn to read and provide materials that will foster the growth and rewards of reading skills. It is important to remember that the child has a natural curiosity, and it is necessary to use it to its greatest advantage.

Parallel to selecting books on a pictorial–print gradient is the consideration of interest. The pictorial–print gradient challenges the child, but the content must stimulate or interest him or her. Hence there is another gradient to consider, that of the child's growing world. Initially, the child's real world is egocentric and limited pretty much to family and home. Gradually, the child's real world expands to include neighborhood, library, school, and an ever enlarging world community. Obviously, the child's reading interests will grow accordingly, and the library needs to be ready to minister to them. The child also has an imaginary, make-believe world, which at times can become quite "real." The library can foster reading development by including in the collection books that appeal to the child's sense of adventure.

Still another consideration that cannot be overlooked is the child's personal vocabulary. Critics accuse television of propagating a society of illiterates, but it cannot be denied that a child from the television era has mastered a far greater vocabulary than his pretelevision predecessor. This means that when the child is ready to read, it is not the Dick and Jane books that will have appeal, but books that contain a more adult vocabulary. Furthermore, with regard to the pros and cons of television's effect upon reading ability, it has been found that at around age 10 the intelligent child who has had an oversized diet of television becomes somewhat saturated with the medium and seeks other channels of communication, namely the printed word. With less intelligent children, this phenomenon occurs a little later. It is for the library to be ready to capitalize on this regenerated interest in reading by having literature of suitable level and interest. Rather than criticizing television and crusading against it, the librarian should use it as a means of promoting reading and filling a void that cannot be achieved by the television tube. Maybe for the group of children who have drifted away from reading but now have a new-found reorientation to it, the librarian will need to be especially aware of books of low level–high interest (i.e., low level vocabulary but more mature content suitable for a 10- to 12-year-old child). The purpose is to have books that can be mastered and still be of interest. Perhaps it would be also wise to take into consideration books that do not take too long to read, for television has conditioned the child to obtaining a complete story in a minimum amount of time.

One other aspect of children's books to consider is that of format. Printing should be large enough for the child to read easily, illustrations need to be colorful, pages durable and easy to turn, and bindings extremely durable. Children tend to be hard on books and give them punishing use. If books do receive heavy use, then the librarian should consider the advantages and disadvantages of prebinding. Basically there are four types of prebinding: (1) reinforced in the publisher's original covers when the book is bound, (2) original binding is resewn with stronger stitching, (3) resewn and reinforced with buckram covers, which can have the publisher's original design, and (4) resewn and rebound in buckram, plastic, or fabrickoid. Obviously, prebinding cost more, but the book will last much longer and will not need rebinding, which involves removing it from the collection. However, if a book is to be prebound the original pages should be strong and durable (i.e., as strong as the heavier binding).

Most of the concerns and considerations discussed here go beyond selection and evaluation and have a profound influence on the success of the library collection. The children's collection should be a treasure for the child, but it must be in a form whereby its wealth can be readily recognized, used, and appreciated.

Assessing and Constructing Book Reviews

There is a twofold purpose discussed here: (1) to know how to assess book reviews and (2) to be able to actually construct a book review. In the process of selecting books, the skilled librarian refers to book reviews for assistance in making acquisition decisions. The librarian does not have time to meticulously read every book acquired, but by following the selection criteria set forth in this chapter, he or she can develop an efficient selection technique, and published reviews help to guide and reaffirm judgments. To be able to construct a book review not only helps to analyze them better, but also provides an indispensable service to library patrons. It is indeed a fortunate patron who has the services of a librarian in selecting a book for a particular requirement and who is able to give an assessment as to how well a book can fill a need.

With regard to assessing book reviews, it is important for the review first to provide a comment on what the book is about. Now the comment about a book is not to be confused with a book report. Often book reviews that are nothing more than glamorized book reports mislead the reader by presenting superficial descriptions of content and fail to reveal more valuable and intrinsic insights. Attention needs to be given to the scope of the book and the manner in which information is treated. A review should give information as to the broadness or narrowness of the topic, as well as the vehicle by which content is developed and characterizations are used to convey meaning.

Next the book review should describe the book's attributes and its literary merits. The reviewer should tell how well the book is put together and the degree to which it achieves its intended purpose. Here is where the reviewer presents a case for the book's strengths and deficiencies. Something should be said of the author's writing style and its contribution to the particular work being assessed.

Along with the author's style, reference should be made of the author's credentials as they relate to the particular book being reviewed. A statement of the author's experience, authority, and knowledge of the book's topic helps to qualify its value. As the author's credential are not usually found in the context of the book, it is beneficial for the reviewer to document his or her source of information. (A detailed investigation is obviously more valuable than information gleaned from the book's preface or dust jacket.) Also, if warranted, information regarding the reputation of the publisher can be given.

Some mention should be made of the book's physical characteristics, e.g., dimensions, number of pages, quality of print and illustrations, and, if applicable, the quality of indexes and bibliographies.

Finally, the reviewer should make an unequivocal statement about the book as a discrete entity. If they are applicable, the reviewer can also include external factors. For example, the reviewer may compare the book to any of the author's previous works or compare it to similar works by other authors. Mention should be made of the book's current and future value. Recommendations should be made as to the type of reader who would most benefit from reading the book and for what purpose.

Although they do not pertain directly to the book being reviewed, the librarian should know something of the reviewer's credentials and reputation. The reviewer should have read the book and know something of the topic. The reviewer should also be responsible for good literary form in the review per se. The review should be authoritative, comprehensive, informative, easy to read, and (it is hoped) free of prejudicial biases.

On occasion, the librarian may find it helpful to construct a book review. Basically there are three reasons for doing so: (1) there is no review available on the book; (2) the librarian disagrees with existing reviews; or (3) a review has to be written for a particular type of reader, e.g., reviewers of childrens book write their reviews for adult readers when in actuality a great service would be provided if they were written for children to provide them with guidance as to whether or not the book is worth reading. It is important to remember when writing book reviews that the purpose is to enlighten the reader as to his or her possible desire, interest, or need to read the book. For the book review to be valid and reliable, the reviewer should read the entire book. A second-best method would be to skim the book, but a review predicated on the skimming technique should be done only by a person extremely skilled in skim reading. If the review is accomplished in this fashion, the reviewer should admit that the review was constructed from knowledge obtained from skimming or a cursory overview.

Obviously, the standards used to analyze book reviews can serve as a guide in constructing them as well. However there are additional factors to take into consideration. When constructing a book review, it is always necessary to keep in mind the importance of comprehensiveness and completeness while at the same time being concise and *brief*. An extensive treatise, regardless of how well done, is seldom appreciated. It is a good practice after completing a book review to reread it to see if it can be further improved by editing it further down. There is actually no prescribed order in which information has to be presented; what is given here is a logical sequence intended to inform, not confuse, the reader. The review must contain a complete bibliographic entry. Something should be said about the type of book being reviewed. If it is a work of fiction, the review should indicate what the plot is about, the theme of the book and how it is conveyed, the setting(s) in which the book takes place, the use of symbolism, what the characters contribute to the book, and the general pace and development of the book. With a work of nonfiction, mention should be made of the contribution the book makes, the accuracy and completeness of information, the scope or emphasis given to exploration of content, and the parameters the book entails. Some insights should be given regarding the author and his writing ability. The review should react to and take a definite stand on any particular positions or points of view advocated by the author. This should be a statement of what the author is attempting to do with regard to how the content is treated and how it can affect or influence the reader. It is important to mention something of the author's writing style. Oftentimes, this can be achieved by quoting a passage from the text; but when this is done, the passage should be representative of the writing style of the entire book. An assessment needs to be made of the book's literary merit. Depending on the reviewer's own disposition and writing style, all this information can be conveyed either objectively or subjectively. Some reviewers find it difficult not to intersperse personal opinion throughout the entire review. But regardless of the reviewer's writing style, the review should conclude with an appraisal of why the book is liked or not liked, as well as a recommendation as to what kind of person would benefit from reading it and why he or she would appreciate it.

When preparing a book review, the writer must always bear in mind for whom the review is being written. It could be for a library administrator, another librarian, a scholar, a general reader, or even a child. It is essential that the writing style be aimed at the intended readership. Some librarians make a practice of putting book reviews on audio cassettes. Audio book reviews, when well done, make interesting listening and seem to lend a more personal touch. In the final analysis, the purpose of a book review is to inform a prospective reader as to what a book is about, present its strengths and weaknesses, and most important, advocate or discourage the reading of the book.

Selected Bibliography

Avant, J. A. "Slouching toward Criticism: A Librarian's Review of Reviews." *Library Journal* 96 (Dec. 15, 1971):4055–4059.

Carter, M. D.; Bonk, W. J., and Magrill, R. M. *Building Library Collections*. 4th ed. Metuchen, N.J.: Scarecrow Press, 1974.

Downs, R. B. *How to Do Library Research*. 2d ed. Urbana: University of Illinois Press, 1975.

Gates, J. K. *Guide to the Use of Books and Libraries*. 3d ed. New York: McGraw-Hill, 1974.

Haines, H. E. *Living with Books*. 2d ed. New York: Columbia University Press, 1950.

Woodkrutch, J. W. "What Is a Good Review?" In *If You Don't Mind My Saying So*. New York: William Sloane Associates, 1964. Pp. 120–123.

Oppenheimer, E. *Book Reviewing for an Audience: A Practical Guide in Technique for Lecture and Broadcast*. Philadelphia: Chilton Company, 1962.

Perkins, E. L. *Book and Non-Book Media: An Annotated Guide to Selection Aids for Educational Material*. Urbana, Illinois: National Council of Teachers of English, 1962.

Sheehy, E. P., comp. *Guide to Reference Books*. 9th ed. Chicago: American Library Association, 1976.

SELECTION AIDS

Books

Books in Print. Annual. New York: R. R. Bowker, 1948–.

Barton, M. N., and Bell, M. V. *Reference Books; A Brief Guide for Students and Other Users of the Library*. 7th ed. Baltimore: Enoch Pratt Free Library, 1970.

Cheney, F. N. *Fundamental Reference Sources*. Chicago: American Library Association, 1971.

Children's Catalog. 12th ed. New York: H. W. Wilson, 1971. (Four annual supplements 1972-1975.)

Cumulative Book Index. New York: H. W. Wilson, 1898-. (Monthly except August, semiannual, and annual cumulations.)

El-Hi: Textbooks in Print. Annual New York: R. R. Bowker, 1970-.

EPM: Educator's Purchasing Master. 3d ed. Englewood, Colo.: Fisher Publishing Company, 1971.

Fiction Catalog. 8th ed. New York: H. W. Wilson, 1970. (Four annual supplements 1971-1974.)

Galin, S. and Spielberg, P. *Reference Books: How to Select and Use Them*. New York: Random House, 1969.

Haviland, V., comp. *Children's Literature: A Guide to Reference Sources*. Washington, D.C.: Library of Congress (U.S. Government Printing Office), 1966. (Supplements 1972-.)

Hodges, E. *Books for Elementary School Libraries: An Initial Collection*. Chicago: American Library Association, 1969.

Junior High School Library Catalog. 3d ed. New York: H. W. Wilson, 1975. (Four annual supplements 1976-1979.)

Katz, W. A. *Introduction to Reference Work*. 2d ed. New York: McGraw-Hill, 1974.

Learning Directory. New York: Westinghouse Learning Corp., 1970-1971.

Paperbound Books in Print. Annual. New York: R. R. Bowker, 1955-.

Pirie, J. W. *Books for Junior College Libraries*. Chicago: American Library Association, 1969.

Public Library Catalog. 6th ed. New York: H. W. Wilson, 1973. (Four annual supplements 1974-1977.)

Reader's Adviser. 12th ed. New York: R. R. Bowker, 1974.

Senior High School Library Catalog. 10th ed. New York: H. W. Wilson, 1972. (Five annual supplements 1973-1977)

Sheehy, E. P., comp. *Guide to Reference Books*. 9th ed. Chicago: American Library Association, 1976.

Subject Guide to Books in Print. Annual. New York: R. R. Bowker, 1957-.

Van Orden, Phyllis. *Elementary school library collection*. 10th edition. Williamsport, Pa.: Bro-Dart Publishing Co., 1976.

Voight, M. J. *Books for College Libraries*. Chicago: American Library Association, 1967.

Walford, A. J., ed. *Guide to Reference Material*. 3d ed. London: Library Association, 1973.

Periodicals

Book Review Digest. New York: H. W. Wilson, 1905-. (Monthly except February and July, cumulations three times a year and annually.)

Book Review Index. Detroit: Gale Research Company, 1965-. (Six times a year with annual cumulations.)

Booklist. Chicago: American Library Association, 1905–. (Semimonthly.)

Books Abroad; An International Literary Quarterly. Norman: University of Oklahoma, 1927–. (Quarterly.)

Choice. Chicago: American Library Association, 1964–. (Monthly.)

Current Index to Journals in Education. New York: Macmillan Information, 1969–. (Monthly, semiannual cumulations.)

Education Abstracts. Paris: UNESCO, Education Clearing House, 1949–. (Monthly, irregular.)

Educational Product Report. New York: Educational Products Information Exchange Institute, 1967–. (Monthly September through May.)

Horn Book Magazine. Boston: The Horn Book, Inc., 1924–. (Bimonthly.)

Index to Book Review in the Humanities. Williamston, Mich.: Phillip Thomson, 1960–. (Annual.)

Kirkus Reviews. New York: Kirkus Service, 1933–. (Semimonthly.)

Library Journal. New York: R. R. Bowker, 1876–. (Semimonthly.)

New Technical Books: A Selective List with Descriptive Annotations. New York: New York Public Library, 1915–. (Monthly.)

New York Review of Books. New York: A. Whitney Ellsworth, Publisher, 1963–. (22 times a year, biweekly except July, August, September, December, and January when monthly.)

New York Times Book Review. New York: New York Times Company, 1896–. (Weekly.)

Publisher's Weekly. New York: R. R. Bowker, 1872–. (weekly.)

Resources in Education. U.S. Department of Health, Education, and Welfare—National Institute of Education. Washington, D.C.: U.S. Government Printing Office, 1966–. (Monthly, cumulated semiannually.)

RQ. Chicago: American Library Association, 1960–. (Quarterly.)

Wilson Library Bulletin. New York: H. W. Wilson, 1914–. (Monthly except July and August.)

Journals in subject fields such as: *English Journal, Social Studies Journal.*

15

Learning Centers

A Definition

Libraries, in providing a service to patrons, allocate spaces for reading and studying. The usual requisite for these spaces is that they be reasonably comfortable and relatively quiet. Oftentimes, they contain nothing more than tables and chairs; and the patron selects materials from the library shelves, finds a vacant chair, and proceeds to use the materials. If the material selected happens to be phonograph record, the patron proceeds to that section of the library where record players are available. Basically, this way of allocating space and, if necessary, the equipment to gain access to information is fine; and indeed the library is providing a service beyond that of being only a depository of information. However, if a systematized information service were implemented, the patron would have, if need be, access to uniquely designed multimedia packages of information to be used in a space designed to work efficiently with the information to be acquired. Hence, the evolution of the learning center, a facility involved with the planning, designing, fabricating, utilizing, and evaluating of information packages that facilitate the learning or acquiring of information on a particular topic using the best media for successfully achieving the task. No longer does the patron proceed to search among shelves for information, rather he is given a package of materials and has available a properly designed space in which to use them.

In varying degrees, school libraries have been implementing the learner center concept for a number of years. Unfortunately, in many schools the librarian has been relegated a subordinate role, that of gathering instructional materials and providing the necessary space for using them. Too infrequently is the librarian involved in planning, designing, or evaluating the instructional packages, especially when the skilled librarian has both the selection aid tools and the knowledge of what types of materials are available that will best achieve the learning objective. Thus, an indispensable contribution to the success of learning is being disregarded. It becomes essential for the librarian to understand and promote the learning center concept as an interrelated system and to be involved in learning packages at the time of their inception.

Learning centers are not solely the province of the school librarian. The proliferation of college extension courses being taken by students living great distances from college campuses is starting to mandate that public libraries be purveyors of the information necessary to complete a course of study adequately. Furthermore, with the growing acceptance of the mediated approach to providing information, it is now being realized that perhaps using several different types of media is the best way to investigate a particular topic. Hence, the need for informational packages and learning centers in which to use them.

Unique Uses of Learning Centers

The learning center can serve as a learning core i.e., the primary place the patron would visit to learn about a particular topic. It can be used as a place of enrichment or in-depth investigation for the patron who has already received basic information from a teacher or textbook and desires or needs to acquire more information. It can also be a facility at which to acquire the facts necessary to understand a topic, this could be acquiring a broader knowledge of a topic, obtaining different perspectives, practicing rote learning, developing expertise, or even having access to the same information, perhaps in different formats more suitable to different types of learning abilities. Again, the librarian must be involved in the planning stages in order to design the learning packages that will be most suitable to the patron's needs.

In facilitating the use of the learning center, the librarian must know something of the patron, or learner, who will be requesting service, his needs, abilities, and objectives. Here is where the librarian will need to work in close concert with the educators who originally initiate the need for learning packages. Planning with educators is crucial for the success of the learning center. A determination must be made regarding specific objectives to be studied and the scope to which they are being investigated, the time allocated to learners to achieve the objectives, the learners' abilities, and how many learners will be involved in a particular unit of study. These data are fairly easy for the school librarian to obtain, but for the public librarian it requires establishing channels of communication between the library and the institution of learning and determining the resources each is able to, or should, provide to the learner. In the case of the patron who is not referred by an educational institution but has an interest in a particular topic, then the librarian, using the interview method, will need to ascertain specific objectives then proceed to design the necessary learning package. It is paramount that the concept of the learning center not be overlooked—that of a systematized information service, including the media and the facility for using them.

In developing the learning center concept and the various uses that could be demanded of it, the librarian needs to take an inventory of resources available. It would be far better to provide excellent service of which the library is capable than to assume the omniscient role of dispensing the means for the whole learning experience. A delineation of roles is necessary between the institution providing instruction and the library, with both knowing who is responsible for core, supplemental, in-depth, and enrichment information. This ascertainment of use will greatly enhance the efficiency of the learning center and eliminate any learning voids or duplication of effort.

Space Allocation

A prime criterion in determining space allocation for a learning center is whether the facility is to be centralized or decentralized. A centralized facility is predicated on the premise that one large space will be set aside and will include a central storage place for learning packages. If the operation is of sufficient magnitude, it could also provide space for a learning center librarian or facilitator. A decentralized facility advocates having spaces in several areas of the library in close proximity to the materials being used. One is not preferred over the other. The library, however, must determine which will function better for its particular requirements. An exploration of the positive features of each is warranted.

The centralized learning facility affords better supervision and control. Everything is in one place; learning packages, equipment, storage, learning spaces. If a librarian is on duty, he or she will be responsible only for the operation of the learning center and can cater to the needs of the learning center patron. Records of usage can easily be maintained. An additional advantage of a centralized facility is that it is multidisciplinary. This means that at particular periods of time the demands for space for the study of a particular subject may greatly increase, which a centralized facility can easily absorb. Conversely, if a particular subject is not being studied, other subjects are being studied, justifying the allocation of space.

A decentralized facility, meanwhile, has the advantage of having spaces adjacent to resources being studied. If the learner has need for information beyond that provided in the learning package, he is already in the physical area where the information is located. Rather than relying on one librarian for all learning center assistance needed, the learner now has access to a librarian perhaps more skilled in his particular area of study. Because some learning packages, by the nature of the discipline being studied, may require only the use of one type of medium, e.g., books, there is no need to have a learning space set up with a multitude of audiovisual equipment that will receive no use.

In either situation, centralized or decentralized, other factors warrant consideration when justifying space needs. As learning materials are assembled into learning packages, storage boxes are needed along with storage shelves. With audiovisual equipment, space for utilization and storage needs to be considered. Projections must be made as to how many patrons will use the facility at peak hours; how many copies of a particular learning package must be made available; and any anticipated rate of increase in use of the learning center over a prescribed period of time. The space requirement of the individual patron must be carefully planned, which will result in a measured space area factor. When multiplied by the number of actual spaces needed, this will give credence to overall space needs.

Individual Space Requirements

When using a learning package, the patron will need space to spread out the various materials being studied. It is suggested that a minimum of 9 square feet of working surface be provided. The area should have some line of demarcation in the form of an inscribed boundary line or partition. This will eliminate the situation of patrons accidentally infringing on each other's learning spaces. Actually, what is needed is some type of learning carrel. By definition a carrel is "a nook near the stacks in a library, used for private study."[1]

[1]From *The American Heritage Dictionary of the English Language. New College Edition.* 1976.

The carrel can be designed to offer visual and audio privacy so that the patron is not disturbed and does not disturb other patrons. Some carrels completely enclose the patron on three sides with a partition about 30 inches high. This provides extreme privacy, but attendant to it is the librarian's inability to supervise the area—it is virtually impossible to observe from a central location whether a particular carrel is occupied, let alone what the patron is actually doing. Many librarians will opt for much lower partitions, about 1 foot high, which provide the patron with sufficient privacy to function with minimal distractions.

Another factor to consider in designing carrels is whether they are to be "wet" or "dry." A wet carrel has access to electricity, a dry carrel has none. A wet carrel is necessary for using audiovisual equipment (slide and filmstrip viewers, motion picture projectors, audio- and videotape recorders). Obviously, a wet carrel housing a videotape recorder will require much more space than a dry carrel used solely for reading. If the media used involve recorded sound, headsets must be provided along with the space to store them. Until a few years ago, carrels being used to listen to recordings required highly absorbent acoustical materials to minimize the disturbance to others; but with the high quality of headsets now available, this is no longer a problem. The problem now is how much equipment should go into a carrel. With the increasingly extensive use of various audiovisual materials, it is conceivable to have a single learning package containing a book, charts, pictures, audiotapes, filmstrips, motion picture films, and videotapes. Such a package would require a carrel with a vast array of equipment.

A decision must also be made whether equipment will be permanently installed, portable, or a combination of both. If each carrel is to have a complete complement of audiovisual equipment, the space requirement for each carrel can become excessive, without considering the cost, which can become exorbitant. Alternatives should be considered: Perhaps it would be better to have a few expensive one-of-a-kind carrels. By careful planning, a proportion of the learning center can be allocated to the expensive one-of-a-kind carrels. Furthermore, it would be difficult to justify placing expensive equipment that would receive only limited use in every carrel.

When formulating space needs for learning carrels, ascertain whether all learning will be conducted individually. Some topics of study lend themselves to learners working in pairs or groups. If two people are working together, obviously a 9 square foot working space will be inadequate. Rather than create a dilemma as to the design of individual space needs, incorporate flexibility into the design concept. Settle on a basic modular space design for a dry carrel and elaborate on its size to satisfy the multiplicity of needs that will be demanded of other carrels in the learning center. Using this formula will eliminate having a plethora of designs and space formulas: e.g., 1 modular space for a dry carrel; 1½ modular spaces for wet carrel; 2 modular spaces for a 2-person dry carrel; 2½ modular spaces for a basic 2-person wet carrel 1½ modular spaces for a one-of-kind carrel; etc.

Flexibility has an added advantage in that it does not require specially designed furniture. A simple table can be partitioned off into the determined modular space units. Too often librarians in their overenthusiasm will purchase uniquely designed learning carrels. No doubt this furniture is beautiful and well made; but for the librarian incorporating a learning center into the library, more often than not it is a venture into immediate obsolescence. This is especially true of carrels containing built-in equipment, which after a few uses may be found to be inadequate to the needs of a particular learning center. Only after field testing a particular carrel design and modifying it until it competently achieves its intended purpose will a librarian be ready to consider the more expensive, custom designed furniture.

In the final analysis, it is for the librarian to determine in the planning stages what a carrel is to contain, how it can be used, and what its space and designment requirements should be.

Designing a Centralized Learning Center

When a learning-carrel space design has been ascertained, it becomes necessary to incorporate it into the overall schema of the learning center; for when planning a learning center it can be truly said that, "the sum is greater than the parts."

Learning packages, because they contain collections of information, will ordinarily require a substantial period of time to use—not uncommonly as long as several hours. This being the case, it is essential that the learning center be a "welcoming" place with an environment conducive to learning. Fundamentally, it should be comfortable, well lighted, and away from any major traffic flow; maintain a relatively low noise level; and contain adequate workspace for each patron. In addition, there should be provision for incorporating whoever else is responsible for maintaining the facility; ample storage space; convenient access to materials; space for files, catalogs, and record keeping; and consideration for ease of monitoring.

It is strongly recommended that the floor be carpeted, for not only does carpet improve the appearance of the room, it also aids tremen-

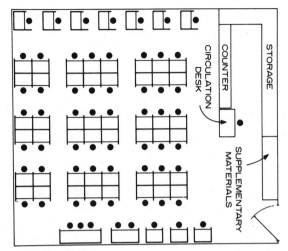

Figure 15.1. Learning center layout A. Carrels adjacent to walls are wet (electric access). Carrels in center of room are dry (no electricity). Large carrel can accommodate large pieces of audiovisual equipment or can be used by 2 or 3 people. Carrel partitions 12 in. high maximum.

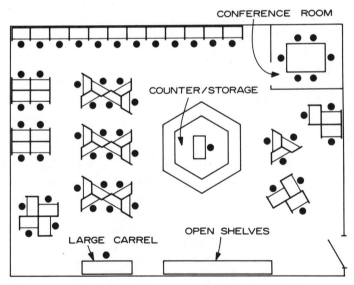

Figure 15.2. Learning center layout B. Carrels adjacent to walls are wet (electric access). Carrels in center of room are dry (no electricity).

dously in noise absorption. Contoured chairs are advised, preferably with seat cushions, especially if patrons are expected to be seated for sustained periods of time. Table surfaces should have finishes that are resistant to marring and scratching. Lighting should be evenly distributed with a 30–50 foot-candle range for illuminating work surface areas. In learning centers with high partitioned carrels, it may be necessary to have a lamp in each carrel. Media that require projection have to be positioned or designed with some type of shadow device that will restrict ambient light from striking the screen and washing out the projected image. Electrical raceways should be placed where people will not be tripping over them. All electrical accesses must comply with minimal inspection code standards, enough planning should be given them so that future needs will not overload the electrical circuits.

Arrangement of furniture should be efficient, but not crowded. Attempts should be made to keep the learning center spacious and uncluttered. Depending on the amount of space available, its shape, the location of doors and windows, a variety of furniture arrangements and configurations can be conceived. Polygonal shaped clusters of carrels can be located away from walls; linear or front-to-front carrels can be placed along walls. (See Figures 15.1 and 15.2.) It is recommended that you experiment with furniture arrangements. Make a floor plan or scale model of the facility and using the formula derived earlier, make 2-dimensional cutouts of carrels, storage shelves, desks, and any other furniture to be installed. These pieces can then be manipulated into an efficient, esthetic design.

Invariably the learning center will be a dynamic facility in a continual state of flux. Learning packages, in all probability will have periods of heavy use followed by extended periods of relatively little or no use. Learning packages of timely or temporary value will be fabricated, used, and then dismantled. A plan needs to be devised and implemented for the circulation of learning packages. Several alternatives should be examined and considered.

The ultimate procedure of circulation is to have carrels set up with complete learning packages and the necessary equipment to utilize them. This procedure is possible when learning packages are scheduled for use during a specified time period. School libraries take advantage of this procedure by setting aside blocks of carrels and assigning students to them during the prescribed calendar periods. At the end of the calendar period, the learning packages are either stored or dismantled and are not available to the student until the next scheduled use. This works fine in a school library where curricula are presented in an orderly time sequence. A public library is not quite as fortuitous; its patrons tend to use the learning center in a more random time order, and a completely set up carrel could possibly go for weeks without being used.

At the opposite end of the continuum of having learning packages set up in carrels is giving each patron two packages, one containing learning materials and the other containing the necessary equipment for using it, and assigning him to a carrel where he can set up and use the material. The librarian must ascertain which circulation method provides the optimum benefits. Obviously, there are many variations, with each having its inherent advantages and disadvantages.

An analysis must consider how many copies of each learning package are needed. This is predicated on the anticipated number of patrons who will be requesting a particular learning package, the calendar time period it will be in demand, and the number of possible requests during any peak usage time. The problem warrants serious investigation, for nothing is more frustrating than telling a patron that the learning package was available only for a prescribed time period and will not be available in the immediate future, or conversely, that because of exceedingly large demands for the learning package it will be several hours or days before it may be available.

To alleviate problems of circulation requires careful planning. Records must be kept. The following procedures are worthy of consideration.

- Develop workable inventory procedures: Know what is on hand; know what materials are available when needed; know what materials are missing and need to be replaced, or are damaged and need to be repaired.
- Prepare a file of all learning packages, their respective contents, and the kinds of equipment necessary to make use of them.
- Maintain a time record of learning packages usage. Include any turndowns or refusals because of unavailability.
- Develop a filing and check-out system. Keep a record of the amount of time a learning package receives during each use.
- Know what supplementary or additional adjunct materials may be requested. This can be easily determined if a bibliography of suggested additional materials is prepared for each learning package.
- Formulate how many learning packages can be competently served by a single expensive one-of-kind item.

Although not a circulation consideration per se, note what types of materials are being circulated in the learning packages. Oftentimes, a learning center will acquire a particular media syndrome. Gradually all materials are of a particular type, e.g., an inordinate number of learning packages contain an audio tape, a filmstrip, and a pamphlet. This is called the sound–filmstrip–pamphlet syndrome. When materials are selected for a learning package, consideration must be given to how well they communicate within a cost effectiveness context and not reflect habit or myopic thinking.

Advantages of Learning Centers and Learning Packages

The learning center provides an environment where the patron can work efficiently with learning materials. Through the use of learning packages, all the material is available in one physical container. No longer is a search required to gather materials for study. Because the librarian is in control of the entire system, the precise information in the best media form is available. Learning packages could be a required adjunct to a formal curriculum or maybe fabricated to serve a perceived community need. (Envision a patron with a gardening problem being able to resolve it with one complete learning package.)

The learning center promotes independent or individualized learning. The patron has access to a learning package which he can use at his own learning rate; furthermore, if the learning package is properly designed, there is little or no need for a librarian to provide assistance with the package. This means that the learning package is a complete, self-contained learning experience. Ideally, the learning center should be used with learning packages; however it also provides a facility where the patron can read or interact with any kind of individual medium available in the library. It is the ideal place to have a computer terminal for patron use.

When designing a learning center or selecting materials for it, know the ability and interest of the patron; the allocation of space and space–time; furniture, equipment and storage requirements. Paramount to all this, the library must have an objective for having a learning center, i.e., what it is that it expects to achieve and how it expects to accomplish it.

Selected Bibliography

Cornmesser, K. *et al. Handbook of Learning Centers: Grades 3–4.* Clarksville, Md.: Board of Education of Howard County, 1972.

Cornmesser, K. *et al. Handbook of Learning Centers: Grades 4–5.* Clarksville, Md.: Board of Education of Howard County, 1972.

Culyer, R. C., III. *Learning Centers and Independent Activities.* Boone, N.C.: Appalachian State University, 1972. (The Vineyard Series, vol. 26.)

Easthope, G. *Community Hierarchy and Open Education.* Boston: Routledge and Kegan Paul, 1975.

Espinosa, L., and Morlan, J. *Easy-to-Make Devices for Learning Centers.* San Jose Calif.: Personalized Learning Associates, 1974.

Forte, I. *et al. Center Stuff for Nooks, Crannies and Corners.* Nashville, Tenn.: Incentive Publications, Box 12422, 37212.

Gall, P. *IPI: An Individualized Approach,* Arlington, Va.: National School of Public Relations Association, 1975.

Glasser, J. F. *The Elementary School Learning Center for Independent Study.* West Nyack, N.Y.: Parker, 1971.

Godfrey, L. L. *Individualize with Learning Themes.* Menlo Park, Calif.: Individualized Books, P.O. Box 591, 1974.

Godfrey, L. L. *Individualizing through Learning Stations. (Elementary School)* San Francisco: Teachers Exchange of San Francisco, 600 - 35 Ave., 1973.

Greenlee, J., and Moore E. *Ideas for Learning Centers.* Palo Alto, Calif.: Fearon Press, 1974.

Gurske, B. and Cote, B. T. *Learning Center Guide.* Sunnyvale, Calif.: CTM Pub. Co., P.O. Box 1513, 1972.

Kapfer, P. G. and Ovard, G. F. *Preparing and Using Learning Packages for Ungraded, Continuous Progress Education.* Englewood Cliffs, N.J.: Educational Technology Publications, 1971.

Kaplan, S. N. *et al. Change for Children: Ideas and Activities for Individualizing Learning.* Pacific Palisades, Calif.: Goodyear Pub. Co., 1973.

Learning Centers. New edition. West Haven, Conn.: National Education Association, 1975.

Morlan, J. *et al. Classroom Learning Centers.* Palo Alto, Calif.: Fearon Press, 1973.

Morlan, J. E. *Classroom Learning Centers: Individualized (Personalized) Instruction.* Belmont, Calif.: Fearon Publishers, 1973.

Morlan, J. E., and Morlan, G. *Creative Writing Learning Centers.* San Jose, Calif.: Personalized Learning Associates. P.O. Box 886, 1974.

Mummert, P. A. *Create Your Own Learning Center,* Buffalo, N.Y.: DOK Publishers, 1974.

Peterson, G. T. *A Sphere for Non-Traditional Approaches to Education,* Hamden, Conn.: Shoe String Press, 1975.

Rapport, V. ed. *Learning Centers: Children on Their Own.* Washington, D.C.: The Association for Childhood Education International, 3615 Wisconsin Ave. N.W., 1970.

SECDC (Special Education Curriculum Development Center). *Classroom Interest Centers.* Iowa City: University of Iowa, 1972.

Thomas, J. I. *Learning Centers: Opening up the Classroom*. Rockleigh, N.J.: Holbrook Press, 1975.

Voight, R. C. *Invitation to Learning: The Learning Center Handbook*. Washington, D.C.: Acropolis Books, 1971.

Waterman, A. and Pflum, J. *The New Open Education: A Program for Combining the Basics with Alternative Methods*. Washington, D.C.: Acropolis Books, 1975.

16

Local Preparation of Information Materials

Rationale

Occasionally, situations may arise requiring that materials be produced locally. Perhaps there is a need for a bulletin board, display, supplementary material not available from commercial sources, unique materials applicable to a particular locality, or existing materials that require embellishments or modification for a distinct patron need. Given such a situation where materials are unavailable, the librarian has the alternatives of informing the patron that the request cannot be satisfied or making the necessary material. If the latter alternative is chosen, a plan of execution must be instituted. For the school librarian, the problem is easily resolved: The request is communicated to the school's media specialist, who is equipped to handle such contingencies. In the case of a public librarian or school librarian not large enough to employ a media specialist, the problem is not quite as easily resolved. The librarian must use his or her own resourcefulness and be responsible for having the materials produced.

First, a determination must be made as to exactly what types of materials can or should be locally produced. This determination is predicated on the degree of skill the librarian is expected to possess in materials production, as well as the equipment necessary to do the job. There are some excellent materials preparation manuals available (see bibliography), that are designed for the nonprofessional in need of a particular skill or procedure, and the results of the end product, with adequate practice, can be of professional quality.

Bearing in mind that local materials preparation is an adjunct service, the librarian should not expect to become involved in sophisticated production activities but rather to produce materials that help fill an information gap not filled by commercially prepared materials. Generally, the materials that can be produced by the librarian assumed not to have professional training in materials production include: dittos, models, transparencies for overhead projection, mounted and preserved materials for display, hand puppets for story-telling, prepared specimens, photographic slides, audiotapes, 8-mm motion pictures, and enlargements of existing materials.

Before becoming involved in materials production, the librarian needs to make a priorities assessment. Time will have to be alloted for making materials, which in some circumstances can consume a considerable portion of the working day. Furthermore, making materials requires the procurement of production tools and equipment. A decision needs to be made as regards the extent to which the library should become involved in materials production. The library should examine its policy to determine if its role is solely to acquire and not produce information or if it is to provide information by whatever means possible. Circumstances, and even the philosophy of the library, may dictate whether materials can or should be locally produced. Locally produced materials can provide a service, but not without incurred costs. If the costs can be justified, a policy of local material production would be strongly considered.

Basic Production Equipment

In order to produce even the basic types of informational materials, the library will need some basic kinds of equipment. The equipment is basic in the sense that it should not require special skills or training in order to operate it. Depending on the extent of involvement, the library engaged in the production of informational materials would need the following equipment.

1. *Photocopier:* To make copies of existing materials. Libraries usually have the coin-operated variety permitting the patron to make his own copy. (Beware of copyright infringement!)
2. *Spirit duplicator (Ditto):* This requires the information being copied to be transferred to a ditto master. A ditto master is good for a run

of about 150 paper copies. Can also make multicolored copy (red, blue, green, purple, black).

3. *Mimeograph machine:* Also requires information be transferred to a master. Mimeograph master is more expensive than ditto master, however results more closely approximate professional printing quality, and the master is good for at least 1000 copies.

4. *Complement of basic drafting equipment (compasses, T-square, triangles, guides, etc.):* To make charts, graphs, diagrams.

5. *Assortment of lettering guides:* To produce professional quality printing (e.g., Unimark, Wrico, Dyno, Rapidograph, Leroy are types of mechanical lettering systems available).

6. *Primary typewriter:* It is a typewriter with a large type font. Ideal for typing information that can be comfortably read at a distance of approximately 10 feet.

7. *Paper cutter, X-acto knives, scissors:* For cutting and trimming paper, cloth, and cardboard.

8. *Thermal copier:* To produce overhead transparencies directly from newsprint or any other black and white materials. Requires the use of thermal transparency material, which is available in black, red, blue, green, and yellow. The copier can also be used for making thermal ditto masters or paper reproductions from black and white originals.

9. *Diazo copier:* A process for making colored overhead transparencies on low photosensitive film. Produces transparencies with vivid, brilliant colors.

10. *Dry mount press:* Used for affixing photographs and other visuals to cardboard for display purposes. Can also be used for bonding reinforcing materials to the backs of large visuals (cloth or cardboard backing for added strength and durability, and laminating the front surface of visuals for protection).

11. *Camera and copystand:* For making pictures and slides. The copystand aids in taking photographs from books and magazines. There is a whole array of cameras and copystands available. Consult your local camera dealer for the best equipment compatible to your needs and ability.

12. *Audio tape recorder (reel-to-reel or cassette):* To record original information to an audio format for the visually handicapped or to duplicate existing audio tapes. Again consult your local dealer for assistance in selection.

13. *Opaque projector:* For tracing and enlarging original materials. Indispensable for libraries with limited budgets, time, and graphic

skills. Can also be used for projecting opaque materials directly onto a screen.

14. *Materials, accessories:* Your local art supply or business office supply dealer can provide invaluable assistance for your particular needs.

This equipment is the type prevalent in facilities involved in the non-professional production and duplication of informational materials. What is actually acquired will be dependent upon the needs of a particular library. The equipment can range from inexpensive, easy-to-operate models to expensive, complex varieties. Libraries possessing the necessary means can become involved with processing information in a television, or video, format. This is a relatively new area of local material production, but it usually requires minimal professional training. It is recommended that prior to becoming involved in the production of information materials, the librarian visit a local school media center and consult with the media director in order to obtain a better understanding of what is involved and practical for his or her particular situation.

Free and Inexpensive Materials

Being able to provide library patrons with locally prepared materials is indeed a worthwhile service. However, it is assumed that the materials to be produced locally are unavailable from commerical sources. This unavailability could be a result of the uniqueness, or special character of the item, its applicability to a very restricted group or locale, or insufficient demand to produce it at a profit. This does not preclude the possiblity that some organizations might produce an item for precisely the same reasons a commercial organization would not produce it. Private organizations, both profit and nonprofit, produce and distribute materials either to promote a product or as a public service. Many of these materials are available to the general public at little or not cost. It could prove to be valuable for the librarian to investigate these resources prior to becoming involved in producing an item locally. A free or inexpensive item could cost much less than the time and materials it takes to make it.

There are selection aids designed solely for providing information on sources, types, and availability of free and inexpensive materials (see bibliography). These selection aids are usually well indexed and contain information regarding types of material, areas of applicability, content, producer, datedness, cost (if any), and an annotation. The materials include books, pamphlets, charts, realia, audio and video recordings, filmstrips, and motion picture films. Some requested items are given to the library, while others are available on a free loan basis. The selection aid provides information regarding copyright use, loan procedures, obtaining multiple copies, and suggested lead time required to receive material.

Along with professional selection aids, the librarian should not overlook resources in the community. There are many excellent private and public organizations ready to provide the library with materials on request. Community agencies, civil government, educational establishments, public utilities, and private businesses have a plethora of materials available and welcome the opportunity for an institution such as a library to distribute their materials. An excellent local selection aid is the telephone directory. In the yellow pages are listed practically every community resource that is likely to have materials available to the library.

As with many other selection aids, those that contain listings of free and inexpensive materials cannot provide complete content descriptions and do not evaluate each item. It is for the librarian, prior to issuing it to a patron, to evaluate scrupulously any free or inexpensive material acquisitions. All acquisitions should be evaluated, but it is critical with free and inexpensive materials in order to ascertain the intended purpose of the material and be sure that its use is not in violation of library policy. Consideration must be given to propaganda, selling a product or service, datedness, authenticity, truthfulness, biases, quality of content, and value. Many of the producers of free and inexpensive materials are sincerely trying to provide a public service, unfortunately, some material may, on occasion, violate the public good and be more concerned with achieving its own profit motives. In summary, the selection aids tell what is available; it is for the librarian to determine what is selected.

Some librarians are reluctant to use free materials for they feel their ulterior purpose is to sell something. A closer examination of free materials will reveal that most of them do serve a purpose; they are prepared by people who, by virtue of their contact with a particular product, possess special knowledge; the materials are generally up to date; and oftentimes they are the only readily available source of information. The librarian should objectively evaluate them for presentation effectiveness, importance, freedom from undesirable bias or advertising, and awareness of how they can be used in the library. In the final analysis, perhaps most important when contemplating local material production is to use the free material selection aids and determine if the materials needed are available from a free or inexpensive source which could well result in a generous savings of time, labor, and material.

Production Criteria

Assuming that you have the necessary production materials and resources and that the material to be produced is not available from any source, there are some basic production and design criteria that should be considered when planning to produce informational materials. The following outline raises questions that are deemed essential in analyzing requests for materials that will be produced locally.

    I. What purpose is the material to serve?

        A. Satisfy a request?
        B. In preparation of an anticipated need?
        C. Provide supplementary or enrichment information?
        D. Function as promotional material?

    II. How is the material to be used?

        A. By one patron? Many individual patrons? Group use?
        B. Anticipated frequency of use? One time only? Many repeated uses?
        C. In the library only? Outside the library?
        D. As an adjunct to existing material? As a discrete entity?

    III. What is the best format to use (e.g., ditto, photographic slide, overhead transparency, mounted visuals, poster, 8-mm film, model, audiotape)?

        A. Will it be manipulated and handled by an individual patron? Used by a group?
        B. Should it be produced in print form, illustration form, picture form, color, sound, motion?
        C. How durable should it be?
        D. Should a combination of formats be used?
        E. Will there be any later problems in storing the materials?

    IV. What is the complexity of producing the materials?

        A. How much time will it take to produce?
        B. How much material will it require?

C. How many pieces of material will be produced?

D. Are any special production skills or equipment required?

After considering these four basic production criteria, the librarian is in a better position to ascertain if local production of materials is warranted.

Design Criteria

If after answering the questions in the preceding section, the decision is to proceed with production, the next step to consider is design factors. Granted the format being used will be a major factor in determining design, regardless of format some basic design details need to be appraised.

The finished product should be neat, clean, and easy to use. In the case of visual materials, they should be comfortable to read and view. The information should be arranged in a design that has a smooth flow and continuity. Any extraneous information that is not essential should be stringently avoided. Remember the purpose is to provide information that is not available; leave the fancy artwork and superfluous detail to the professionals. The use of good texture, color, perspective, arrangement, and layout greatly enhance the quality of the material.

Audio materials should be easy to hear and comprehend. They should not be too lengthy; and when used with visual materials, they should collaborate, not compete, with the visuals. The librarian does not have to be an artist; making materials that are esthetically pleasing does not require a special talent. However, taking a little extra concern and time for quality will be well worth the effort.

It is strongly advised that the librarian who is a novice in the production of materials read Morlan's *Preparation of Inexpensive Teaching Materials* in order to gain a better understanding of what is entailed and can be accomplished.

Evaluation Standards

Evaluating locally produced informational materials can be summed up in one term—cost effectiveness (CE). Too often materials are produced without regard for cost. Incidentally, the biggest cost, and that which is most often overlooked, is the cost in time or labor to produce material. If it takes 1 hour to produce an item, then realistically the time cost is 1 hour's labor. A professional librarian should be critical of the time factor involved in producing materials; perhaps the task can be done more economically by a staff paraprofessional. The librarian who claims that tasks such as producing materials can be done at no labor cost in spare time needs to make a close examination of the library's operations system, for an obvious inefficient use of staff time exists.

The effectiveness half of the cost effectiveness term refers to how the finished product will perform. An assessment must be made regarding extent of use. As an exaggeration, if an item takes 3 hours to produce at a labor cost of $3 per hour and consumes $1 in materials, then the item costs $10. If the item is going to be used one time only by one patron for supplemental information, it has rather limited effectiveness. It is doubtful that a librarian would purchase a $10 book for such narrow use. Simply stated, the effectiveness of an item justifies the cost.

The librarian should regard the CE not solely as a phase to be aware of when planning to produce material but rather as a mathematical ratio. The cost half of the ratio is easily computed as a real dollar figure; the effectiveness half of the ratio has to be constructed in terms of units. The librarian will have to formulate a chart of effectiveness value expressed as units. There is no set criteria as to what constitutes effectiveness or what unit value should be assigned to them. It is for the librarian to generate criteria of anticipated effectiveness. Each library has peculiar needs, as well as the scope of services it provides; therefore, value of effectiveness will vary among libraries. As an example of effectiveness value, assume that one of the criteria would be patron use. Now if a patron were to use a locally produced item one time to obtain original information, then it could be assigned a unit of value of 1; if 10 patrons were to use it, the item would have a unit value of 10. The critical decision to be made by the librarian is what is the minimal acceptable ratio of dollar cost to unit effectiveness that will determine if an item is to be produced? Once this ratio is determined and a chart of effectiveness units is prepared, all future decision regarding local production of materials becomes purely objective and justifiable. If a request for locally produced materials is below the minimum CE ratio, it is automatically rejected; conversely, if it is above the minimum ratio, the librarian can expect the item to receive profitable use.

Some basic effectiveness criteria can be offered here; however, it is for each librarian to assign unit values and add or delete criteria that are germane to his particular library situation. (See Figure 16.1.)

1. *Patron usage:* Anticipated number of patrons who will use the material.
2. *Timeliness:* Because of the nature of the information, it has immediate time value and is unobtainable by any other means.
3. *Datedness:* The material will be of value over a specified period of time.
4. *Use:* To be used as basic or original information, supplementary information, promotional materials (e.g., bulletin boards, displays, etc.).
5. *Service:* Very specific use or general broad use. Serve a need to handicapped patrons.
6. *Consumption:* Material will be consumed, either written on or per-

---

Date of request:
Name:
Occupation:
Date needed:
Description and purpose of material needed:

How is material to be used:

  Individual____   Group____   Display____

Recommended format:

Ditto____   Mimeo____   Photos____   Slides____
  Audiotape____   Overhead transparency____   Poster____
  Model____   Other_____

Extent of use:

  Once____   Repeated____   Heavy short time____
  Long time____

Office Use Only

Availability of material for other sources:
  Commercial   Yes____   No____
  Free and Inexpensive   Yes____   No____

Cost of materials:
Time to produce:
Are materials and time available   Yes____   No____
CE ratio:
Priority of request: Immediate____   Can be deferred____   Explain:
Decision to produce: Yes____   No____

Figure 16.1. Request for locally produced materials.

manently kept by patron (applies to situations involving multiple copies, e.g., dittos).

7. *Demand:* Material requested by patron(s) or recommended by library staff.

An item that has survived the scrutiny of the CE ratio needs to be evaluated as regards format, durability, and multiple copies. Is the request in the best material format? Assuming some versatility in production capability, is the material (1) being made in a media form that is best as regards use, and (2) best as regards local skill and production capability? For example, if the information is for group use, then perhaps an audiotape and slide series should be considered, say, in preference to dittos with graphic data or illustrations. If the material is to receive considerable handling, it must be durable; a positive correlation exists between extent of use and durability. Multiple copies may be necessary either because of the material's limited durability or requests made by many patrons at one time.

Finally, all requests must be analyzed within a space–facility–staff context. Space must be allocated to conduct the activity for producing materials. The necessary equipment for production must be made available. Skilled staff need to be provided time to producing materials. Local production of materials is not a perfunctory task to be taken lightly. Locally produced materials can fill an information gap, but the librarian needs a specific, detailed policy to implement.

Selected Bibliography

Bergamini, E. S. *Sight and Sound Tape Directory.* New York: Drorbaugh Publishing Co., 1974.

Bowker, M. K. *Easy Bulletin Boards No. 2,* Metuchen, N.J.: Scarecrow Press, 1974.

Brown, J., and Lewis, R. B., eds. *AV Instructional Technology Manual for Independent Study.* 5th ed. New York: McGraw-Hill, 1977.

Brown, J. C. *Cartoon Bulletin Boards,* Belmont, Calif.: Fearon Press, 1971.

Bullard, J. R., and Mether, C. E. *Audiovisual Fundamentals: Basic Equipment Operation and Materials Production,* Dubuque, Iowa: William C. Brown, 1974.

DeKeiffer, R. E., and Cochran, L. W. *Manual for Audiovisual Techniques,* Englewood Cliffs, N.J.: Prentice-Hall, 1962.

Faier, S. B. *Anyone Can Create a Lively Bulletin Board,* Wilkinsburg, Pa.: Haves School, 1968.

Garland, K., *Graphics Handbook,* New York: Van Nostrand, Reinhold, 1972.

Kemp, J. E. *Planning and Producing Audiovisual Materials.* 2d ed. San Francisco: Chandler Publishing Co., 1975.

Kinder, J. S. *Using Instructional Media.* New York: D. Van Nostrand, 1973.

Making the Most of Charts: An ABC of Graphic Presentation, Washington, D.C.: U.S. Government Printing Office, 1970.

Minor, E., and Frye, H. R. *Techniques for Producing Visual Instructional Media.* 2d ed. New York: McGraw-Hill, 1977.

Morlan, J. E. *Preparation of Inexpensive Teaching Materials.* 2d ed. San Francisco: Chandler Publishing Co., 1973.

Morlan, J. E., and Espinosa, L. *Electric Boards You Can Make,* San Jose, Calif.: Personalized Learning Associates, 1974.

Nelson, L. W. *Instructional Aids.* 2d ed. Dubuque, Iowa: William C. Brown, 1970.

Romiszowski, A. J. *The Selection and Use of Instructional Media,* New York: Halsted Press, 1974.

Spear, M. E. *Practical Charting Techniques.* New York: McGraw-Hill, 1969.

Taylor, C. W., and Williams, F. W., eds. *Instructional Media and Creativity.* New York: John Wiley, 1966.

Wittich, W. A., and Schuller, C. F. *Audiovisual Materials.* New York: Harper & Row, 1976.

SELECTION AIDS

Index To Instructional Media Catalogs. New York: R. R. Bowker, 1974.

Perkins, F. L. *Book and Non-Book Media: Annotated Guide to Selection Aids for Educational Materials.* Champaign, Ill.: National Council of Teachers of English, 1972.

Rufsuold, M., and Guss, C. *Guides to Educational Media.* 3d ed. Chicago: American Library Association, 1971.

17

Selecting the Proper Medium

Designing a Policy and Program of Equipment Selection

Media selection for the library cannot be a haphazard process. It must be predicated upon a specific policy that takes into consideration patrons' needs, budget, physical space, personnel requirements, and philosophic goals of the library. Once formulated, the policy for media selection will have to be examined periodically and perhaps revised to reflect utilization trends and technological developments.

Patrons' needs, both real and perceived, regarding media utilization must be carefully identified. The ultimate success of the media selection policy will certainly have as a criterion for measurement the extent to which it is actually used. It is therefore essential to develop a profile of user's characteristics and assess propensities toward any particular types of media. However, this should not preclude consideration of a medium not presently in the library collection, as it could be well received by patrons once it is in the collection. The assessment should include patrons' frequency of use and where the media are used and under what conditions, e.g., individual or group, in or out of the library.

It is a hard reality, but one that cannot be obscured, that the library operates on a budget; without it there is no library. The parameters for selecting media must operate within budget constraints. The flexibility exists in determining how much of the budget will be allocated for each type of medium. Of course, no librarian ever has enough budget to get everything that should be acquired. Obviously, limits must be set; and it is the good librarian who can design a justified needs priority that functions within budget while making the best contribution to the library program. Lacking well-developed media selection criteria, it becomes difficult to justify the purchase of one $400 film in preference to 40 books or 30 periodical subscriptions. Operating within budget requires that the library develop a balanced collection with regards to types of media and kinds of information required. It is much too easy, and perhaps safe, to expend the greatest portion of the budget, for example, on books of a particular genre and be completely oblivious to other media needs. Such an approach will result in the library providing a rather narrow or limited service and will never achieve the full potential of serving all the information needs of its community. There could even be a causal relationship whereby increasing media service to patrons results in obtaining larger budgets. The librarian must determine which media are capable of fulfilling a particular information need then employ the systems approach discussed in Chapter 2 to determine which media will yield the greatest cost benefit.

Physical space for media, though usually not a great concern, should nevertheless be given consideration with regard to both storage and use space. It would be well to mention at this point that along with selecting media the library should have a prescribed policy for weeding out media, for weeding is actually a process of *selecting* media out of the collection. Weeding can provide considerable relief to strains on need for space. It is readily apparent, when considering storage space, that an inverse ratio usually exist between the cost of an item and the storage space it requires (a $400 film requires less storage space than 40 $10 books). In regard to space necessary for utilization, many kinds of media can be used in the same alloted space whether it be a reading area, carrel, or learning center; however, some media require the use of equipment that makes additional demands on space requirements, and some media are usually viewed in group settings which make a different kind of strain on available space. It is indeed regretable when media are acquired and there are inadequate provisions for their use. The library needs to know the characteristics and peculiarities of space requirements of media being considered for acquisition, then determine if the media can always be used to their best advantage in the library.

Personnel requirements for maintaining media involve a variety of skills. The collection requires maintenance; books must be kept in good repair, periodicals bound, films cleaned and inspected, equipment maintained, etc. In smaller libraries, perhaps one person may have all the responsibilities of maintenance, while in larger libraries, personnel may be hired to perform specific maintenance tasks. In either case, it is an inescapable fact that maintenance chores need to be performed. The extent to which they can be achieved could very well influence which types of media can be selected. The librarian must be cognizant of the maintenance needs of the various types of media being considered for selection.

To be meaningful, the library's philosophic goals should not be regarded as a collection of nebulous euphemistic phrases. They should be respected as the guides and procedures by which the library is to serve its community. If the library's philosophic goal is to be a depository of information for private citizens, then perhaps its media needs may differ from those of a library whose goal is to provide information in its most usable form. Philosophy is not sacrosanct; when no longer useful or consistent with the needs of the community it serves, it should be modified; however, until such time, it should be strictly adhered to, for without it the library has no mission or sense of direction. When media are selected in agreement with philosophical goals, the library maintains the posture of a dynamic, growing institution providing a valuable service to the community.

Any policy and program of media selection should cover an extended time period. It is recommended that the policy and program be projected for 5-year periods. This means that any media being selected should fit into a 5-year acquisition plan. For example, the librarian should project how many films the library anticipates acquiring over a period of 5 years then acquire films within the projected figure. The purpose of this projection is to keep a balance within the collection and also to perform with the library's goals. This does not imply that in the case of films 20% should be acquired each year, but rather that whatever the number of films acquired, they comply with the 5-year projection. If all the films for the 5-year period are acquired within the first year, no additional films will be acquired for another four years. With a 5-year policy, budget planning is greatly facilitated; the library can perform much better within its budget; and media acquisition goals can be more realistically realized.

A 5-year planning program, once instituted, should be examined annually and revised if necessary in light of changes not anticipated at the time of the original projection. Such revision should not alter the media selection program but result either in shortening or lengthening the period of realization or incorporate a change in needs for media because of technological developments or patrons' demands.

Selecting the Medium That Best Fills the Need

A recurring theme throughout this text is that whatever materials the librarian acquires for the collection their ultimate value must be measured on how well they serve the needs of library patrons. It must also be firmly understood that library patrons are not just those people who actually use the library but also the vast numbers of other people who are entitled to use it but perhaps never, or rarely, do so.

The task of the librarian in regard to ascertaining patrons' needs is to (1) identify the specific community the library serves; (2) list the general or predominant traits of the community, which include the various activities its members pursue (e.g., vocations, avocations, interests, leisure time activities); (3) indicate the educational, cultural, political, and social attitudes possessed by the community; and (4) determine what services can be provided both to serve and to attract people to the library. It is essential that the librarian be cognizant of these needs, for nothing can be more frustrating than to know that a bond issue has failed or the budget has been cut. It is debilitating, for example, for the librarian to be informed that more people visit the local zoo than the public library. These unfortunate circumstances result when the community does not see a need for its library.

Item 1 of the task, identifying the specific community which the library serves, is readily apparent, for it is determined by whoever provides the finances, whether it be the taxpayer or the student paying tuition. Information regarding Item 2, community traits, in the case of a public library can easily be obtained from the chamber of commerce; with educational libraries the information can be gathered from faculty. It is considerably more difficult to obtain information regarding Item 3, the educational, cultural, political, and social attitudes possessed by the community. Valid and reliable data can best be obtained by conducting a survey.

The survey, to be valid, must obtain responses from both users and nonusers of the library. User response can easily be obtained by having the patron fill out the survey whenever in the library. Surveying the nonuser is a bit more complicated, but it can be done by telephone, mail, or door-to-door canvassing. The telephone survey will be less expensive to administer than door-to-door canvassing and will yield a higher return than a mail survey. All methods are costly, it is for the individual library to decide which method it prefers to undertake and whether the information it is attempting to gather is best achieved by using a particular method. The objective checklist type of survey is easier to administer, tabulate, and analyze than a subjective, essay, or short-answer type of form. Furthermore, a checklist type survey takes the least time to answer.

The librarian must keep the survey as brief and succinct as possible, asking only those questions that provide information regarding user and nonuser needs for information which the library can provide. The following are items to be considered for inclusion in a survey.

1. *Vital information about the individual responding:* Sex, age, occupation, level of education, frequency of library use
2. *Information acquisition habits:* Newspapers and periodicals read, hours daily of television viewing, number of books read, frequency of film viewing
3. *Information preferences:* Scholarly, scientific, pleasure, hobbies, vocational, arts
4. *Information needs:* Reference, enrichment, enjoyment, leisure
5. *How library can improve service:* More communication to potential users, special programs, special services

Figure 17.1 is a suggested form that incorporates the above information.

The survey will provide the librarian with a profile of library patrons, both actual and potential, that are to be served, their information habits, and what the library means to them. The respondents to the survey should be a cross-sectional representation of the community; and, as mentioned earlier, the local chamber of commerce can provide information regarding the composition of the community.

Item 4, services that can be provided both to serve and to attract people to the library, can be partially ascertained by examining Part V of the survey. Displays, booktalks, bookmobiles, special events and activities, etc. are the means by which services can be implemented. The survey will indicate the type of medium most frequently used (or preferred), what type of information patrons expect to obtain from the library, and the extent to which patrons require library materials. The librarian, with the information obtained from the survey, is now ready to try a pilot program to test the reliability of the survey. A campaign can be embarked upon that provides patrons with materials in formats for which preferences are indicated, informing patrons of the campaign and observing results. If the survey is properly conducted, it would be safe to hypothesize that materials selected would receive greater use by more patrons during the campaign than prior to it. The patrons must

In an effort to improve the library's service to you please respond to the following:

I. Sex: Female   Age: 3–12   Level of Education:
       Male   13–19   Grade   K–8
                         20–35   9–12
                         36–55   College
                         56+

   Occupation: Frequency of library use
                              Average at least:
     Professional
     Producer   A. Once a month
     Distributor   B. Once a year
     Service   C. Once in 5 years
     Unemployed   D. Never

II. How do you acquire information?

Daily newspaper	Number read	1	2	3+
Magazines, periodicals	Weeklies, monthlies	1	2	3+
Television	Hours of daily viewing	1–2	3–4	4+
Books	Number per year	1–3	4–10	10+
Motion picture films (not on television)	Number per year	1–3	4–10	10+

III. Types of materials read, viewed, listened to: education, pleasure, vocational, hobbies, other.

IV. Purpose of getting information: reference, enrichment, enjoyment, leisure, other.

V. How can library improve its service to you?

     Inform you of services and material available
     Offer special interest programs and services
     Group activities, e.g., booktalks, films, seminars
     Other

Figure 17.1. Survey of community needs for library service.

be informed that their perceived needs from the library have been acknowledged and something has been done about them. When patrons become aware that they are providing actual input regarding the types of materials being acquired by the library, then undoubtedly patrons will feel they are not just using materials selected by nonidentifiable librarians but rather are involved in the development of the library collection. This process of informing patrons that their requests are acted upon requires a good follow-up public relations program which should involve the cooperation of local channels of mass communication (newspaper, radio, television) providing adequate news coverage and interesting by-line human interest stories of the patrons and their library.

Categorizing Informational Media

When an information format is selected, a determination must be made as to which medium will provide the best communication. The selection process cannot be performed out of the context in which the information will be employed. Relationships exist between the needs and abilities of the user, the objectives intended to be achieved by the information, the method in which the information is to be used, the facilities available for utilizing the information, and finally the equipment (hardware) that may be needed to gain access to the information.

In order to make intelligent decisions regarding which format to choose for a particular type of information, one should have a basic understanding of the characteristics of the various types of information media.

Print (Paper)

Printed information in its most prevalent form usually does not require the use of equipment to be accessible to the user. Granted, microforms in the main contain printed information requiring magnification equipment to be used; however, the majority of printed information is available in a paper (hard copy) format. Paper print includes books (soft and hard cover), periodicals, newspapers, posters, charts, maps. The design of paper print information places emphasis on individual use. The information is presented by the use of alphanumeric characters, line graphics, and pictures. Within the paper print category, there are differences in the quality of materials containing the information. Newspapers are of low quality paper intended primarily for information printed in black and white which will be used only for short periods of time. Periodicals are made of a more durable finish of paper, for color as well as black and white information, and intended for use over longer periods of time than newspapers. Books are made to be most durable. Generally, they contain many more pages than a newspaper or periodical and require a quality binding. By nature, books are intended for long periods of use, and entire collections are built using books.

Another general characteristic is that of size. A correlation exists between size and expected period of use. Newspapers are largest and have the shortest usage expectancy; periodicals are next in size and usage expectancy; and books are smallest with the longest usage expectancy. Coupled to usage expectancy, newspapers are usually read in one sitting, periodicals are generally read over longer periods of time, while books usually take several days for the average person to read and may be reread at some future time. The usage expectancy also reveals another characteristic, namely, that newspapers contain daily news that is primarily of immediate value, periodicals contain items or themes of current or timely interest, whereas books often have timeless value.

Audio

Audio information requires equipment to make it accessible. The prevalent formats are radio, disc recordings, and audiotape recordings. Sound information can be used by one individual through the use of headphones or by large groups through the use of amplifiers and speakers. Information can be the spoken word, natural sounds of the environment, or music. In the case of musical sounds, stereophonic information is the preferred format, while a monaural format more than suffices for the spoken word. Audio media have the advantage of recording original information, e.g., actually hearing the voice of President Kennedy. Also, audio information can convey more emotion, inflection, and meaning; thereby possessing more realism than the printed word. Music provides its own elements of entertainment, enjoyment, and appreciation. To insure the fidelity of the audio message, care must be taken in the quality of equipment selected and the acoustical environment in which it is used.

Still Projected Media

Still projected media include slides, filmstrips, overhead transparencies, and microforms. Depending on equipment available, still projected materials can be viewed independently or in groups. Slides and filmstrips require a darkened room, while overhead transparencies can be used in a lighted room. They all have the advantage of projecting a single visual for as short or long a period as needed. Slides can be arranged in any order desired, while filmstrips are arranged in a prescribed sequence. Overhead transparencies are best suited for live presentations, with the presenter being able to write on the transparencies, use overlays, and in general have complete control of how the information is presented. Microforms are intended for individual use and have the unique characteristic of being able to store an extraordinarily large amount of information in a relatively small space area. Another type of still projection is that of opaque projection which uses printed paper material and enlarges the image by projecting it onto a screen. The characteristic of the opaque projector is that it can project only paper originals that are no larger than 10 inches square and requires an extremely well darkened room. (Note: Opaque projectors are now available, that can be used in lighted rooms but the price of this type of projector is rather expensive when compared to regular opaque projectors and overhead projectors.)

Audio–Still Projected Media

This category includes sound filmstrips, sound slide sets, sound on slides, and any other types of projected visuals that are accompanied by audiotapes or disc recordings. They have an advantage over still projected visuals in that the projected image does not require an explanation via a printed caption or a live person to explain it. But, by virtue of having sound accompaniment to the projected visual, the information is locked into a time-viewing sequence whereby the visual is viewed only as long as it takes to present the accompanying sound. Automated sound projection equipment is available that will, by an inaudible electronic cue on the audio recording, advance the visuals at the conclusion of each audio sequence.

Silent Motion Projected

This category is composed of silent motion picture films. Information presented in this fashion should have the characteristic of not requiring audio or extensive verbal accompaniment. Many of the super 8-mm single concept filmloops commercially available are of the silent variety. The information they contain can be adequately communicated in a silent visual motion modality.

Sound Motion Projected

This category is the most versatile as regards capability, for it can combine the characteristics of the five preceding categories. But by virtue of its capability, it is also the most expensive to acquire. (A feature of all visuals is that they can be produced either in black and white or color; however, information is considerably more expensive in color than in black and white.) The two modes of gaining access to sound motion materials are via either sound motion picture projector or television receiver. The motion picture projector can project information on a small screen for individual use or on a huge screen for a large audience. Television is intended for small screen viewing, i.e., 17- to 24-inch diagonal screen. Video projectors are available that project a television image from about 50 inches wide all the way up to the size of a large theater screen. At present, it is unlikely that such an application will find its way into the library. Sound motion media posssess a type of completeness in that they do not require supplementary communication aids while being presented. However, this does not preclude the possibility that the viewer, after attending a sound motion presentation, could request additional information in another format.

Models, Realia, Mockups, and Dioramas

Items in this category have the unique characteristic of being three dimensional. Of all the categories, it is the only one capable of providing a kinesthetic experience. The user can actually handle and get a "feel" for the information. Items in this category can be motionless, manipulated, or (by internal mechanisms) actually moving and operational. These kinds of media can provide a concrete experience by allowing the user to become actively involved in their function or view them in their entirety. The material can be miniaturized, enlarged, or cut away to show location and operation of internal parts. When selecting materials that will actually be handled, it is essential that they be evaluated for wear and durability.

These seven categories are not mutually exclusive; there is an obvious overlap, with the possibility that some types of media are applicable to more than one category. When selecting informational media, consideration needs to be given to their appropriateness and to any adaptation that must be made to a particular medium for it to be of value in the environment(s) in which it could possibly receive use. Not to be overlooked is the possibility of a combination of media being used to satisfy a particular information request. There is an omnipresent dilemma of which information format is best to acquire. Characteristics of formats must be assessed and compared as a step in the process of selection. The librarian needs a working knowledge of all the characteristics germane to the various information media available, and the decision of selection must ultimately satisfy the criterion of cost effectiveness, i.e., is the library getting its money's worth, or would the selection of a different information format have yielded a more beneficial cost effectiveness ratio?

Environments in Which Media Are Used

Knowing the use characteristics of various media is important, but the librarian must also know something of the physical environment requirements for properly using them. Viewing a film in a room that cannot be properly darkened can be frustrating to the viewer and severely retard the quality of the message being transmitted by the film.

When assessing environments for using media, it is immediately apparent that physical spaces in the library can accommodate a variety of media and, in some cases, accommodate them simultaneously. Some of the newer equipment designed expressly for individual use can be adequately used in an ordinary room without inconveniencing either the user or other occupants in the room using other types of media. For example, a patron can view and hear a slide and tape presentation on a small unit with rear screen projection using a set of headphones. This allows the patron to view the slides without the need for room darkening, and the headphones provide sound without disturbing, or being disturbed by, anyone else in the room.

Table 17.1 charts media characteristics in relation to physical environments required. The information that each column assesses is as follows:

1. *Number of users:* How many people can actually use the material at one particular time? This can be complex, as some material, depending on the equipment being used, can be used individually or in groups. Where a particular medium can be used in either way, it is repeated on the table, and its characteristics are charted both for independent and group use. *Group* is defined as four or more people.
2. *Requires equipment:* A device is needed in order to gain access to the information.
3. *Requires light control:* The room must be adequately darkened in order to view the material.
4. *Requires noise control:* The room must be free from sound (noise) distractions.
5. *Makes sound:* The material itself makes sounds that would disturb nonparticipants.
6. *Utilized in one sitting:* The material is designed to be consumed in its entirety in less than 2 hours.
7. *Carrel beneficial:* It would be more advantageous if the material were used in a carrel or private, individual space.
8. *Requires private room:* To be properly used, a private room is necessary

Table 17.1.   Media Characteristics and Environmental Requirements

Medium	1 Number of users	2 Requires equipment	3 Requires light control	4 Requires noise control	5 Makes sound	6 Utilized in one sitting	7 Carrel beneficial	8 Requires private room
Printed page	1	No	No	No	No	No	No	No
Microforms	1	Yes	No	No	No	No	Yes	No
Slides or filmstrips silent	1	Yes	No	No	No	Yes	Yes	No
Slides or filmstrips silent	Group	Yes	Yes	No	No	Yes	No	Yes
Slides or filmstrips sound	1	Yes	No	No	Yes	Yes	Yes	No
Slides or filmstrips sound	Group	Yes	Yes	Yes	Yes	Yes	No	Yes
Audio recording disc and tape	1	Yes	No	No	Yes	Yes	Yes	No
Audio recording disc and tape	Group	Yes	No	Yes	Yes	Yes	No	Yes
Motion picture films silent	1	Yes	No	No	No	Yes	Yes	No
Motion picture films sound	1	Yes	No	No	Yes	Yes	Yes	No
Motion picture films sound	Group	Yes	Yes	Yes	Yes	Yes	No	Yes
Television	Group	Yes	No	Yes	Yes	Yes	No	No
Television	1	Yes	No	No	Yes	Yes	Yes	No
Flat visuals, e.g., maps, charts, pictures	1	No	No	No	No	Yes	No	No
Flat visuals	Group	No	No	No	No	Yes	No	Yes
Overhead transparencies	Group	Yes	No	No	No	Yes	No	Yes

As indicated in Table 17.1, a variety of media can be used simultaneously in the same physical environment. It is for the librarian selecting media for in-library use to make provisions for the right kinds of space and environmental controls. When material is charged out of the library, problems of a different kind are generated. Now the concern is not for space but for making certain the patron has access to the necessary hardware. For some media, equipment (hardware) must be made available. If it is provided by the library, it needs to be lightweight, portable, relatively easy to operate, and durable enough to withstand the rigors of being frequently moved. Perhaps more perplexing is the situation when the patron uses his or her own equipment. The librarian really has no way of knowing the condition or quality of the patron's equipment. A disc recording played on a record player with a badly worn phonograph needle will be returned in poor condition. If 16-mm sound film is played on a double sprocketed silent-only projector, it will completely destroy the sound track. It is advisable for the library to provide the patron who will be using his or her own equipment with a list of do's and don'ts for using media. Many libraries, in anticipation of occasional destruction of material, charge patrons a use fee, which in effect is a type of insurance to help defray expenses for replacing damaged material. The librarian should check out a patron's ability to use equipment before he or she takes mediated material out of the library.

Basic Criteria for Selecting Equipment

Selecting the right piece of equipment for library use is no easy task. Too often equipment is acquired which for any number of reasons receives little or no use. The anticipated use and value of such equipment is never realized, and the librarian is burdened with regrets ex post facto. Decisions for selecting equipment must be based on an intelligent investigation. With the plethora of brands and types of equipment on the market, making the ultimate decision of which equipment to acquire, as well as which to reject, necessitates the use of a basic set of selection criteria. The librarian will find that a positive correlation will exist between the degree to which the criteria are developed and used for selecting equipment and the eventual value of the equipment to the library.

The criteria of equipment selection are purpose, cost, extent of usage, skill of patron (difficulty of usage), life expectancy (amortization), standardization, maintenance, and new developments (obsolescence).

Purpose

Purpose is not an evaluative criterion; it is used rather to delineate precisely what it is that is needed. It takes heed of such questions as (1) What is it needed for? (2) What kinds and quantity of material are in the library collection with which to use it? (3) Where and how will it be used? These are obvious questions, but often it is by overlooking the obvious that poor decisions are made. As an example, if you were considering acquiring a microform reader, Question 1 (need) would answer the obvious, i.e., to be able to magnify and read the microforms in the collection. But do you want to have it readable as information projected on a screen or information printed on paper? Question 2 (kinds and quantity of material) refers to format, e.g., if your microforms are in microfiche and microfilm formats, then the purpose may be to gain access to more than one format; quantity refers to actual number of materials in the collection, which may necessitate buying two less expensive pieces of equipment in preference to a more expensive and refined mode:. Question 3 (where and how it will be used) addresses the concern for space needs and portability. Again to use the example of selecting a microform reader, if it is to be used in a brightly lighted, busy room, the brilliance of the projected image and quietness of operation become paramount. If the microform reader is expected to be moved around extensively or even charged out of the library, light weight and compactness are essential.

Cost

Every librarian must and should be concerned about cost. Although libraries are not intended to be profit-making institutions, nevertheless the librarian must work within a budget and is measured on how well he or she manages it. Actually, the best way to measure cost is on a comparative basis, i.e., which make or model is least expensive; and, more important, exactly why does it cost less? Here the librarian should actually use and compare different models *in the environment in which they will be used* and challenge the sales representative as to why a model costs more or less than another model (a reputable salesperson will willingly provide this information).

Extent of Usage

Usage is synonomous with wear. The librarian should project anticipated usage. If a piece of equipment will receive only infrequent use, perhaps the acquisition of a less expensive model is justified. However, the librarian should have an idea of how many times a piece of equipment should be used before it has paid for itself. Coupled with quantity of use is frequency of use and when the frequency occurs. Knowledge of the frequency variable will help to ascertain how many pieces of a particular type of equipment should be acquired.

Skill of Patron

Not to be overlooked is the patron's ability to operate or use equipment. If the library staff is to operate the equipment, patron operation is of no concern but attention must be given to making staff available for equipment operation. Selecting equipment to be operated by patrons must take into consideration whether patrons will be occasional users or frequent and repeated users of the equipment. If equipment is difficult to operate, plans to provide staff for instruction will have to be an integral aspect of patrons using it. If this is the case, perhaps it may be best to opt for more expensive automatic equipment. Also to be considered is the possibility of an inexperienced patron doing damage to the equipment, to the informational materials, or even to himself.

Life Expectancy

Although libraries are seldom allowed to set up plans for amortization of equipment, the librarian should set up some type of plan for depreciation in order to provide for eventual repair or replacement. There are two main aspects of life expectancy to be considered: frequency of use, with a view of the equipment eventually wearing out, and the actual number of years the equipment should be expected to perform. No piece of equipment can be expected to last forever, and the perceptive librarian will make the necessary life expectancy projections at the time of selection.

Standardization

If more than one piece of a particular type of equipment is to be acquired, standardization is a prime consideration. Finding a multitude of different kinds of equipment can be confusing to the patron, who may be expected to operate all of them. Add to this is the problem of maintaining an inventory of basic replacement parts for the various types of equipment. Give this criterion considerable thought, for once the decision on standardization is made, the librarian should be able to live with it. Furthermore, it will eliminate the need to go through an extensive study every time an additional piece of a particular type of equipment needs to be acquired.

Maintenance

Practically every piece of equipment requires some maintenance. When selecting equipment, determine whether maintenance can be done by the librarian or requires the services of a trained technician. If a trained technician is required, should that person be employed by the library, or would it be best to have the equipment serviced by a representative of the company that sells it? If the decision is for the latter, is such service readily available? Nothing can be more frustrating than having a piece of equipment in need of repair and waiting many days for service. Determine if company service is available in your community. Also investigate the possibility of service maintenance contracts, exactly what they entail, and how much they cost. Try to be acutely aware of the quality of construction of equipment. It should be sturdy and durable. If simple maintenance can be done by the librarian, determine if special tools are required and replacement components easily accessible to an untrained person. Find out what kind of an inventory of replacement parts should be on hand, how much they cost, and the anticipated frequency of replacement.

New Developments

With the accelerating rate of technological developments, it is necessary to be aware of obsolescence. It is certainly a disappointment to purchase an expensive piece of equipment that is expected to receive many years of service and soon after find out that a far superior model is available. Investigate the state of the equipment art thoroughly; then a valid commitment can be made to use a particular piece of equipment for a specified period of time regardless of technological developments occurring in the interim. Incidentally, it is just as foolish to take an ultraconservative stance and decide to wait for something better to come along. This is analogous to riding a horse and buggy while waiting for the ultimate form of automobile. Be aware of what is happening; attend conferences where the latest equipment is displayed; check with other libraries in an effort to determine their equipment plans.

These eight criteria are not all of equal value and can vary in value among different libraries. However, careful consideration should be given to them when selecting equipment. If a large amount of expensive equipment is to be purchased, it is a good idea to engage the services of a qualified consultant. Even in this case, the eight criteria stated here should be met to your satisfaction. Ultimately, the burden of decision rests with you. Do not skirt the criteria or try to disguise their implications. Be objective; it is really a case of "To thine own self be true."

Selected Bibliography

Alexander, L. T., and Yelon, S. T. *Learning Systems Design.* New York: McGraw-Hill, 1974.

Allison, M. L. *New Education Materials.* New York: Citation Press, 1968.

Bretz, R. *The Selection of Appropriate Communication Media for Instruction.* Santa Monica, Calif.: The Rand Corp., 1971.

Brown, J. W.; Lewis, R. B.; and Harcleroad, F. F. *AV Instruction: Technology, Media and Methods.* 5th ed. New York: McGraw-Hill, 1977.

Dale, E. *Audiovisual Methods in Teaching.* 3rd ed. New York: Dryden Press, 1969.

Davidson, R. L. *Audiovisual Machines.* Scranton, Pa.: International Textbooks, 1969.

Ducote, R. L. *Program and Function Study.* Glenn Ellyn, Ill.: College of DuPage, Instructional Resource Center, 1967.

Eboch, S. C. *Operating Audiovisual Equipment.* 2d ed. San Francisco, Calif.: Chandler Publishing Co., 1968.

Gambee, B. L. *Non-Book Materials as Library Resources.* Chapel Hill: University of North Carolina, 1967.

Haney, J. B., and Ullmer, E. J. *Educational Communications and Technology.* 2d ed. Dubuque, Iowa: William C. Brown, 1975.

Komoski, K. ed. *Educational Products Information Exchange (EPIE).* New York, 1977.

Riddle, J.; Lewis, S.; and MacDonald, J. *Non-Book Materials: The Organization of Integrated Collections,* Ottawa: Canadian Library Association, 1970.

Rosenberg, K., and Duskey, J. S. *Media Dictionary for Teachers and Librarians,* Littleton, Colo.: Libraries Unlimited, 1975.

Treasure Chest of Audio-Visual Ideas, Plainville, Conn.: Kalart Co., 1976.

SELECTION AIDS

Audiovisual Equipment Directory. Fairfax, Va.: National Audiovisual Association, 1977.

Dale, E., and Trzchbiatowski, G. *A Basic Reference Shelf on Audiovisual Instruction.* Stanford, Calif.: ERIC Clearinghouse, 1967.

Edling, J. V. *A Basic Reference Shelf on Instructional Media Research.* Stanford, Calif.: ERIC Clearinghouse, 1967.

Winchell, C. *Guide To Reference Books.* 8th ed. Chicago: American Library Association, 1970.

Wynar, B., ed. *American Reference Books Annual.* Littleton, Colo.: Libraries Unlimited, 1977.

Subject Index

DUE